Analyzing
Interest Groups

The New Institutionalism in American Politics
Series Editor, Kenneth A. Shepsle

Analyzing Congress
by Charles Stewart III

Analyzing Policy: Choices, Conflicts and Practices
by Michael C. Munger

Analyzing Politics: Rationality, Behavior and Institutions
by Kenneth A. Shepsle and Mark S. Bonchek

Analyzing Interest Groups: Group Influence on People and Policies

SCOTT H. AINSWORTH

UNIVERSITY OF GEORGIA

W·W·NORTON & COMPANY

New York   *London*

To my parents, Kenneth and Audrey

The text of this book is composed in Galliard
with the display set in Modern MT Condensed
Composition by Professional Book Center
Manufacturing by Courier Companies, Inc.
Book design by Jacques Chazaud

Library of Congress Cataloging-in-Publication Data
Ainsworth, Scott H.
    Analyzing interest groups : group influence on people and policies /
Scott H. Ainsworth.
        p. cm. — (The new institutionalism in American politics)
    Includes bibliographical references and index.

    ISBN 0-393-97708-0 (pbk.)

    1. Pressure groups—United States. 2. Pressure groups. I. Title. II. Series.

JK1118 .A56 2002
322.4'3'0973—dc21   2002071902

W. W. Norton & Company, Inc. 500 Fifth Avenue, New York, NY 10110
www.wwnorton.com

W. W. Norton & Company Ltd., Castle House, 75/76 Wells Street,
London W1T 3QT

1 2 3 4 5 6 7 8 9 0

Contents

List of Figures and Tables

Figures

Tables

Preface

Interest groups have long captured the attention of both social science scholars and casual observers of politics. Scholars and laymen alike are often suspicious of interest group activity, but their critiques of interest groups are not always well structured or carefully reasoned. Even among scholars, critiques are often instinctive rather than analytical. As scandals develop, people tend to assess and judge group activity on a case-by-case basis. Event-driven, case-by-case analysis leads to a slow accumulation of isolated facts and details, but it does not always lend itself to an overall understanding of interest group politics or the effects of groups on American democracy.

Goal for This Book

The goal of this book is twofold: (1) to provide a comprehensive view of interest group politics and (2) to offer a means of analyzing interest groups. A comprehensive view of interest groups requires an awareness of the various contexts in which groups operate. Groups operate in a variety of institutional contexts, including each branch of government and in electoral and grass-roots politics. To understand interest group activity, one must know something of these varied institutional contexts. An awareness of historical context informs any sort of debate about politics or political science, and virtually every chapter in this book refers to the historical context in which groups operate. Finally, a comprehensive view is also aided by including a wide range of examples. For instance, the experiences of the NAACP and the Civil Rights movement, Greenpeace and the Sierra Club, the NRA, the AARP, some Welfare Rights Organizations, early farm groups, and veterans organizations are used to exemplify key theoretical concepts.

The second goal of this book is to offer a consistent and coherent means to analyze interest groups and group activities. Throughout the book, the discussion of interest group politics is intertwined with formal theoretic analysis, including some game theory, social choice theory, and spatial models of voting. The formal theoretic approach does not stand apart from or supplant the concerns of traditional group scholars. For instance, I believe that to appreciate the full importance of the work of Mancur Olson, the most prominent formal theorist to write in the interest group subfield, one must know the work of traditional pluralists such as David B. Truman. The aim is not to advance formal theory, but to introduce a bit of formal theory to help us to understand interest groups better. Therefore, the substantive importance of the formal presentations is emphasized, and empirical implications and tests complement the key formal theoretic arguments. Indeed, throughout the book, the focus is on interest groups, not on formal theory.

Acknowledgments

Upon completing this book, I realized that it would be impossible to acknowledge all the people whose efforts have improved it. Countless people have inspired my thinking about the ideas addressed here. Though I risk committing an embarrassing oversight, some people do deserve special mention. Friends and colleagues from my graduate and undergraduate school days continue to inspire me. In particular, I regularly revisit the ideas first introduced to me by Bob Salisbury in a class entitled "Pluralism and Its Critics." I cannot imagine having written this work without that class or without my interactions with Bob. As an undergraduate, I had the good fortune of taking several classes and one independent study with the late William H. Riker. To me, Riker always stressed that the purpose of formal theory was simply to understand politics better. More than anyone else, Riker affected how I view the connections between politics, political science, and formal theory. Friends and colleagues here at the University of Georgia and at professional conferences have offered helpful comments on a wide range of projects, and many of those comments have affected how I present ideas in this book. At the University of Georgia, members of the lunch bunch and the Friday afternoon committee members deserve special mention.

I wanted this book to be appropriate for upper level undergraduate and graduate-level interest group classes, so I gave it several practice runs. Numerous undergraduate and graduate students at the University of Georgia were forced to read earlier versions of this book. For sharing their thoughts and comments, those students deserve thanks. For working beyond the call of duty, one graduate student deserves special thanks. Thad Hall, now at The Century Foundation in Washington D.C., made numerous suggestions over an extended period of time, all aimed at strengthening this book. Kevin Esterling had the courage to assign the first part of this book to his under-graduates when he was teaching at Dartmouth. Kevin graciously shared his thoughts as well as the comments and concerns of his Dartmouth students. Jeff Berry, Kevin Esterling, Jay Goodliffe, Mark Hansen, and Anthony Nownes shared with me their ideas on course content and structure. Syllabi from a wide array of people allowed me to view the range of topics addressed in interest group classes and to catch glimpses of how many of the topics in this book are addressed by others.

Many people have read and commented on all or part of this book. Alan Gitelson read the first two chapters, giving particularly detailed comments and sage advice about the structuring of the introductory sections of a book. Stefanie Lindquist and John Anthony Maltese, two of my University of Georgia friends and colleagues, read parts of Chapter 7 and helped me to develop and clarify several arguments. Indeed, it would be hard to overstate my reliance on the sound advice of my good friend and colleague John Maltese. Susan Nees read numerous chapters, helping me to clarify my prose at many junctures. Christine DeGregorio, Kevin Esterling, and Beth Leech read and commented on the penultimate draft of this book. Christine and Beth stressed the importance of getting the book and each chapter started in the proper fashion. Christine and Kevin reinforced the importance of presenting formal theoretical models throughout the text. Indeed, Kevin outlined a clear and precise means for me to add a little more formal theory to the final draft. Each of these reviewers deserves a special thanks for helping me to avoid countless mistakes, big and small. Of course, the usual caveats apply.

The folks at W. W. Norton also deserve thanks. Roby Harrington and Steve Dunn approached me several years ago, asking me to consider this project. For convincing me that a book such as this was warranted, I thank them. During the completion of this project, I worked most closely with Leo Wiegman. His timely and careful reading of the entire manuscript was most helpful and most appreciated. His breadth of knowledge and his feel for the structuring of an extended argument is impressive. Upon the completion of a book, many authors thank their family members in one way or another, perhaps because book projects have a way of encroaching on other, much more important family projects. Susan, Samuel, and Benjamin certainly deserve special thanks for their patience and good will. Their wide array of projects has certainly enriched my existence. I hope that in some small way this book will benefit them. Finally, it is with great love and admiration that I dedicate this book to my first and my most cherished and influential teachers, my father and mother.

I

Groups and Individuals

—1—

Interest Groups and the Changing Nature of Political Science

Virtually every introductory book in political science starts with an aphorism to describe politics. Politics may be the "authoritative allocation of value" or a question of "who gets what, when, and how."[1] Regardless of one's favorite aphorism, it is difficult today to depict politics without including a role for interest groups. After all, organized interests are all around us. Adult Americans are more likely to be associated with an interest group than they are likely to vote in a presidential election. Organized interests are often deemed to be all-powerful agents able to alter standard government policy. Yet few understand how groups organize and operate, how individuals interact with groups, how groups affect our lives. The exploration of these questions will be the focus of this book.

Virtually every day, newspapers and magazines provide quick snapshots of group activities. But just as family photos fail to capture fully the richness of a vacation or reunion, many vignettes of interest group activity fail to capture the essence of the group, often omitting crucial details, blurring concepts, or skewing issues. Adding snapshots or vignettes may provide richer detail, but a collection of vignettes cannot elucidate how groups operate, why some groups are powerful when others are not, or why a group might succeed or fail. Snapshots of interest groups are only meaningful after we find some way to organize them to help illustrate enduring elements of politics.

To use a sports analogy, consider the following: Suppose you had to learn a new sport—one you'd never seen or heard of. Endless snapshots and highlight clips would be helpful, but they would also leave much out. They would not help you understand the rules of the game. The highlights for the day or week would not help you understand what a typical play or an average game would look like. Finally, they would not offer any information about the strategic interactions that led up to that single moment captured on film. Sports fans enjoy highlights because they already know the rules of the game, they have a sense of average play versus spectacular play, and they understand some of the strategy involved in the game. That is, the sports fans (perhaps unconsciously) can think systematically about the highlights.

Interest groups are fascinating for several reasons, but two deserve special emphasis here. First, the study of organized interests and interest group pluralism has been at the center of key intellectual developments in political science. A careful analysis of the changing views of organized interests provides a detailed history of the changing field of political science.[2] A study of interest groups, therefore, provides a thorough overview of political science. Second, groups are indeed powerful, but they cannot always rely on the sheer size of their membership for their strengths. Many powerful groups in the United States are relatively small. Such groups intrigue us because they skew the basic majoritarian elements of our government. In the simplest majoritarian setting, two alternatives vie against one another and the winner receives a majority of the support, that is fifty percent + 1 or more. Simple majority-rule settings maintain some basic notions of fairness.[3] Groups fascinate (and frustrate) us because they do not fit neatly into a majoritarian view of politics. If the basic notion of majority rule remained undisturbed by the presence or actions of interest groups, then few individuals would ever complain about groups. However, interest group theories of politics are almost by definition nonmajoritarian. Although some groups are wealthy, most do not have extensive financial resources. Concerns about the wealth of groups are certainly prominent around election time, but grassroots organizations are seldom rolling in money, and many organized interests are short-lived due to financial shortfalls. Certainly, some groups are powerful because they are large or wealthy, but many groups are effective even in the face of small memberships or meager financial resources.

Institutionalism

The study of political science has undergone tremendous changes during the last one hundred years or so. Indeed, politics was not deemed worthy of *independent* study prior to the late 1800s or early 1900s. For instance, politics and governments might be studied by historians, philosophers, and economists, but there were no separate political science or government departments at universities and colleges prior to the late 1800s. The first political scientists were institutionalists who focused their analysis on the constitutionally mandated governmental systems, or political institutions. Laws, constitutions, and legal procedures and precedents were emphasized, especially as they related to the courts, Congress, and the executive branch. Given this focus on formal governmental institutions and procedures, many of the earliest academic departments dealing exclusively with political studies were called departments of government rather than departments of politics or political science.

Early political studies were doctrinal and rich in historical detail. The term *thick description* has often been used to describe such detailed, fact-filled descriptions of human events. The thick description of institutionalism led to an accumulation of facts and details, but a systematic understanding did not always emerge from the vast trove of sometimes disconnected information. In any political environment at any moment, there is an infinite number of facts that can be gathered, an infinite number of possible snapshots. As more and more details are accumulated, the need for a systematic analysis increases. After all, "scientific activity is not the indiscriminate amassing of truths [or facts]; science is selective and seeks the truths that count most."[4]

Interest Groups and Pluralism

The earliest political studies did not look at interest groups because groups were not constitutionally mandated institutions. By the 1940s and 1950s, the focus of political scientists' attention was changing. Pluralism provided a welcome counter to the dry, legalistic institutionalism common in the early part of the century. The earliest pluralists wanted to turn scholars' focus away from the formal institutions and toward people and groups. Pluralists emphasized the multiplicity (or plurality) of interests in society and inspired scholars to study the political bargaining that occurred between groups. Such bargaining occurred throughout the three branches of government, but pluralists often looked beyond the formal, constitutionally mandated institutions of Washington, D.C., to include groups outside of institutions traditionally conceived. Public policy was thought to be the product of group pressures brought forth during the bargaining. Pluralists argued that the best way to understand the governmental process was by studying interest groups and the bargaining between them, not through the study of legal doctrine. For the pluralists, the interest group system was central to the representation of individuals and the formulation of policy.

Pluralism offered many avenues of study and seemed to mirror the dynamics of American politics. Scholars investigated group behavior and group interactions with governmental officials, emphasizing the bargaining, maneuvering, and strategizing that emerged in the absence of large, stable majorities. Indeed, some scholars argued that the continual bargaining and ever-changing coalitions in a pluralist setting might provide an element of stability that a permanent majority-minority division with set winners and losers might not.[5] Whenever there was no dominant and enduring majority, the pluralists' emphasis on coalitions of smaller groups and political bargaining seemed most relevant. For a large number of pluralists, the governmental process was best described as balancing the various interests expressed by groups and coalitions of groups.[6]

Some scholars were so enamored of pluralism that they considered it an antidote to all sorts of societal ills. These scholars moved from describing politics from a pluralist perspective to prescribing pluralist solutions.[7] For prescriptive pluralists, enhanced participation, especially from traditionally underrepresented groups, improved the governmental process. Such pluralists were quick to recall James Madison's admonitions in the tenth Federalist Paper about controlling the "tyranny of the majority."[8] Prescriptive pluralists argued that pluralism ensured the dispersion of power among organized groups. They deemed the inclusion of more and more interests beneficial as a brake on majority tyranny as well as other forms of concentrated power. To many pluralists, greater inclusion was considered a part of the natural process of political development. Greater inclusiveness in negotiations was beneficial because voicing interests and concerns enhanced the deliberative process.[9] The outcomes of deliberation and bargaining often allowed groups to dominate policy areas where their interests were particularly strong.[10] Why should a society weight individual views on all issues equally when certain issues are of greater concern to some groups than others? Why not weight preferences in proportion to the concern evinced? Pluralism seemed to allow for finely calibrated political inputs, while elections and voting were coming to be viewed as crude measures of public opinion.

Critics of Pluralism

Most critics of pluralism were not opposed to studying groups per se, but they did dispute the purported benefits of prescriptive pluralism. Some of these critics argued that the deliberations and bargains inherent in pluralism were really quite limited.[11] Seldom were all interests included in the deliberative process, and often deliberations addressed only minor issues.[12] At no time were fundamental issues—are American politics too elitist, too prone to socialism, or too enamored of the free market—addressed within the traditional pluralist paradigm. These fundamental concerns about the nature of American politics and society did not arise within the pluralist paradigm. Perhaps attempts to secure broad-based input on minor or inconsequential issues were simply a ruse to avoid debating fundamental concerns about the nature and structure of government. In short, most critics were unconvinced of the inclusiveness of pluralism. Pluralism appeared elitist, and it favored the status quo. Rather than dispersing power, pluralism seemed better designed to concentrate it in the hands of the upper classes.

Some of the most trenchant criticisms of pluralism were made by E. E. Schattschneider, who bemoaned the elitist elements of pluralism, claiming that the "flaw in the pluralist heaven is that the heavenly chorus sings with a strong upper class accent."[13] Although largely remembered for this one catchy phrase, Schattschneider's critique of pluralism was much more extensive. Schattschneider was also concerned about the *persistence* of bias, which he traced to the political rules and structures that affected the mobilization of interest groups.[14] That is, biases in outcomes in our interest group society were inevitable because of the rules governing the political process. Schattschneider's work shows that the institutionalists' emphasis on rules and procedures has relevance to group theories of politics because the mobilization of bias is connected to the rules and procedures of the governing process.[15]

Schattschneider's frustration with political science was not centered solely on the pluralists. He also lamented the general lack of scientific rigor in political science and the absence of *an operating theory* of politics.[16] An operating theory can, however, be built from key principles. Schattschneider stated that "conflict, competition, leadership, and organization are the essence of democratic politics" and that at "the root of all politics is the universal language of conflict."[17] Conflict occurs because "the winners get so much more than the losers."[18] Conflict may occur among individuals with very different political tendencies or among members of the same organizations. Indeed, conflict and cooperation coexist in organizations because the members often have mixed motives: a "thousand men want power for a thousand different reasons."[19] For Schattschneider, individuals were strategic and calculating because of the conflict inherent in politics. Indeed, Schattschneider viewed favorably "a little cool calculation" on the part of individuals maneuvering for greater influence.[20]

Formal Theory: An Operating Theory of Politics

Suppose one wanted to study a particular group's influence on public policy. One could collect facts about the group (its wealth, founding and history, governmental and community relations), its membership (their wealth, length of membership, status in their communities, relations with government officials), its allies, and its adversaries. One might even collect facts about groups that chose not to mobilize in opposition to the policy. The number of facts and the amount of information that one might consider is unlimited. But simply collecting facts is not particularly helpful. How one sifts the facts, sorting meaningful from unmeaningful, depends on one's theoretical approach.

An operating theory of politics, as Schattschneider called it, would limit one's search for information and help one select and organize facts. Rather than merely amassing facts, an operating theory would indicate which bits of information to seek from the start. Some facts would be highlighted and others would be bypassed. A limitless world would be constrained, and the gathered facts would be organized. Theories force us to focus on a manageable set of facts and relations in a rigorous and consistent way. A formal theoretic approach highlights decision makers' *strategic, goal-oriented* behavior. It proceeds deductively and allows one to highlight the interactions among decision makers in both the cooperative and competitive aspects of politics. By using deductive models built from a clear set of assumptions, one can abstract lasting lessons from individual case studies of group politics.

The focus throughout this book is on interest groups, but within each chapter some formal theory will be introduced to highlight a fundamental aspect of interest groups. The discussion will range widely over the many topics engendered by a careful analysis of interest groups, but it will remain focused on its commitment to displaying theory as an organizing principle. I will introduce some game theory and social choice theory because those theories are particularly well suited to analysis of the "universal language of conflict," which Schattschneider placed at the root of politics, and especially interest group politics.

Notes

1. These widely coined expressions are from David Easton, *The Political System* (New York: Knopf, 1953), 129–133, passim, and Harold Dwight Lasswell, *Politics: Who Gets What, When and How* (New York: Meridian, 1958), passim.
2. See, for instance, G. David Garson's *Group Theories of Politics* (Beverly Hills: Sage Publications, 1978) and Frank R. Baumgartner and Beth L. Leech's *Basic Interests: The Importance of Groups in Politics and in Political Science* (Princeton, NJ: Princeton University Press, 1998).
3. The fairness conditions maintained by majority rule are carefully specified by Kenneth O. May in "A Set of Independent Necessary and Sufficient Conditions for Simple Majority Decision," *Econometrica* 20 (1952): 680–84. Other careful analyses of majority rule include William H. Riker's *Liberalism against Populism* (San Francisco: W. H. Freeman, 1982) and Kenneth A. Shepsle and Mark S. Bonchek's *Analyzing Politics* (New York: W. W. Norton, 1997).
4. David Hackett Fisher, *Historical Fallacies: Toward a Logic of Historical Thought* (New York: Harper & Row, 1970), 5.
5. Nicholas R. Miller develops this argument in "Pluralism and Social Choice," *American Political Science Review* 77 (1983): 734–47.
6. Although he did not entirely reject the role of the government as referee, David B. Truman argued that the government acted as more than just a referee for competing interests. Inevitably, the analogy was stronger than the objections to it, and many scholars still refer to the government as the ultimate referee. Truman, *The Governmental Process*, 2nd ed. (New York: Knopf, 1971), xxv, xxxi.
7. The distinctions between descriptive and prescriptive pluralism are made by Jeffrey M. Berry in *The Interest Group Society*, 3rd ed. (New York: Longman, 1997).
8. James Madison, "Federalist #10," in *The Federalist Papers*, ed. Clinton Rossiter (New York: New American Library, 1961).

9. Jane Mansbridge makes this argument in "A Deliberative Theory of Interest Representation," in *The Politics of Interests*, ed. Mark P. Petracca (Boulder: Westview 1992).

10. This process is seen in Robert A. Dahl's *Who Governs* (New Haven: Yale University Press, 1961).

11. Peter Bachrach and Morton S. Baratz, "The Two Faces of Power," *American Political Science Review* 56 (1962): 947–52. Bachrach and Baratz, "Decisions and Nondecisions," *American Political Science Review* 57 (1963): 632–42. E. E. Schattschneider, *The Semisovereign People* (New York: Holt, Rinehart, & Winston 1960). Jack L. Walker Jr., "A Critique of the Elitist Theory of Democracy," *American Political Science Review* 60 (1966): 285–95.

12. In *Who Governs*, longtime Yale political scientist Robert A. Dahl examined various local community organizations. Some critics wondered whether Dahl's conclusions about a local Parent Teacher Association (PTA) offered meaningful insights into other issues or other larger, more powerful organizations. Could a study of the local PTA offer insights into the governmental process?

13. Schattschneider (1960), 34–35.

14. Robert Dahl also recognized the importance of rules. "Constitutional rules are mainly significant because they help to determine what particular groups are to be given advantages or handicaps in the political struggle." *A Preface to Democratic Theory* (Chicago: University of Chicago Press, 1956), 137.

15. Schattschneider (1960), 71.

16. E. E. Schattschneider, *Equilibrium and Change in American Politics* (College Park: Bureau of Governmental Research, College of Business and Public Administration, University of Maryland, 1958), 7, emphasis added.

17. Schattschneider (1960), 139, 2.

18. E. E. Schattschneider, *Party Government* (New York: Holt, Rinehart, & Winston, 1942), 37.

19. Schattschneider (1942), 36. In his criticism of the nineteenth century conservative Edmund Burke, Schattschneider argued that no political party was "an association of men who have agreed on some principle." Schattschneider (1942), 37.

20. Schattschneider (1942), 41. Also see E. E. Schattschneider, *Two Hundred Million Americans in Search of a Government* (New York: Holt, Rinehart, & Winston, 1969).

~2~

Why Do Individuals
Join Groups?

Introduction

Prior to serving as secretary of state for President George W. Bush, Colin Powell gained considerable media attention due to his popularity during the Persian Gulf War. Upon his retirement from the army, Powell was courted by both the Democratic and Republican parties for a possible political career. He was considered presidential, or at least vice presidential, material. However, for the eight years of the Clinton presidency, Powell largely avoided partisan politics.

Instead of partisan politics, Powell turned his attention to volunteerism and the plight of needy children here in the United States. Volunteerism received considerable media attention in 1996 and 1997 due in large part to the efforts of Powell. Powell's organization, America's Promise, secured some successes, but in other areas, it also suffered failures. Although America's Promise received commitments for assistance from 325 corporations for an extensive advertising campaign, few corporate donations have actually been received. Some corporations agreed to promote volunteer efforts among their own workforce, but their intentions and practices in these areas are dubious. For instance, First Union Corporation promoted a literacy program, but it allowed its volunteers to tutor any child, whether needy or not: one's *own* children even counted. Indeed, one could simply go on a field trip with his or her own children. Of course, the shortcomings in corporate programs may not tell us anything about the volunteers themselves. What about the volunteers' efforts and sacrifices? More often than not, the "volunteers" remained on company time while they "donated" their services. "For all of its good intentions, the effort by Powell and America's Promise may become a case study in the limits of private charity."[1]

Why did such an overwhelmingly popular figure pursuing such a worthy goal face such difficulties? Powell could not surmount what is commonly referred to as the collective-action problem. To be successful, some endeavors require the collective efforts of many people. Collective action is necessary, but coordinating disjointed individual actions into a collective effort is difficult in itself. If individuals who choose to do nothing are able to benefit from the collective efforts of others, problems emerge. Simply put, the freeriding of some individuals may hurt the collective efforts. The term *collective-action problem* is simply a catchall phrase for the *coordination* and *freeriding* problems associated with collective action. In this example, a clear understanding of the collective-action problem might have provided Powell a better sense of the difficulties that America's Promise would face.

This chapter assesses why individuals join groups and how groups overcome their collective-action problems. The two most prominent scholars to address these issues are David B. Truman and Mancur Olson. Truman's impact on political scientists' study of groups is difficult to overstate.[2] References to some of the more compelling arguments first introduced by Truman are made throughout this book. Olson's *The Logic of Collective Action* was a direct attack on Truman's views on our interest group society.[3] Olson and other scholars have been critical of Truman's assessment of pluralism and American democracy. Indeed, numerous scholars were concerned about the array of interests represented in our pluralist society.[4] Who actually participated in the interest group community? Simple observation seemed to suggest an upper-class, elitist bias. Olson also addressed unequal participation in the interest group community, but he derived his conclusions deductively from a model of the collective problem rather than from direct observation. Olson, therefore, was in a position to *explain* the empirical regularities observed by others.[5]

This chapter begins with a discussion of Truman's view of the role of groups in society and discusses Olson's criticisms of Truman. The chapter concludes with an analysis of some of the implications of Olson's work, and a discussion of the concerns of some of Olson's own critics.

David B. Truman and the Formation of Interest Groups

To understand interest groups, one must consider how the individuals directly or indirectly involved with groups interact with one another.

Individuals and groups

"Man is characteristically human only in association with other men."[6] For Truman, all of the defining features of human existence are group related.

Regular social interactions at home provide the basis of the family unit or group. Ultimately, even for the family unit, the biological ties are less important than the daily social interactions. Regular association with individuals outside of the family provides the basis for the natural establishment of groups in society. Groups emerge out of regular interactions at school, work, or play. The effect of any group on a member depends substantially on the frequency of the interactions. Given the importance of regular interactions for groups, Truman concludes that the family unit is the most important group in society. Different group affiliations provide different socialization, affecting how one views the world. In such fashion, group affiliations structure our ideology, education, recreation, circle of friends, and every other aspect of our human nature.

Truman distinguished interest groups and political interest groups from the primary social groups—such as one's family. For Truman, each of the following two conditions are necessary for an interest group and together they are sufficient for interest group formation.

Condition 1: Shared Attitudes
Condition 2: Claims upon Others

Shared attitudes lead to the common interests that are fundamental to interest groups. One might even equate interests with groups; that is, there could be no group without its interests, and no interest without its group.[7] For Truman, the second condition is also necessary for an interest group. The claims upon others make it clear that the groups pursue their narrow, self-interested goals even at the sake of others' well-being. Debtors and creditors and developers and environmentalists seldom view the world in the same fashion, and they frequently make costly demands or claims upon one another. Only when these claims upon others are made through governmental bodies are the interest groups truly *political* interest groups.

Suppose a neighborhood association in a new suburban development asks the developer to reserve four or five lots for a playground. The association is voicing a shared attitude and making a claim upon the developer, hence the neighborhood association is an interest group. The association becomes a political interest group when it asks the local government to adopt statutes that *require* the developer to reserve land for a playground. In this instance, the government does not determine whether a playground will or will not exist. After all, the neighborhood association (or some individual) could purchase the lots and build the playground regardless of the government's decision. The government does determine how the costs of the playground (if there is to be one) are distributed. For instance, the government could mandate that the developer bear the costs of the playground, or suggest that the neighbors pool their resources to fund the playground project.

The government's role in the distribution of the costs of public projects has received wide attention since the pathbreaking work of Ronald Coase.[8] Coase was the first social scientist to study systematically the effects of property rights on social, political, and economic transactions.[9] If property rights are well established and negotiation costs are relatively low, then Coase (and now many others) suggested that the government has only a small role in resolving private disputes. One might think that the developer in the earlier example would have well-established property rights, leaving the neighborhood association little room for political or legal recourse. Suppose, however, the developer's brochures and the community's charters promised a neighborhood "especially designed for young families" with "plenty of fun spaces for kids to play"? In this case, the neighborhood association might have a right to expect a playground. The distribution of the playground's costs then becomes a zero-sum situation, which means that the winners win exactly what the losers lose. Either the developer covers the bill for the park or the neighborhood association does. Any compromise simply redistributes some of the costs from one party to the other.

Such compromises may or may not be fair or reasonable, depending on how one views the property rights involved. When legal, political, or economic rights are not well defined, there is a natural gravitation toward political or legal adjudication. Interest groups become political interest groups because rights are not well established and negotiation costs are high.[10] Political interest groups force the government to take an active role in the balancing of interests and the adjudication of conflicting claims. Because the focus throughout this book is on political affairs, unless otherwise noted the terms *group* and *interest group* will refer to what Truman referred to as a political interest group.

Truman's disturbance theory

The array of interest groups staking their claims and seeking political adjudication is ever changing. Truman recognized that new groups were always emerging and that many groups faded away with time. Truman's disturbance theory tied changes in the group environment to social, economic, technological, or political disturbances. Technological change, for instance, affects the group environment by strengthening some groups and weakening others. Computer technologies affected the unions representing lead typesetters and printers as well as the unions and trade associations in the computer and software industries. Truman argued that any fundamental disturbance that affected the interactions within or between groups led to the demise of some established groups and to the creation of completely new groups. Ultimately, as a society's social and economic interactions became more complex and complicated, its group affiliations became more complex and complicated.

In his *Devotions upon Emergent Occasions*, the seventeenth-century English poet John Donne wrote that "No man is an island entire of itself, every man is . . . a part of the main." Truman argued that this very interconnectedness of human relations is what led to group affiliations. Truman envisioned individuals as inherently human only when they interacted in groups with other individuals. Only social misfits, such as hermits, renegades, and outlaws, would choose to live alone. Group affiliations with others were contextually or sociologically predetermined and led to shared attitudes. Just as individuals generally do not choose their race or gender attributes, they do not choose group affiliation. Individual choice, therefore, was not a concern for Truman. Some group scholars presented this argument in an especially stark fashion, arguing that any truly individual concern or individual activity is "of trifling importance *in interpreting society*."[11] For the pluralists, and in particular for Truman, society was entirely associational. If one wanted to understand society, then he or she needed to study groups and group behaviors rather than individuals' activities.

Mancur Olson and the Formation of Interest Groups

Rather than simply noting the numerous differences in Truman's and Olson's *conclusions* about groups, it is as important to highlight the differences in their views of how to conduct social science. Truman was a behavioralist, and as such, he based his analysis on the direct observation of events and people around him. His analysis was strictly empirical. Olson's analysis was formal theoretic, more deductive than inductive. That is, his work was logically derived from a small set of assumptions. Olson's approach highlighted the logical consistency or inconsistency in one's work.

Individuals and groups

For Olson, there was a fundamental contradiction in Truman's analysis. Recall Truman's second condition for interest groups—claims upon others. Obviously, interest groups are narrowly focused on their own well-being. The sense that "groups act to serve their interests presumably is based upon the assumption that the individuals in groups act out of self-interest. If the individuals in a group altruistically disregarded their personal welfare, it would not be very likely that collectively they would seek some selfish common or group objective."[12] In short, if groups pursue narrow self-interests, then certainly the individual members of the groups must be sensitive to their own narrow self-interests. Therefore, individual concerns and individual choice must be incorporated into the analysis of interest groups. Starting with this simple assumption, Olson proceeded deductively to develop his theory of collective action.

Individuals' benefits from joining

What sort of narrow self-interests might emerge as one considers whether to join a group? Individuals pursuing their narrow self-interests might join a group depending on the sorts of benefits provided by the group: magazines, bumper stickers, t-shirts, lobbying campaigns, public rallies. Olson carefully distinguished between the different kinds of benefits that groups provide in their attempts to induce individuals to join. Group benefits are essentially either private or public goods. Private goods are characterized by two conditions: rivalrous consumption and excludability. Both conditions are straightforward. Rivalrous consumption precludes two or more people from using the good at the same time without there being some diminution in the value of the good. Excludability insures that one can prevent others from using or benefiting from the good. Your breakfast and the shirt on your back are private goods. In contrast, public goods have nonrivalrous consumption and are nonexcludable. Many people can consume the same good without any depreciation in the value of the good because they are nonrivalrous. In addition, no one can be prevented from using or benefiting from the good because they are nonexcludable. There are many public goods all around us. National defense and clean air are public goods. Old-fashioned television broadcasts (as opposed to cable or pay-for-view) are public goods. My television reception is unaffected by millions of other viewers, and once I purchase a television I cannot be prevented from watching network broadcasts. Table 2.1 summarizes the characteristics of private and public goods.

TABLE 2.1
Private and Public Goods

		Rivalrous Consumption	Excludability
Group Benefits	Private Goods	yes	yes
	Public Goods	no	no

Two common misperceptions about public and private goods deserve attention. First, the provider of the good does not determine whether the good is public or private. Certainly, governments do provide public goods, but they also provide many private goods in the form of contracts and entitlements. Consider the bidding process that takes place before any government roads, bridges, or airports can be built. The government's selection of a bid bestows a private good on the chosen construction company, even though the construction project itself may yield a public good. The government *contracts* for roads, bridges, or fighter jets are themselves private goods.[13] In addition, governments are not the only providers of public goods; individuals, private firms, and interest groups also provide public goods. The private homeowner with the spare lot who maintains a small soccer field for neighborhood children provides a public good. The second misperception is that everyone need value a public good. National defense is a public good provided by the national government, but it is not equally valued by all citizens. Some citizens may not value it at all. As noted earlier, television broadcasts are public goods because they are nonexcludable and have nonrivalrous consumption, regardless of how easy it is to find broadcasts that are of absolutely no value.

Groups provide both private and public goods. Private goods may consist of buttons, decals, or bumper stickers. These may seem to be trivial goods, but consider our display of these items. Prominent displays of group-related items indicate our desire to associate with and belong to the group. Buttons, t-shirts, and bumper stickers help to advertise what we believe and to define for others who we are. However important they might be, buttons and bumper stickers are not very expensive. Many groups publish their own magazines. Some of the glossiest nature magazines are affiliated with groups. The *Audubon* and *National Geographic* magazines come immediately to mind. Some of the most widely distributed magazines are affiliated with groups. *Modern Maturity* is produced by the AARP, formerly also known as the American Association of Retired Persons. Many of the most respected academic journals are published by groups. The American Medical Association's (AMA) *JAMA* may be the most widely recognized, but it is hardly alone. Professional associations of economists, political scientists, and sociologists publish the best journals in their fields as well. In exchange for modest dues, one may secure a highly professional publication or a simple newsletter. Discounts on goods and services are frequently secured through group membership. Discounts on insurance are most common. The American Farm Bureau Federation (AFBF) sells insurance to any member, regardless of their farming status. At one time, Cook County, Illinois, had as many as seven thousand AFBF members. Many of these memberships were linked to the discounted insurance rates because the Chicago area provides little opportunity for farming. The National Rifle Association (NRA) provides accidental death insurance and discounts on moving expenses. The array of private goods available through interest groups is astonishing. If one wants to wear the button, read the magazine, or secure the discounts, he or she must join. Olson referred to private goods offered by groups as selective incentives because they are selective, available only to joiners.

What sort of public goods do groups provide? Keeping in mind that one may not value all public goods, groups provide a public good every time they affect public policy. Whether they lobby to pass, defeat, or amend legislation, groups are providing a nonexcludable good with nonrivalrous consumption. For instance, the legislation that leads to cleaner air or water affects everyone, whether they have joined a group pushing for the legislation or not. Interest groups are vulnerable to freeriding because the public goods they provide are vulnerable to freeriding. We can still benefit from the group's provision of the public good whether we contribute or not. Given Olson's assumption about individuals' goal-oriented behavior, one inexorably runs head long into the collective-action problem.

The homeowners' game

Consider again the neighborhood association in the new suburban development seeking an area for a playground. Suppose two private homeowners have agreed to maintain a donated lot as a small playground and ballpark. Of course, such informal agreements are not binding. Each homeowner faces two choices: contribute fully to the maintenance of the park or freeride. Depending on the choices made by the two homeowners, one of four possible outcomes occurs. The homeowners cannot choose outcomes directly. Table 2.2 depicts the choices faced by the homeowners and the four possible outcomes. Suppose the park has a value of P if each contributes fully and one half of P ($P/2$) if one contributes fully and the other freerides. Of course, there are costs to contributing, which can be represented by C. To make things more concrete, let $P = 3$ and $C = 2$.

TABLE 2.2
The Homeowners' Game

H2

		Contribute	Freeride
H1	Contribute	$P - C, P - C$	$P/2 - C, P/2$
	Freeride	$P/2, P/2 - C$	$0, 0$

Note: The payoffs for H1 are on the left, and the payoffs for H2 are on the right.

Consider the perspective of homeowner one, H1. Suppose H1 thinks that the second homeowner, H2, will choose to contribute. H1 must choose either to contribute or freeride. Assuming that H2 will contribute, one can read down the first column and find that H1 could secure a payoff of $P - C$ by contributing and a payoff of $P/2$ by freeriding. Note that $P/2$ is greater than $P - C$, so if the second homeowner is contributing, the first prefers freeriding. Suppose now that the first homeowner presumes the second will freeride. Reading down the second column, one sees that H1 could secure a payoff of $P/2 - C$ by contributing or 0 by freeriding. Once again, H1 prefers freeriding to contributing because $P/2 - C$ is less than 0. Regardless of the choice made by the second homeowner, the first homeowner prefers to freeride. The game is perfectly symmetric, so the same reasoning applies to the second homeowner. She too prefers to freeride regardless of the choice made by the first homeowner. Neither homeowner is opposed to the park, per se. However, for every possible scenario, each homeowner prefers to freeride. For this interaction, freeriding is a dominant strategy.

This sort of interaction between the homeowners is often referred to as a prisoners' dilemma game. The game is very simple, with just a few components. There are only two homeowners, or players, and each player has only two possible choices, or strategies. Even with such a simple structure, much can be learned. Even though individuals share the same interests and value the same goals, they may not choose to join or contribute to the provision of a public good. Interests are not sufficient for group formation because of the freerider problem.

A slightly more advanced game

Much can be gleaned from simple games, like a prisoners' dilemma. However, more complex games often allow for greater subtlety and a richer set of results. In the prisoners' dilemma there are only two players facing two choices. In addition, there is no strategic interdependence between the players because each player has a dominant strategy that she prefers regardless of the choice of the other. In this section, we analyze the interactions between a whole group of individuals facing a collective-action problem. Each individual still faces just two choices: contribute or freeride.

What do we need to know about this group of individuals? Does it matter how large the group is? For this game, the group can be of any arbitrary number. Oftentimes, N is used to represent this arbitrary number. To refer to individual members of the group, we often use the letters i or j. Such labels are simply shorthand for longer names, such as Robert Zimmerman. Each of the N individuals in the group must choose whether to contribute or freeride. To highlight a particular individual's choice or strategy, one might say that individual i chooses a strategy s_i. As before, a contribution is costly. Suppose the costs, c, are greater than zero and less than one and that the benefit, b, from the public good is equal to one.

Public goods are either discrete or continuous, depending on whether they must be provided in an all-or-nothing fashion or bit by bit. In the prisoners' dilemma example, the park could be entirely built yielding a benefit of P, or half built yielding a benefit of $P/2$. If partial victories are possible, as in the playground example, then the related public good is continuous. Cleaner air is a public good that can be provided bit by bit. A bridge over a river is more discrete—it either reaches the other side or it fails. At times the distinctions between discrete and continuous goods are murky. The passage of legislation may be considered discrete because the legislation passes or fails, or it may be considered continuous if the amending process allows for numerous adjustments. For the present game, the good is discrete. Therefore, the group is either successful and the good is provided or the group is unsuccessful and no good is provided. For this example, there are no partial victories. If at least some minimum number of contributions is made, then the group can provide the public good. The actual size of that minimum number, or threshold, is unimportant as long as it is greater than or equal to one. For shorthand, we use ω to represent this threshold.

Table 2.3 illustrates the decisions faced by any player i and the possible outcomes to the game. At the most basic level, one either contributes or freerides. Of course, only those individuals who value the public good would ever consider contributing, but not all who value the good will necessarily contribute. Some may freeride. Whether it is rational for an individual to contribute depends on what actions the *other* individuals are taking. That is, there is strategic interdependence.

TABLE 2.3
N-Person Contribution Game with a Threshold of ω

Let	Player i's strategies	Number of contributions from all players except i		
$b - c > 0$		$< \omega - 1$	$= \omega - 1$	$\geq \omega$
$1 > c > 0$				
	Contribute: $s_i = 1$	$- c$	$b - c$	$b - c$
$b = 1$				
	Freeride: $s_i = 0$	0	0	b

b, benefit derived from the public good

c, cost of contributing to the public good

s_i, strategy for individual i

ω, threshold, or minimum, number of contributions needed for the provision of the public good

One might imagine various outcomes to this game, leaving individuals better or worse off. However, in some outcomes, no individual can alter his or her strategy to make himself or herself any better off. These outcomes are specified as equilibria. If (given the strategies chosen by everyone else) no one has any incentive to change his or her strategy, then the game is in equilibrium.[14] Identification of equilibrium outcomes allows social scientists to make predictions. One should not anticipate an outcome in which one or more individuals have an incentive to change their strategies. For any threshold number of contributions ω, where $\omega \geq 1$, there are two kinds of equilibria of interest.[15] In the first, no one contributes and no public good is provided. The promise of the collective good has not been sufficient to overcome the collective-action problem. This has come to be thought of as the Olsonian equilibrium because of the ubiquity of freeriding. In the second kind of equilibrium, ω individuals contribute and $N - \omega$ individuals freeride. As long as ω is less than N, there are numerous equilibria of this sort. To be exact, there are $\binom{N}{\omega}$ equilibria of this sort, and in each of these equilibria the public good is provided because the threshold number of contributions was made. To calculate $\binom{N}{\omega}$, one simply needs to determine all the ways in which one can select ω people out of a group of N people. Suppose N is 3 and ω is 2, then $\binom{N}{\omega} = 3$. The general formula is $N! / \omega (N - \omega)!$, where $N!$, read as N factorial, is equal to $N \times (N - 1) \times (N - 2) \times (N - 3) \times \ldots \times 1$. Obviously, the Olsonian solution to the collective-action problem is not the unique equilibrium to simple participation games. Olson highlighted one equilibrium to a situation that contains many. Given Olson's focus on the vulnerability of public goods to freeriding, it was only natural for him to investigate the various means by which group leaders might try to obviate the collective-action problem through the sale of selective incentives or with other ploys.

The by-product theory and Olson's solutions to the collective-action problem

Selective incentives, as private goods, are invulnerable to freeriding; whereas a group's public goods are vulnerable to freeriding. Therefore, Olson concludes that a group's public goods can be provided as *by-products* of the sale of their selective incentives. The selective incentive provides the inducement to join and the revenue to supply the public good. Although the selective incentive provides the inducement to join, one should not think that individuals necessarily value the selective incentive more highly than the public good. The relative values of the public and private goods are irrelevant to the issue of freeriding. Certainly, group members are apt to say that goals such as world peace, a clean environment, or a stable economic market are more important than bumper stickers and buttons. However, freeriders are apt to make the same assessment: world peace *is* more important than a bumper sticker. As it happens, the provision of world peace is vulnerable to freeriding and the bumper sticker is not.

For some critics, Olson's by-product theory seemed to belittle the grand concerns of groups and group members. Didn't the existence of collective efforts indicate that people were inherently altruistic and community oriented? Did selective incentives provide the only solution to the collective-action problem? Olson also wrote of the effects of group size, the presence of high demanders, and coercion on the collective-action problem. Olson argued that the collective-action problem would be most onerous for large rather than small groups. For instance, automobile manufacturers avoided the collective-action problem because they were so few in number. They could readily coordinate their actions, and they could see the impact of their efforts because the benefits of their efforts were concentrated. In contrast, automobile consumers faced much greater obstacles in their collective efforts. Whenever collective benefits are concentrated, collective efforts are easier; and whenever benefits are widely disbursed, collective efforts are harder.[16]

There are high and low demanders for private and public goods. High demanders simply put a higher monetary value on the good in question than low demanders. For private goods, high demanders simply spend more than low demanders. Clothes horses buy more clothes and spend more money than their beatnik throwbacks. If there is a smooth functioning marketplace, the supply of clothes will accommodate the aggregate demands of the high and low demanders. For public goods, the relationship between high and low demanders is very different. A high demander may value the public good so much that he or she does not mind footing the entire bill or a very large portion of it. If a high demander provides a public good, the low demanders can freeride. That is, there is little or no collective effort. One individual provides the public good, while everyone else freerides. Olson connected the presence of high demanders for public goods to small groups with concentrated benefits. Large groups, Olson argued, were most likely to have low demanders who would only be willing to contribute small amounts to the provision of some public good. Contrast the automobile consumers and manufacturers. If the manufacturers lobby for particular safety regulation standards, millions of dollars are at stake for a small number of producers. Suppose consumers want safer cars. Although there are millions of consumers each of whom might value safer cars, the benefits are widely disbursed rather than concentrated.

To this point, the selective incentives discussed have all been positive, but Olson argued that selective incentives could be either positive or negative. Coercion or social pressure, Olson argued, greatly affected individuals' decisions about joining. Social pressure can be intense. Consider, for example, the college student who returns home for a break, bringing with him college awards and good will but little money. Suppose this student has so much good will that he volunteers to take Grandmother to her weekend church service. Grandmother beams, and everything is fine until a collection plate is passed. For the student not to contribute at this point is to risk losing his spot in Grandmother's heart, but a quick glance into his wallet indicates that there is only a single $10 bill. Knowing that it is best not to make change from within the collection plate, our poor student must decide whether to contribute $10 and return to school absolutely broke or to contribute nothing. It is difficult not to contribute to a collective effort when everyone, including Grandmother, is watching. Anxiety in such situations is due to social pressure.

Lighthearted examples of coercion are more difficult to find. Often labor and trade groups as well as professional societies seek legal sanctions to make membership all but mandatory. Unions seek closed shops, wherein union support is compulsory for all workers. The argument for a closed shop is straightforward: if unions fight for safer work conditions and a higher wage, then all workers benefit whether they are union members or not. The goods provided are public goods and thereby nonexcludable. Because all benefit, all should be forced to support the collective efforts. Debates about the rectitude of open and closed shops are beyond the scope of this book, but such debates are enhanced by Olson's discussions of freeriding and collective efforts. Professional societies have secured considerable influence over accreditation processes and licensing procedures, making membership all but necessary for one's professional standing. Most states require practicing lawyers to be members of the state's bar association.[17]

Neither social pressure nor coercion would be necessary if individuals naturally gravitated toward groups. Coercion plays little role in Truman's analysis because, according to him, group affiliation requires no prompting. For Truman, shared attitudes and claims upon others are necessary and sufficient for an interest group's existence. However, for Olson shared interests are certainly not sufficient for group formation because of the collective-action problem. Depending on the value of the selective incentives, shared interests about the public good may not even be necessary. If individuals join the National Geographic Society because of the magazine or the American Farm Bureau Federation because of the low insurance rates, then there may not be shared attitudes about the public goods involved. The selective incentives may be more important than the public good. Many late-rising commuters who are prone to speeding claim that joining the State Highway Patrol Association for the small bumper sticker is well worth the price. The phenomenal growth in the AARP from under one million in 1965 to over ten million by 1980 and over thirty-three million today is often tied to the group's impressive array of selective incentives.[18] Any copy of the AARP's *Modern Maturity* is filled with information about special medical insurance policies, Medicaid and Medicare, tours and vacations designed for the elderly, mutual funds, IRAs and tax advice, and discounts for all sorts of goods and services. Other groups now offer their members mutual funds with various screens to select investments. The Humane Society teamed with Smith Barney to offer a mutual fund that avoided investments in meatpackers and companies working with animal by-products, and the Sierra Club has considered developing its own mutual fund.[19]

Truman and Olson found considerable worth in each other's work, but genuine disagreements persisted. In particular, Olson insisted that if groups are self-interested, then certainly the individual members in them must be as well. Truman might counter that groups structure our interests, making it difficult for selfish individual interests to take root. After all, humans long for group affiliation, and one of the costs of affiliation is conformity to the group.[20] The word *conformity* suggests that the groups structure our interests. Does the individual precede or supersede the group or does the group dominate the individual? Truman asserts that studying individuals in isolation is meaningless. "The human being upon whom we fasten as individual *par excellence* is moved and regulated by his association with others; what he does and what the consequences of his behavior are, what his experience consists of, cannot even be described, much less accounted for, in isolation."[21] What, however, is the relation of the isolated individual to formal theory or game theory?

The focus of formal theory is certainly on individuals and individuals' choices, but there is an explicit analysis of the strategic interactions between individuals. In a game theoretic setting, two or more individuals' decisions are studied and the interactive effects of their choices analyzed. Game theory highlights individuals' choices, but it does not disassociate individuals from one another. Whether or not someone should contribute in the game presented in Table 2.3 depends on what the other players have done. If no one else has contributed, then contribution is not warranted; but if $\omega - 1$ individuals have contributed, then making a contribution is a rational choice.[22]

Evidence and Empirical Concerns

On empirical grounds, the evidence for Truman's and Olson's work appears mixed, working well in some venues but not in others.

The demise of groups

Truman's emphasis on the link between complexity and technological advancement and group proliferation seemed appropriate for some professional societies. For instance, Oliver Garceau's study of the medical community ties the proliferation of smaller and smaller groups of specialists to the advancement of medical technology.[23] As family doctors became less common, the AMA simply could not represent the particular concerns of an increasingly broad array of specialists. The AMA remains as an umbrella organization, but numerous smaller medical associations represent the more specialized medical fields. Truman and Garceau provide a rationale for the emergence of new groups, but they do not specify how the groups actually get started. Critics of Truman remained concerned with how one goes from shared interests, technological changes, and disturbances to the nuts and bolts of group formation. These critics argued that too often widely shared interests were not adequately represented by an established group.

Many scholars admired the straightforward logic inherent in Olson's work but remained unconvinced by the overall modeling endeavor. Ironically, Olson first published his work during the mid-1960s, a period of steady interest group growth. More and more groups were being founded, so the logic seemed to fail on empirical grounds. The general consensus among scholars is that there were more groups and an increase in group activities in the 1960s and 1970s.[24] There has, however, always been both growth and decay in the interest group environment, though data on a group's founding are much easier to find than data on a group's demise.[25] Looking at the 1990s, some scholars suggest that the growth in Washington-based group activities is moderating.[26]

Though not conceding to Olson's reasoning, Truman acknowledged that the inability of groups to attain their full membership potential might be explained by Olson's work on freeriding. For instance, public opinion polls suggest that the vast majority of U.S. citizens consider themselves environmentally friendly, but few environmental interest groups have more than 500,000 members. The Sierra Club has about 500,000 members; Greenpeace, USA has about 500,000 members; Audubon has just over 500,000 members; and The Nature Conservancy has just under one million members. The National Wildlife Federation stands alone with almost 4.5 million members. The sheer volume of freeriding suggests that groups fail miserably at attempts to reach their natural clientele. Given that Olson argued that large groups typically overcome collective-action problems with selective incentives, subsequent studies explored the sources of groups' funds and individuals' incentives for joining collective efforts. These studies did not always lend much support to the Olsonian view of the centrality of selective incentives for overcoming the collective-action problem. For instance, many groups distribute selective incentives, but the late University of Michigan political scientist Jack Walker found that many groups' financial footings depended very little on the sale of selective incentives.[27] Groups may use selective incentives, but their impact on group budgets is often minimal.

In sum, Truman failed to recognize the difficulties associated with group formation. Quite simply, group formation requires more than Truman's emphasis on shared attitudes suggests. Olson's formal theoretic modeling characterized the collective-action problem quite nicely. Of course, the collective-action problem is surmountable in various ways, but Olson's emphasis on the dominant role of selective incentives met with mixed success. The collective-action problem is an onerous one that few groups attack with a single weapon. Selective incentives provide just one of many possible sources of revenue.

Groups' revenue sources

Jack Walker's survey of more than five hundred voluntary associations reveals important insights into groups' sources of revenue. Walker uses the term voluntary association to emphasize that his survey did not include corporations or trade unions. Eighty percent of the sampled groups required members to come from a certain profession or industry. These occupationally based groups were further broken down depending on whether their members came from the public or private sectors. Members of the National Tank Truck Conference, the National Soybean Producers Association, and the Motorcycle Industry Council all came from the private sector. The members of the National Association of Counties and the National Association of Student Financial Aid Administrators came from the public sector. Groups with members from the private and public sectors included The Society of American Foresters and the American Planning Association. Among the occupationally based groups, there were groups with members from the private sector, the public sector, or both the private and public sectors.

Only twenty percent of the groups were not occupationally based, and had no qualification for membership. These groups are generally thought of as public interest groups or citizens groups. Examples range from groups promoting civil liberties, environmental causes, or good government, such as the American Civil Liberties Union, the National Wildlife Federation, or Common Cause. The members of these groups have no natural occupational base. Walker found that few citizen groups offered typical selective incentives. Within this category, the AARP was the clear anomaly, offering a wide array of selective incentives. On average, only fifteen percent of the citizens-based groups offered insurance and only thirty percent offered group trips. In short, citizen groups raised very little money from the sale of selective incentives, and generally less than one half of all group revenues were generated from dues or other special membership fees. However, eighty-nine percent of the citizen groups noted that they received aid from sources outside of the group. In other words, only eleven percent of the citizens groups relied solely on their members for revenue. Groups received support from foundations, government agencies, and other groups.

Table 2.4 illustrates how varied groups' sources of revenue are. Annual dues are most important for groups with members from the private sector, and least important for citizens groups. As Table 2.4 indicates, support from beyond the group's members is most important for citizens groups. Over forty percent of citizens' groups' revenue comes from outside of the direct membership. In Olson's terms, these outside supporters of groups are similar to high demanders who benefit from the broadened support for various policy agendas. Unlike Olson's high demanders, patrons from outside the groups never become intimately involved in the group's affairs.

TABLE 2.4
Average Percentage of Group Revenue
Obtained from Various Sources

	Occupationally Based Groups with Members from the			Citizen-based Groups
	Profit Sector (%)	Profit and Nonprofit Sectors (%)	Nonprofit Sector (%)	
Routine contributions from members or associates	89.2	73.8	63.3	47.4
Nonmember sources (Total)	2.9	18.6	24.2	42.9
Individual gifts	1	3.8	3.5	17.2
Foundations	0.2	3.2	4.2	12.8
Government	1.2	9.3	14.6	8.9
Other associations	0.5	2.3	1.9	4

Note: Member and nonmember contributions do not add up to 100 percent. Miscellaneous income provides the balance.

Walker notes that the for-profit groups in his sample often had a small group of contributors providing the bulk of the operating finances. Although he does not possess systematic data on this issue, Walker suggests that dues burdens were seldom shared equally among members. Walker notes that for some years, the bulk of the National Association of Manufacturers' revenues has come from a small handful of firms. It might seem odd that only a small group of firms provide so much of the revenue for one of the largest representatives of manufacturers. In this instance, the large contributors are high demanders in the precise sense that Olson used the term. Kay Lehman Schlozman and John Tierney record another interesting aspect of corporate memberships in trade associations: the largest corporations are members of dozens of trade associations. For instance, General Electric, one of the largest corporations in the United States, is a member of over eighty trade associations, in industries as diverse as mining, aerospace, and home appliances.[28] In later chapters, the ability of corporations to lobby through numerous distinct channels is explored in much greater length. However, it should be clear that in any one of these trade associations, General Electric has the ability to become a dominant high demander.

Government support for groups

The presence of government agencies as supporters of, indeed high demanders for, various groups deserves further explanation. Governments have frequently urged groups to facilitate the coordination and communication of constituents' interests. Governments were especially active in this regard during the progressive era in the early part of the twentieth century. Professional associations and groups of civic-minded individuals were considered an important counterbalance to the parties' spoils system, which had wreaked havoc on any notion of public officials as policy experts. During the height of the spoils system in the late 1800s and early 1900s, expressions of political loyalty were more important for government bureaucrats than displaying any sort of overall competence. The lack of any accepted standards of training or competence for professionals further heightened these problems. For instance, in the absence of standards in legal training, the difference between filling a judgeship with a lawyer or a nonlawyer was seldom clear. Parties were adept at preserving partisan loyalties, whereas professional associations and new public interest groups focused on establishing clear standards to distinguish their own expertise from the ineptness of novices and hacks. Government recognition of specialized licensing boards helped to clarify standards and legitimized professional associations of doctors, lawyers, engineers, and others. "The greatest single spurt in the creation of new licensing boards . . . came between 1911 and 1915."[29] The impact on professional associations was often profound. Over the period from 1900 to 1910, the AMA went from a regionally oriented association of only eight thousand members to a national association of seventy thousand.[30] Writing during this general time, two distinguished political scientists, Mary Follett and E. Pendleton Herring, linked the emergence of groups with the advent of governmental expertise and the professional administration of public policy.[31]

Sometimes government officials simply like to mobilize their supporters. The 1914 Smith-Lever Act mandated that the state and federal governments would share the costs of the development of the county agent system. County agents, which are still in existence today, provided advice to farmers about the latest technological advances in agriculture. Many states required those counties wanting an agent to establish a local farm bureau. These farm bureaus operated as private interest groups. States wanted to facilitate the communication of information from agricultural schools to farmers, and many state governments felt that an effective farm organization would best accomplish that task. The emergence of today's American Farm Bureau

Federation is, therefore, directly tied to the Smith-Lever Act and the actions of state governments.

Government officials have also influenced the organization of business and labor interests. The government's Army Corps of Engineers organized the Rivers and Harbors Congress, which represents large construction contractors and barge companies. The Chamber of Commerce was created largely at the behest of Charles Nagel, secretary of commerce and labor under President William Howard Taft, who wanted to be able to speak to the entire business community about various policy concerns. The Wagner Act of 1935 facilitated the growth of the labor movement by formalizing unions' roles in collective bargaining and by allowing for closed shops.

Finally, all levels of government have used groups in the delivery of goods and services. Unlike the federal or state governments, local groups have an established infrastructure and established contacts to reach target populations. Governments are most apt to establish formal contracts with groups that are active in the area of social services. Indeed, the federal government is increasingly contracting with groups for the delivery of social services.[32] Throughout the 1960s, numerous pieces of federal legislation coordinated public and private organizations in the distribution of governmental goods and services. Grants in aid programs and citizen participation requirements were elements of virtually every piece of President Lyndon Johnson's War on Poverty. For many government officials of that era, increased participation at the local level enhanced democracy and improved public policy. For such individuals, increased pluralism became a prescription for societal ills, and federal legislation that mandated "maximum feasible participation" at the local level were generally lauded.[33]

New Insights

The empirical implications of the collective-action problem can be directly and indirectly tested in various ways. Direct, empirically based tests are often considered essential for the advancement of scientific knowledge. Direct tests, however, remain a luxury not always afforded social scientists (or astrophysicists or paleontologists). Often one must resort to indirect tests. A series of direct and indirect tests may yield greater and greater or less and less faith in an underlying model. In addition to empirical tests of formal models, sometimes one comes to favor a particular model because of the new insights it yields about broader issues. That is, one may be able to push the model even further and follow the argument wherever it leads. In this section, I argue that the collective-action problem for groups allows one to think more broadly about interest group competition and the unequal mobilization of interests.

Interest group competition

The traditional notion of interest group competition suggests that opposing interests are the competing interests. Labor interests oppose business interests and environmental interests oppose various commercial and agriculture interests. Pluralists typically consider the existence of opposing interests as essential to the overall balance in public policy. Certainly this sort of competition is important for interest groups, but the collective-action problem suggests that there might be another equally important element of group competition. Simply put, groups must compete for members, and when groups compete for members they compete with (ostensibly) like-minded groups rather than opposition groups. If one follows the argument inherent in Olson's work, interest group competition looks quite varied. Does competition among like-minded groups overwhelm the traditional sort of interest group competition envisioned by pluralists? Probably not, but instances of this sort of competition are easy to find. As a prominent board member of the Sierra Club, David Brower held considerable sway over a large portion of Sierra Club members. Brower's break with the Sierra Club to form the Friends of the Earth led to a direct competition for membership. Other examples will be highlighted in Chapter 4. In short, opposing interests may compete over policy goals, but like-minded groups compete for members. There are, for instance, many environmental groups, and few environmentalists are in a position to join them all.[34]

Of course, group scholars have long known the importance of farming the membership, continually nurturing the member–group relations. Given the difficulties associated with securing new members, retaining the existing members becomes particularly important. Lawrence Rothenberg's work on the retention decision of Common Cause members provides the most careful analysis of this issue.[35] Rothenberg argues that potential members have unclear impressions of the benefits provided by a group. However, most groups keep dues very low, making it possible for individuals to try out one group or another. After one joins a group, he or she learns more about the group's public goals and its more narrowly focused private benefits. Individuals engage in experiential search, joining various groups but retaining their memberships only in those groups that suit their needs particularly well. Rothenberg found that retention among Common Cause members was greatest among long-term members. Those individuals who were members for only a year or two were much more likely to drop out than longer-term members. The collective-action problem is ongoing because there are always some individuals leaving groups. Retention remains a concern because it is very difficult for groups to reach their natural clientele, and no group wants to start from scratch, year after year facing the same massive collective-action problem. Continuing members provide a buffer against a full-scale collective-action problem.

Differential impact of the collective-action problem

Scott Gartner and Gary Segura's formal theoretic model of interest mobilization addresses the differential impact of the collective-action problem.[36] The differential impact of the collective-action problem is a direct implication of Gartner and Segura's decision to separate the decision to identify with a group from the decision to join the group. Truman's notion of individuals' natural group affiliation is ignored by Gartner and Segura. Indeed, Gartner and Segura turn Truman's analysis on its head. Rather than positing that individuals have natural group affiliations, Gartner and Segura "begin with the simple observation that before people can organize . . . on behalf of a group, they must, at the very least, recognize themselves as being part of a group or sub-population that shares a set of interests."[37] The presence of a collective-action problem implicitly suggests that individuals recognize some common interests. Gartner and Segura admit that this contention would be "ludicrous" if group affiliations were "apparent, enduring, and immutable."[38] More importantly, they argue that individuals may choose to hide group affiliations because of societal oppression.

Gartner and Segura are particularly concerned with the mobilization of oppressed minority groups. Choosing to identify with an unpopular group in society often comes at considerable cost. When identification with a group creates a risk of personal harm, it seems reasonable to think of such groups as oppressed. Gartner and Segura refer to American communists during the McCarthy era, European Jews during World War II, black Americans, and homosexuals as oppressed groups. Unfortunately, no region of the world is without its story of the oppression of one group or another. How does such oppression affect the collective-action problem? The immediate reaction is to assume that oppression limits collective efforts because it makes such efforts more costly. Sensitive to such costs, individuals would be less apt to identify with oppressed groups and less apt to join such groups. This conclusion, however, requires a few crucial caveats. What Gartner and Segura cleverly note is that some individuals may be oppressed whether or not they formally identify with a group. That is, there is a chance of oppression whether one chooses to mobilize or not. Identification may be a choice for a communist or a homosexual because they are generally "invisible," but it is less of an individual choice for blacks or Hasidic Jews, who are more visible—literally. The novelist Ralph Ellison's commentary on the plight of blacks in America portrayed blacks as invisible in a figurative sense.[39] Blacks, for instance, were seldom acknowledged in simple day-to-day social interactions. After years of being ignored, one begins to feel invisible and disconnected to the rest of society. Clearly, Ellison and other writers following his lead used invisibility in a different sense than Gartner and Segura. Gartner and Segura write that "being able to observe that someone is black or gay is not the same; the homosexual has made a choice [to be visible] . . . while the African-American makes no such choice."[40]

Several implications of Gartner and Segura's work deserve attention. Readily visible minority group members may suffer from intolerant majorities. Clearly, the decisions about group identification and group mobilization are partly a function of one's degree of visibility and the likelihood of oppression. Therefore, the marginal cost of mobilizing if one is readily visible is lower than if one is invisible, which means that efforts to uncover members of unpopular, invisible groups may lead to greater mobilization rather than less. Ultimately, the question of whether to join is affected by whether one bears the costs of identification regardless of joining and how group membership affects the costs of majority oppression. Observed mobilization rates are not necessarily good indicators of a group's success at solving the collective-action problem. The mobilization rates for visible groups can be determined because the relevant pool of potential group members is also visible. For invisible groups, mobilization rates are more difficult to determine because one cannot determine the relevant pool of invisible potential members. Finally, Gartner and Segura argued that nonmember support for oppressed groups is much more likely for visible groups than for invisible groups. Nonmembers who support visible groups will not be mistaken or misidentified as members. Early white supporters of the NAACP did not have to worry about oppression in their day-to-day lives. Nonmembers are less likely to support invisible groups because misidentification remains a problem. That is, if one supports communists' rights to be politically active, then one may very well be mistaken for one. Indeed, during the McCarthy era, communists and communist sympathizers were treated as one and the same. More recently, at the start of the AIDS epidemic, Americans attached a tremendous stigma to anyone with AIDS. No matter how sympathetic individuals might have been toward those with the disease, social pressure may have prevented many from identifying with groups working on behalf of AIDS patients.

Conclusion

Given the existence of so many groups, is the collective-action problem truly that onerous? One's answer depends on two related concerns. First, does one wish to highlight the joiners of groups or the freeriders? If one focuses on joiners, then obviously freeriding is not an insurmountable problem. Few groups, however, mobilize more than five to ten percent of their natural clientele.[41] If one focuses on the freeriders, then groups appear much less successful in their struggles to resolve the collective-action problem. To answer that patrons and high demanders pick up the slack is to suggest that the best way to solve a collective-action problem is through *individual* rather than collective efforts.

The second concern is related to the first. Certainly there are many groups that have resolved the collective-action problem, but are all interests equally well mobilized? Truman acknowledged that some interests might not be represented by groups. Indeed, he suggested that potential groups were quite common, but that they existed in a *"state of readiness,"* and that other groups operated "as if such potential groups were organized and active."[42] Furthermore, unorganized interests were not necessarily unrepresented interests because the existing groups had to work within established rules of the game; if they violated key rules, potential groups would emerge to reestablish order.[43] Most scholars writing about unmobilized interests are much less sanguine than Truman. E. E. Schattschneider is probably best remembered for having argued that politics was about the mobilization of bias and that the group environment possessed a distinctively upper-class tinge.[44] Unmobilized interests were indeed unrepresented interests. Jack Walker's data on the role of wealthy patrons supports his concerns about elitist tendencies in both the public and private sectors.[45] What, however, is the cause of the unequal mobilization of interests? Perhaps some interests are never promoted because of elitism, which is to say because of biased political structures. Another reason may be the collective-action problem, which is tied to the inherent nature of human interactions. Schattschneider and Walker, along with Olson and Gartner and Segura, expressed concern about the unequal mobilization of interests. Although there are clear differences in the arguments of Schattschneider and Walker, they each raise concerns about elitism and tie the persistence of elitism to various political institutions. One could, therefore, resolve the unequal mobilization of interests by reforming political institutions. In contrast, for Olson and Gartner and Segura the unequal mobilization of interests remains because it is tied to human nature. As long as individuals are goal oriented, the collective-action problem does not go away. It may be obviated, but it cannot be eliminated. Put slightly differently, reforming political institutions may reduce the unequal mobilization of interests, but no reforms can totally eliminate the unequal mobilization of interests.

Olson and Walker offered various solutions to the collective-action problem faced by groups. Selective incentives, social pressure, and wealthy patrons may all come into play, but important questions remain unanswered: who puts together the package of group benefits for members and who solicits the contributions from the wealthy patrons? The focus of the next chapter is on interest group entrepreneurs. Perhaps some individuals naturally coalesce and spontaneously or unconsciously solve the collective-action problem. More often than not, interest group entrepreneurs, such as Colin Powell, play a key role in the resolution of collective-action problems. Interest group entrepreneurs perform three functions: They exchange a set of goods for group membership; they provide information that solves what formal theorists have called a coordination problem; and, finally, some interest group entrepreneurs have been able to act as both agents and ombudsmen for group members and government officials. Each of these functions affects the abilities of the group to resolve the collective-action problem and maintain a healthy membership base. The discussion of entrepreneurship in the next chapter leads naturally to an extended analysis of internal group organization and decision making in Chapter 4.

NOTES

1. All details on America's Promise are drawn from Mark Stricherz's article entitled "Any Volunteers" (*The New Republic*, January 5 & 12, 1998), 12–13, and Reed Abelson's "Charity Led by Gen. Powell Comes Under Heavy Fire" (*New York Times*, October 8, 1999), A-12.
2. Truman's *The Governmental Process*, first published in the early 1950s, relied heavily on work by Arthur Bentley and provided an eloquent explanation and extension of Bentley's *The Process of Government*. We know as much as we do about the work of Bentley largely because of Truman's (re)discovery of his work. Truman's title was itself a graceful acknowledgment of Bentley's influence. Arthur Bentley, *The Process of Government*, ed. Peter Odegard (Cambridge: Harvard University Press, 1967, originally published 1908).
3. Mancur Olson, *The Logic of Collective Action* (Cambridge: Harvard University Press, 1965).
4. See, for instance, Schattschneider (1960) and Walker (1966).
5. Even Truman acknowledged that Olson's work provided a theoretical foundation for certain tendencies "noted largely in empirical terms." Truman (1971), xxix.
6. Truman (1971), 15.
7. Bentley (1967), 211.
8. Ronald H. Coase, "The Problem of Social Cost," *Journal of Law and Economics* 3 (1960): 1–44.
9. Volumes of work have addressed these issues. Other excellent readings on this subject include Thrainn Eggertsson's *Economic Behavior and Institutions* (Cambridge: Cambridge University Press, 1990); Richard A. Posner's *Economic Analysis and the Law*, 2nd ed. (Boston: Little Brown, 1977); and Itai Sened's *The Political Institution of Private Property* (Cambridge: Cambridge University Press, 1997).
10. It is important to note that Truman also writes of the "inevitable" gravitation of groups toward government. Truman argues that groups seek to supplement their power and resources with the support of larger, more encompassing institutions. Governments are the quintessential "encompassing institution." See Truman (1971), 104–06.
11. Bentley (1967), 215, emphasis added.
12. Olson (1965), 1.
13. For excellent analysis of the types of goods provided by governments and of the role of groups in the demand for publicly provided goods, see Kenneth Godwin, Nancy Kucinski, and John Green, "The Market for Publicly Supplied Goods," a paper presented at the Southern Political Science Association Meeting, Savannah, GA (1993).
14. This type of equilibrium is often called a *Nash equilibrium*, in honor of John F. Nash, a Nobel laureate in economics, whose pioneering work in this area yielded some of the most fundamental results in game theory. Nash's personal life and his long battle with schizophrenia provided the storyline for the Academy Award–winning film, *A Beautiful Mind*.
15. In addition to pure strategy equilibria, there are also mixed strategy equilibria in which individuals place some probability on contributing and then essentially

flip an appropriately weighted coin. More information on these games is available in Thomas R. Palfrey and Howard Rosenthal's "Private Incentives in Social Dilemmas," *Journal of Public Economics* 35 (1988): 309–32; Scott Ainsworth and Itai Sened's "Interest Group Entrepreneurs: Entrepreneurs with Two Audiences," *American Journal of Political Science* 37 (1993): 834–66; and the following chapter.

16. This argument is most fully developed by James Q. Wilson in *Political Organizations* (New York: Basic Books, 1973).

17. Associations themselves used to restrict accreditation or certification to members, but as Jack Walker notes: "a decision by the Supreme Court in 1978 [largely] prevented the practice." Jack L. Walker Jr., "The Origins and Maintenance of Interest Groups in America," *American Political Science Review* 77 (1983): 397. Walker refers to Supreme Court decision *National Society of Professional Engineers v. United States,* 435 U.S. 679 (1978).

18. See, for example, Walker's (1983) discussion on p. 396.

19. John H. Cushman Jr., "Sierra Club Considers a Mutual Fund to Lure Investors" (*New York Times,* Friday, July 20, 2001), A-17.

20. Truman (1971), 19.

21. John Dewey as cited by Truman (1971), 17.

22. The game theoretic presentation in Table 2.3 is not drawn from Olson's work. For Olson, whether it was reasonable to study individuals in isolation depended on the size of the group involved. In large groups, no individual's impact on the group is likely to be noticed. Olson's analysis was similar to the sort of reasoning used in standard microeconomics. In a competitive marketplace no one individual's supply or demand affects the market equilibrium price. Individuals in such settings could be studied in isolation. In small groups with a high demander, individuals' behaviors do affect one another. The high demander's contribution allows the low or moderate demanders to freeride. There are clear interactions between individuals. In intermediate sized groups, the interactions between individuals are most explicit. In intermediate sized groups, there is no single high demander, but instead there is a small group of moderate demanders. If any member leaves the group, the effect is immediate and noticed by all.

23. Oliver Garceau, *The Political Life of the American Medical Association* (Hamden, CT: Archon Books, 1961).

24. Work by Frank Baumgartner and Jack Walker found that individuals' group-related activities most likely did increase since the 1950s. See: "Survey Research and Membership in Voluntary Organizations," *American Journal of Political Science* 32 (1988): 908–28.

25. Anthony Nownes is one of the few scholars directly addressing the death of groups. See his paper entitled "Toward a Theory of Public Interest Group Collapse and Death," presented at the Midwest Political Science Association meeting in Chicago, April 27–30, 2000.

26. Berry (1997), 24.

27. Walker (1983).

28. Kay Lehman Schlozman and John T. Tierney, *Organized Interests and American Democracy* (New York: Harper & Row, 1986), 72–73.

29. Corinne Lathrop Gibb, *Hidden Hierarchies: The Professionals and the Government* (New York: Harper & Row, 1966), 42, is quoted from Jack H. Knott and Gary J. Miller's *Reforming Bureaucracy: The Politics of Institutional Choice* (Englewood Cliffs, NJ: Prentice Hall, 1987), 63. Also see James A. Monroe's *The Democratic Wish: Popular Participation and the Limits of American Government* (New York: Basic Books, 1990).

30. Knott and Miller (1987), 63.

31. Mary P. Follett, *The New State* (Gloucester, MA: Peter Smith, 1918), and E. Pendleton Herring, *Group Representation before Congress* (Baltimore: Johns Hopkins University Press, 1929).

32. Definitive work in this area is by Steven Rathgeb Smith and Michael Lipsky, *Nonprofits for Hire: The Welfare State in the Age of Contracting* (Cambridge: Harvard University Press, 1993).

33. In addition to Smith and Lipsky's work, there are a number of other excellent works in this area, including: Jeffrey M. Berry, *Feeding Hungry People* (New Brunswick, NJ: Rutgers University Press, 1984); Jeffrey M. Berry, Kent E. Portney, and Ken Thomson, *The Rebirth of Urban Democracy* (Washington, D.C.: The Brookings Institution, 1993); Frances Fox Piven and Richard A. Cloward, *Poor People's Movements* (New York: Pantheon, 1977); Jeffrey M. Berry, *Lobbying for the People* (Princeton, NJ: Princeton University Press, 1977); Saul Alinsky, *Rule for Radicals* (New York: Random House, 1971); John H. Mollenkopf, *The Contested City* (Princeton, NJ: Princeton University Press, 1983); David Street, George T. Martin Jr., and Laura Kramer Gordon, *The Welfare Industry* (Beverly Hills: Sage Publications, 1979); Tom Wolfe, *Radical Chic and Mau Mauing the Flak Catchers* (New York: Farrar, Straus, and Giroux, 1970).

34. Ronald G. Shaiko's *Voices and Echoes for the Environment* (New York: Columbia University Press, 1999) highlights this aspect of group competition for environmental groups.

35. Lawrence S. Rothenberg, "Organizational Maintenance and the Retention Decision in Groups," *American Political Science Review* 82 (1988): 1129–52.

36. Scott Sigmund Gartner and Gary M. Segura, "Appearances Can be Deceiving: Self Selection, Social Group Identification, and Political Mobilization," *Rationality and Society* 9 (1997): 131–61.

37. Gartner and Segura (1997), 132.

38. Gartner and Segura (1997), 133.

39. Ralph Ellison, *Invisible Man* (New York: Modern Library, 1992).

40. Gartner and Segura (1997), 133.

41. Most scholars adopt a five percent rule.

42. Truman (1971), 35, 52.

43. See, for instance, Truman (1971), 159.

44. Schattschneider (1960).

45. Walker's concern for elitism is clearest in his 1966 article.

~3~

Interest Group Entrepreneurs

Introduction

During the late 1990s, Greenpeace, one of the most active environmental groups in the nation and the world, lost more U.S. members than many environmental groups ever dreamed of attracting. While it was losing about 800,000 members and securing only fifty percent of its projected U.S. donations, the Sierra Club and the Wilderness Society were holding steady at about 600,000 and 250,000 members.[1] One might argue that the "whales are pretty well saved . . . [and that] the Clinton White House [was] . . . generally friendly to the environment."[2] Perhaps Greenpeace had simply lost its mission. But this argument fails to explain why other groups maintained their memberships during the environmentally friendly Clinton years. Others have argued that Greenpeace was simply unable to handle their explosion in membership when French military frogmen sank the group's flagship Rainbow Warrior in 1985. Indeed, the group roughly doubled in size in the 1980s.[3] This argument implies that Greenpeace's woes are due to the internal incompetence of its own group entrepreneurs. Staff members have been particularly hard hit by the recent woes. "After forty-eight hours of daredevil dangling on ropes from a bridge in Seattle, trying to block outgoing trawlers in a . . . protest against overfishing, Greenpeace staff members returned to solid ground, only to be told that the environmental group had just laid three of them off." Those three members were not alone. Greenpeace cut more than three hundred of its four-hundred-person staff. One former staffer said, "'It's like if you take a bunch of priests and tell them they're laid off because of cutbacks.'"[4] The romance of group activity does not maintain a bottom line.

Interests are the fundamental building blocks of an interest group society, but interests alone do not create an interest group society such as the one we see in the United States. How are the interests of many individuals organized into a common voice and maintained as a viable interest group? How do people learn to solve collective-action problems? Surely, this is a fundamental issue for social and political entities. What roles do interest group entrepreneurs undertake? What differentiates the entrepreneur from the average member? Group entrepreneurs might be colorful leaders, but they are first and foremost risktakers who endeavor to overcome the collective-action problem to create organized groups. If one detects any differences in the influence of organized versus unorganized groups, then the potential for group entrepreneurs to have an independent effect on the group environment is enormous. If organization is not a natural or easy process, then group entrepreneurship merits careful investigation.

Some individuals fail to recognize or appreciate the importance of entrepreneurship and organization, simply arguing that wealthier interests are stronger than poorer interests. As the sociologist Doug McAdam succinctly stated, "resources do not dictate their use, people do."[5] Whether some interests are wealthier than others misses the point—the question is how do people employ the resources they have available to them? In his book, *The Group Basis of Politics*, Earl Latham argued that

> there is an observable balance of influence in favor of organized groups in their dealings with the unorganized, and in favor of the best and most efficiently organized in their dealings with the less efficiently organized . . . organization represents concentrated power, and concentrated power can exercise a predominating influence when it encounters power which is diffuse and not concentrated, and therefore weaker.[6]

If "concentrated power" merits careful study, then clearly interest group entrepreneurship and group organization also merit careful study.

At numerous times in this book, I am apt to state and restate the argument that the collective-action problem is surmountable. It is, however, important to keep in mind that a surmountable problem is still a problem. Of interest are the means to obviate the problem. In this chapter, I delineate three functions that interest group entrepreneurs perform to obviate the collective-action problem. First, interest group entrepreneurs direct the exchange of a set of goods and benefits for group membership. Second, interest group entrepreneurs provide information that solves what formal theorists have called a coordination problem. Finally, some interest group entrepreneurs have been able to act formally or informally as agents for group members who need to communicate with government officials. For those readers interested in a hands-on approach to group entrepreneurship, this chapter concludes with a discussion of some of the tools for today's entrepreneurs.

What Are the Marks of Entrepreneurship?

Interest group leaders run and maintain ongoing groups and associations, just as managers run and maintain business firms and corporations. In contrast, entrepreneurs start a business or organization from scratch. Running any sort of profit or nonprofit organization is difficult, but the initial start-up and the early years are usually the most difficult. Interest group entrepreneurs face a more daunting task than do the leaders of extant interest groups, and, for a business entrepreneur, starting a new car company is more difficult than running an existing one. There is something unique about entrepreneurship that separates it from everyday management concerns. Bean-counting managers are not entrepreneurs. Entrepreneurship requires considerable initiative and risk taking, but it is difficult to pinpoint exactly what entrepreneurs do.

Economic models of entrepreneurship

Given that the term *entrepreneur* has a distinctively economic ring to it, one might think that entrepreneurship is nicely explained in traditional economic literature. Economists have generally analyzed entrepreneurship as a special factor of production or as a special production schedule.[7] As a factor of production, entrepreneurship is just one more input used to produce goods and services, such as cars and car insurance or computers and online help desks. By special production schedule, economists envision entrepreneurs as the embodiment of special recipes. That is, the entrepreneurship is epitomized by the special combination of inputs that make the "special sauce." Unfortunately, these models of entrepreneurship presume that entrepreneurship is as easily adjusted as any other part of the production process. But adding just a little more entrepreneurship is akin to planning spontaneity. If someone works part-time, his or her hours are reduced. No one works part-time by slowing down brain synapses while maintaining full-time work hours. Levels of entrepreneurship cannot be easily adjusted because an individual's entrepreneurship is not readily divisible. Such economic models are flawed because they treat entrepreneurship no differently than any other *ordinary* factor of production, and entrepreneurship is not ordinary.[8]

From these models, one sees that the notion of entrepreneurship makes little sense unless there is some sort of temporary disturbance that the entrepreneur uses to secure personal gains *beyond* those anticipated in the marketplace. Entrepreneurs must bear risks that other factors of production do not. Entrepreneurs win or lose as there are differences in the anticipated returns and the real returns.

Political models of entrepreneurship

Interest group scholars commonly use the term *entrepreneur* to refer to someone who discerns latent preferences and mobilizes those individuals who previously had remained unorganized. Disturbance or disequilibrium in a pluralist setting is evidenced by the imbalance of organized interests. As long as some interests remain unmobilized, there is no complete equilibrium of interests in the society. That is, the concerns of some groups are being ignored, so the equilibrium of interests is inherently biased and incomplete because the mobilization of interests is incomplete.[9] In the interest group setting, the success of entrepreneurs depends on this unequal mobilization of interests. Unless one envisions all collective-action problems solved, opportunities always exists for political entrepreneurs. But what exactly do interest group entrepreneurs do? Three models are explored.

Salisbury's Exchange Theory

Robert Salisbury was the first scholar to argue forcefully that group entrepreneurship wields an "independent effect" on groups and the group environment.[10] Entrepreneurship demanded attention because it affected which interests were unorganized, partially organized, or best organized and represented. Simply put, organized interests were deemed more powerful than unorganized interests. Attention to entrepreneurship, therefore, was one way to address the nagging concerns about the unequal representation of interests. Due to the immense impact of Truman's work, like Olson, Salisbury carefully delineated the major problems with Truman's analysis of group formation. For Salisbury, organization was not the "automatic fruit" of social and political processes; groups emerged from the efforts of successful entrepreneurs.[11]

The proliferation and homeostatic hypotheses

From Truman's work, Salisbury teased out two theories of group formation: the *proliferation hypothesis* and the *homeostatic hypothesis*. Elements of these hypotheses from Truman's work were alluded to earlier in Chapter 2. The proliferation hypothesis suggests that the increasing complexity and interdependence in society leads to the natural development of more and more groups. Simply put, as society becomes more complex, groups proliferate to reflect that complexity. A society dominated by hunters and gatherers will have a simpler group environment than a society with manufacturers of all sorts, a myriad of service industries, and a highly developed agricultural sec-

tor, as well as a few hunters and gathers. The reasoning behind the proliferation hypothesis is straightforward: groups need a clientele from which to
draw members. In addition, there seems to be some evidence for this hypothesis because those states with more diverse economies and populations
tend to have larger and more diverse group environments.[12]

Given its simplicity and the empirical regularities that seem to support it,
what are the drawbacks of the proliferation hypothesis? The hypothesis is
better suited to *describe* a group environment than to *explain* group formation. Indeed, Salisbury noted potential cause-and-effect problems. Throughout much of his text, Truman worked from the assumption that groups affect every aspect of our daily existence and every aspect of our social
structures. The proliferation hypothesis suggests something very different:
new social or economic conditions lead to new interests, which in turn lead
to new groups. For Truman, sometimes groups affect society and sometimes
society affects groups. Clearly, the connections between the group environment and the larger social environment are quite complex, but these complex
relations are exactly what entrepreneurs work to exploit.

What about the homeostatic hypothesis? At any one time, the group environment maintains some sort of equilibrium. If some exogenous shock, such
as a stunning technological advance, alters that equilibrium, then new groups
emerge to restore some semblance of balance. The emergence of a few new
groups often spurs the development of yet more groups. The development of
new groups ends only after all these groups reestablish some sort of balance.
Consider the advent and proliferation of motorized scooters on which the
rider stands rather than sits. Scooter manufacturers claim they will revolu-
tionize transportation. Banned from the streets in many cities, scooters may
or may not be welcomed on sidewalks and bike paths. If slow-footed pedes-
trians feel at risk, they may mobilize to protect their walkways from the motorized intruders. The emergence of the Pedestrian Group of America (PGA)
may lead to counter mobilizations among scooter riders, bicyclists, and car
drivers as each group tries to stake out its territory. Like the proliferation hypothesis, the homeostatic hypothesis seems straightforward. There is, however, some ambiguity. The revolution in transportation is the disturbance
that leads to new groups, but these new groups themselves create disturbances in the balance of interests, which lead to more groups. Once again,
there is a cause-and-effect problem. Disturbances lead to groups, and groups
lead to disturbances. In addition, not all disturbances lead to changes in a
group environment. Why do some disturbances affect the interest group environment whereas others do not?

Salisbury's dissatisfaction with these aspects of Truman's descriptions of
interest group formation led him to develop his *exchange theory* of group formation. Salisbury suggested that group entrepreneurs exchange a set of
goods for group membership. "Entrepreneurs/organizers invest capital to
create a set of benefits which they offer to a market of potential customers

... and as long as enough customers buy, i.e., join, to make a viable organization, the group is in business."[13] In this analysis, capital is the entrepreneur's money invested up front before any group exists. Entrepreneurs provide material, solidary, and expressive benefits in exchange for membership dues. Material benefits are identical to selective incentives. They are pure private goods. Material benefits are the easiest to produce and in some ways are the easiest to promote because the terms of the exchange are clear. Solidary benefits are derived from interacting with other like-minded people. Many group functions promote camaraderie and lead to long-term friendships. Solidary benefits are very important for more socially minded people and organizations, but they are not easy to insure. The group's meeting, picnic, or weekend retreat may or may not be much fun. A promise of solidary benefits is not as sound as the promise of material benefits. Although expressive benefits are often equated with the public goals of a group, expressive benefits do not necessarily depend on the successful provision of the public good. Expressive benefits are derived from expressing those beliefs that one holds dear. They are the intrinsic rewards one gets from doing the right thing.[14] Entrepreneurs may speak of such benefits, but, like the solidary benefits, they are difficult for an entrepreneur to guarantee.

Implications from Salisbury's work

Each of the benefits highlighted by Salisbury is exclusive. One has to join the group before securing material, solidary, or expressive benefits. Entrepreneurs emphasize the exclusive rewards, not the public good that one may enjoy with or without membership. Groups are distinguished by assessing the particular blend of benefits that they provide. Different kinds of groups rely on very different blends of these benefits. Among the exclusive benefits, the material benefits often have the most impact because they are immediately tangible. Solidary and expressive benefits are almost ephemeral. How long after the rainy picnic does the feeling of solidarity and comraderie last? Salisbury noted that those groups that emphasize expressive benefits tend to be the most fleeting. For expressive benefits to have lasting impact, one has to continue to express something. After some length of time, one might begin to consider the impact of such expressions. However, the provision of the public good is not emphasized at this point. Expressive benefits are related to the public good, but they do not depend on its successful provision.

Salisbury's exchange theory noted the parallels between the purchasing of group memberships and the purchasing of any other sort of good. An everyday understanding of economics suggests the following: purchasing power is affected by income or wealth and the costs of goods. The higher our income, the more we can purchase; and the lower our income, the less we can purchase. In a similar vein, as the price of a good increases, we usually demand less of it. Income constraints on purchasing power force us to face tradeoffs.

If someone spends all of his income on books, there will be no money left for leisure activities (baseball tickets and beer or outdoor concerts and brie). Since the publication of Salisbury's work, there has been an ongoing debate about whether people purchase group memberships in the same way they purchase other goods. Are they sensitive to income levels? Are they sensitive to changes in relative prices?

Truman's disturbance theory suggested that the disruptions caused by bad economic times promoted group formation. Of course, declining incomes come with bad economic times, so essentially Truman was arguing that as incomes dropped, demand for group memberships increased. If Truman is correct, then demand for political involvement is not affected by changes in income in the same fashion as everyday private goods. In contrast, Salisbury argued that, with agricultural groups, good times lead to group growth. More recent work by political scientist John Mark Hansen explored these issues in more depth.[15] Hansen argues that just as groups provide different kinds of benefits, our sensitivities to income and price changes are affected by what we want from the group. Demand for the intangible solidary and expressive benefits are income elastic, meaning that small changes in income lead to large changes in demand.[16] Demand for the intangible benefits are also price elastic. Small changes in price create large changes in demand. However, price elasticity is affected by the relative costs of available substitutes. Solidary and expressive rewards are widely available, and no group has a lock on their provision. The neighborhood pool, the corner coffee shop, and the newspaper room at the library also offer solidary benefits.

Of course, groups also provide tangible benefits, whether they are selective incentives or public goods. Here too, members are sensitive to the existence of substitutes. Perhaps some other group would provide an equally informative magazine for less money, or perhaps the local newsstand provides a nice alternative. What about the public good? For Hansen, the public good remains prominent, but the acquisition of a new public good is very different from the loss of an established public good. Suppose that for ten dollars, you could secure a new public good worth one hundred dollars, or for ten dollars you could prevent the loss of a public good worth one hundred dollars. In each instance, the costs and the benefits are equivalent, but at least since the work of psychologists Daniel Kahneman and Amos Tversky, scholars have argued that potential losses loom larger than potential gains.[17] Therefore, bad economic times that threaten the provision of an established good may lead to an increase in group membership levels.[18] In essence, Hansen connected a group's frequent use of scare tactics to Kahneman and Tversky's more formal results about attitudes toward risk. It is easier to mobilize the elderly when a group talks about "the end of Social Security as we know it." During the pro-growth and anti-regulation years of the Ronald Reagan presidency, environmental groups were quite successful at maintaining their ranks. Indeed, some environmental groups increased their ranks during that long period of major legislative losses.

There are no simple conclusions to draw from some of these arguments. Clearly, groups' reward structures interact with individuals' personal economic circumstances in very complex ways. Just as individuals are sensitive to the relative prices of private goods, they may be sensitive to the relative prices of public activities. One of the most eloquent, extended statements about people's movement between the public and private spheres of activity was made by the economist Albert O. Hirschman. In *Shifting Involvements,* Hirschman argued that people always combine some private marketplace activities with some public political activities in their quest for goods and services and sound public policies.[19] Of most interest to Hirschman was the manner in which people shifted their involvements from the public to the private sphere or from the private to the public sphere. In general, as failures occur in one sphere, people tend to shift to the other. However, the extent of one's willingness to shift depends on the substitutability of the private and public goods. For instance, one could address the issue of unsafe cars through private or public means. Ralph Nader's early success as a consumer advocate highlighted the issue of automobile safety. In the public sphere, one could support Nader's efforts to ensure greater car safety; in the private sphere, one could purchase a large heavy sport utility vehicle, which in some circles is considered a "suburban assault vehicle." In this instance, price and income elasticities remain quite prominent. The benefit from the private solution is very focused and very expensive. The public activity is much less expensive, but its rewards are less certain and more diffuse.

Hansen's emphasis on the role of threats might reasonably be coupled with Hirschman's analysis of shifting involvements between the public and private spheres. For instance, Hansen noted that studies of The League of Women's Voters indicated that members were more likely to have children than not and were often concerned about public education issues. Hansen found that when education funding decreased, League membership increased. Members responded to the threat to education. However rather than fighting the decrease in public funding, one could consider private education. The cost of local League involvement is bound to be much lower than the cost of a private education for one or more children. However, the League's rewards would be diffuse, whereas the rewards of private schooling are focused on one's own children. This suggests that the League should have seen the lowest percentage increases in membership in those areas where private schooling was readily available, already widely used, and less expensive.

Entrepreneurs and Coordination

Recall that the collective-action problem has two components: a freerider problem and a coordination problem. Until now we have focused primarily on the freerider problem. What do social scientists mean by coordination?

Game theoretic models of coordination

At this juncture, a bit of game theory is helpful. As noted previously, game theory allows us to analyze how two or more individuals' independent choices lead to a collective outcome. As is often the case when tackling something new, learning about game theory is easiest if you just jump in and worry about the more arcane details and definitions later. Fortunately, simple coordination games readily illustrate the potential roles for communication and leadership in situations where players have *mixed motives*. When players face mixed motives, they want to cooperate, but they recognize that some forms of cooperation are better for them than other forms. In coordination games, players recognize the need to avoid certain outcomes while still debating which outcome is best. In the end, players may or may not successfully coordinate their actions. In Table 3.1, Player 1 must choose among three strategies (*X, Y, Z*), and Player 2 must choose among three strategies (*A, B, C*). For every possible combination of Player 1 and 2's strategies, a different outcome is obtained. The payoffs for Player 1 are on the left, and the payoffs for Player 2 are on the right.

TABLE 3.1
2-Person Coordination Game with Mixed Motives

Player 2

		A	B	C
	X	6, 2	2, –3	–1, –1
Player 1	Y	5, –3	3, 3	1, 1
	Z	–1, –1	0, 0	2, 2

Of course, Players 1 and 2 prefer some outcomes more than others, but they do not, per se, choose outcomes. Players can only choose strategies or actions, and at this stage they cannot communicate with one another. Some outcomes are unstable in the sense that either Player 1 or 2 would change her strategy to secure a better payoff. Consider outcome (*Z, B*). Given Player 2's choice of strategy, Player 1 would change from Z to Y. The outcome (Z, B) yields a payoff of 0 for Player 1, whereas (Y, B) yields a payoff of 3. If Player 2 is set on choosing strategy B, then Player 1's best response is to choose Y. When neither player can alter her strategy to secure a better payoff, the outcome is called an equilibrium. All other nonequilibrium outcomes are unstable in the sense that some player is not responding optimally to another's strategy. Determining whether an outcome is an equilibrium is fairly easy. Focus on outcome (X, A). If X is Player 1's best response to A and if A is Player 2's best response to X, then (X, A) is an equilibrium. Note that the strategy combinations (X, A), (Y, B), and (Z, C) are all equilibria. But which of these three equilibria prevails? One equilibrium, (Z, C), is worse for both players, suggesting that the players may manage to avoid it. Of the remaining equilibria, the players prefer different outcomes. Conflict remains because Player 1 prefers (X, A) whereas Player 2 prefers (Y, B). Therefore, Players 1 and 2 have mixed motives. If communication were allowed, then Player 1 might promise Player 2 that she would share the spoils of the (X, A) equilibrium. However, even if such a promise were made, Player 2 would remain wary if there were no means to enforce the promise. If promises to deliver side payments are credible, then the (X, A) equilibrium may be favored by both players. The players certainly want to avoid inferior equilibria such as (Z, C) as well as outcomes such as (X, C), but they still face mixed motives because there is no clear best equilibrium for both players.

   In the coordination game in Table 3.2, there are two equally good equilibria, (U,L) and (D,R), but they are secured through different courses of action. Player 1 might focus on the upper left-hand corner whereas Player 2 focuses on the lower right-hand corner. If the players focus on or anticipate being in different equilibria, then suboptimal outcomes prevail. Depending on the players' abilities to communicate, even players who want to cooperate with one another may fail to coordinate with compatible strategies. In many game theoretic models, communication and leadership derive their influence from their bearing on the coordination of players' actions.

TABLE 3.2
2-Person Coordination Game

Player 2

		L	*R*
	U	3, 3	0, 0
Player 1			
	D	−1, −1	3, 3

Understanding simple coordination games enhances our understanding of numerous social and political concerns. For instance, both governmental laws and social norms structure and channel our actions. Laws may strictly proscribe certain actions. For instance, simple traffic laws are used to help enforce speed limits. After allowing for a five- or ten-mile-per-hour fudge factor, knowledge of the traffic laws may keep us from excessive speeding. However, we monitor our speed even more closely if the radar detector indicates that there are police nearby. If we fear speeding tickets, we slow down. The point is that speed limits require an enforcement mechanism. There are, however, other traffic laws that need little if any enforcement from police officials. Most drivers stay to the right. Few drivers barrel through stop signs or red lights. Even though some people never want to stop on a yellow light, most drivers generally obey the traffic signals. Indeed, drivers obey the signals even in the absence of law enforcement officials. The stop signs and red lights are obeyed simply because there are so many other cars recognizing their own right of way. Two points deserve attention. First, rather than proscribing certain actions, signal lights are effective because they *coordinate* action. Second, direct communication between the drivers is not necessary to coordinate their actions.

Another look at the contribution game[20]

Though not introduced in a game theoretic sense, coordination problems have been central to interest group studies for years. The essence of an interest group society is that groups aggregate and coordinate individuals' otherwise lone voices. The question is how do interest group entrepreneurs affect coordination problems? Before I can answer this question fully, I need to do three things. First, I will recap the contribution game from Chapter 2. Next, I will introduce the notion of a mixed-strategy equilibrium. Finally, I will add two players to the original game, a government and an interest group entrepreneur.

The participation game in the second chapter had a group of N individuals independently deciding whether to contribute to the provision of a public good. If a certain threshold number of contributions was made, then a public good was provided. In the previous chapter, I surveyed only the pure strategy equilibria. The pure strategies were contribute and freeride. The coordination problem loomed quite large because of the numerous equilibria. Recall that for games of this sort for any threshold number of contributions ω, where $\omega \geq 1$, there are $\binom{N}{\omega}$ equilibria.[21] In the first equilibrium, no one contributes and no public good is provided. In the remaining pure strategy equilibria, ω individuals contribute and $N - \omega$ individuals freeride. In each of these equilibria the public good was provided because the threshold number of contributions was made, but how the players determined who contributed and who did not remained unspecified. The coordination problem persisted.

Working from the same participation game from Chapter 2, I now compli-
cate matters just a bit to highlight the role of interest group entrepreneurs in
the resolution of coordination problems. In the previous chapter, the players
simply chose to contribute or not. Here, I restrict players to mixed strategies.
Rather than choosing to contribute or freeride, in a mixed strategy one
chooses to contribute with some probability. Perhaps a player contributes
with a forty percent probability and does not contribute with a sixty percent
probability. The only restriction on the weights used in mixed strategies is
that they add up to one. Whether the player actually contributes depends on
the roll of the dice or the flip of a coin. Maybe he or she contributes, maybe
he or she doesn't. There are many ways of understanding mixed strategies.
Sometimes there is no single best pure strategy, so players "mix it up a bit,"
sometimes choosing one pure strategy, sometimes another. If all players
choose the same mixed strategies by placing the same weights on contributing and freeriding, then the players' actions differ simply because the flip of
the coin dictates different courses of action.

It is now time to add two additional players. First, a government is added.
In Chapter 2, who actually provided the public good was never specified. If
the threshold was met, the public good was just somehow provided. Now,
suppose that a government provides a public good if enough people petition
for its provision. Like contributing, petitioning is costly, so once again people
have an incentive to freeride if they can. The government's success is determined by its wise provision of goods and services. But the government is not
omniscient and may, therefore, make two types of mistakes. It may provide a
public good that few people desire or it may fail to provide a good that many
people desire. Though perhaps not one hundred percent accurate, the petitions do contain some information about the desirability of the public good
in question. Operating as best as it can with its incomplete information, the
government must decide how to respond to petitions. The government
chooses some threshold number of petitions at which it will provide the
good and below which it will not. Establishing a very low threshold risks the
first type of mistake, and establishing a very high threshold risks the second
type of mistake. The rest of the players must choose the weights to place on
petitioning and not petitioning. The government and the other players respond to one another in this game as one might imagine. If the government
chooses a relatively low threshold, the other players' weights placed on petitioning are reduced. If the government establishes a relatively high threshold, the weights on petitioning are increased. There is also an equilibrium in
which no one petitions.

Next, an interest group entrepreneur is added. How does an interest
group entrepreneur enter into this fray? Traditionally oriented political scientists often referred to groups as linkage organizations. In this game theoretic
model, the entrepreneur establishes a link between the government and the
other players. At some set cost, the entrepreneur decides whether to lobby

the government for the provision of the public good. The entrepreneur's payoff is a function of the number of petitioners, so the entrepreneur is very concerned about inducing high rates of petitioning. Indeed, it may not pay for the entrepreneur to set up shop if the number of people concerned about the public good is too small. By the same token, it may not pay to set up shop if everyone focuses on the equilibrium with the lowest threshold and the lowest rate of petitioning. The entrepreneur makes a profit only when enough people petition to cover the fixed costs of lobbying the government.

The presence of an entrepreneur affects the government and the other players in similar ways. Everyone knows that the entrepreneur is rational. She will not enter into business in anticipation of losing money. She *anticipates* a profit. Since the entrepreneur's payoff is a function of the number of petitioners, her profits are most readily secured when there is a large number of people who desire the public good in question. If the entrepreneur envisions few people valuing the public good and fewer yet petitioning, the best strategy is to avoid entering into this particular fray. In this sense, an entrepreneur's mere presence or absence provides information to the government as well as to the potential petitioners. Indeed, the mere presence or absence of an entrepreneur becomes something of a self-fulfilling prophecy. The entrepreneur's absence suggests that there are few individuals who value the public good, so few that the entrepreneur would only lose money if she tried to set up shop. The presence of the entrepreneur indicates that she is betting capital on the existence of a large number of politically active public good beneficiaries. In the presence of an interest group entrepreneur, the government focuses on a high threshold and the other players adopt a mixed strategy with a large weight on petitioning. The entrepreneur reduces the coordination problem whenever covering her fixed costs requires an equilibrium with a high rate of petitioning.

There are two main results to keep in mind at this point: (1) there are numerous equilibria in contribution games and (2) that the mere presence of an interest group entrepreneur often provides a focus away from those equilibria with low levels of participation. Unlike the Salisbury model, this model is not exchange based, so even in the absence of selective incentives, interest group entrepreneurs may help to solve the collective-action problem. The entrepreneur does, however, provide valuable information to the government and the other players. The entrepreneur provides the government with an indication of how many people are interested in a public good, while at the same time coordinating petitioners' actions. In the presence of an interest group entrepreneur, the government is less likely to supply a public good when too few people stand to benefit from it or fail to supply a good when many people would benefit from it.

As in the Salisbury model, the entrepreneur must invest precious capital. In essence the entrepreneur makes a capital investment by lobbying the government, which hardly seems to support Olson's by-product theory. Lobbying, however, has an informational component that suggests that it may be a reasonable investment for an interest group entrepreneur, rather than a mere by-product. In addition, this model suggests that joining a group may be formally linked to attempts to secure a public good. The more empirically oriented work by John Mark Hansen discussed in this chapter found that groups' increases in memberships are often linked to successful lobbying campaigns that culminated in the provision of a collective good.[22] The game theoretic work presented here and Hansen's finding that individuals may join groups in anticipation of the successful provision of collective goods dovetail nicely.

The coordination of individuals' actions remains an enduring feature of all civil and social settings. At least since the time of de Tocqueville, scholars have marveled at the ability of some leaders to inspire collective action, but few people have written clearly on the matter because they have seldom specified a collective-action or coordination problem. For instance, de Tocqueville wrote of "self interest rightly understood," but he never fully explained what it was or how it operated.[23] "It is held as a truth that man serves himself in serving his fellow creatures, and that his private interest is to do good" for himself and others, but "I shall not . . . enter into the reasons."[24] De Tocqueville recognized that "every man may follow his own interest," but he strove to argue that there was still a rational basis for regarding others. Consider two individuals facing the coordination problem in Table 3.2. The individuals' well-being may be enhanced when they consider the concerns and actions of the other. In Table 3.2, neither player can simply choose the upper-left or lower-right outcome. The players must learn to coordinate their actions to secure the most favorable outcomes. This section has shown how entrepreneurs affect individuals' sense of success and narrow self-interest in the face of collective-action and coordination problems.

Group Entrepreneurs as Government Agents

One of the more striking empirical findings detailed in the second chapter is that many groups receive start-up funds from the government. The benefits to groups of such direct assistance are clear. Some groups also secure indirect benefits from government loan and entitlement programs. Working one's way through government entitlement forms can be difficult, and individuals often seek help from nongovernmental, group sources. In the first part of this section, I discuss the ability of group entrepreneurs to act either formally or informally as government agents, facilitating the processing of individuals' claims for entitlements. Increasingly, groups provide services for the government for a fee. Government contracts or fees for services are particularly common in the area of social services. In the second part of this section, I discuss the effects of the government's use of contracts with groups.

Welfare Rights Organizations

Sometimes there is a disjuncture between legislators' intentions for a policy and the implementation of a policy. Legislation allowing for the distribution of entitlements does not insure the actual distribution of funds. During the 1960s and 1970s, such a disjuncture was especially acute in the area of welfare policy. During that time, interest groups called Welfare Rights Organizations (WROs) were organized around the resolution of individual grievances against government welfare agencies. Two problems were particularly troublesome. First, recipients and potential recipients of welfare entitlements possessed limited information about the programs aimed at helping them. Like much federal legislation, the federal welfare programs were to be implemented jointly by the federal and local governments. Of course, federal mandates and local compliance are two very different things. The second problem to overcome was the local resistance to the federal welfare policies.

The local resistance problem stemmed from a familiar source. Simply put, social welfare agencies have financial constraints. For political and economic reasons, social service agencies tended to be underfunded and overworked. Caseloads could be tremendous, so there was no need to advertise for welfare clients. In addition, local officials had a strong incentive to keep welfare costs down by making welfare assistance difficult to obtain because the Social Security Act of 1935 mandated that the Aid to Families with Dependent Children (AFDC) program costs were to be shared by local governments. The reticence of the local officials ensured that few potential recipients knew of the special-grants programs under AFDC, which allowed individuals to secure funds to address unforeseen circumstances.[25] The lack of information among recipients and potential recipients was astonishing. During the mid-1960s, the number of people receiving welfare equaled only one-half of those eligible.[26] Among recipients, on average only one-half of the benefits for which they were eligible were actually disbursed.[27] Lack of information about the full range of existing programs and the reluctance of local officials to expand welfare rolls affected the value of seeking aid and the opportunities for group entrepreneurs.

The local resistance fostered competition among claimants seeking the same grants and services. Only so many claims for aid could be processed by an overburdened system. Therefore, the expected value of one's own claim for a grant depended in part on the amount of competition it faced from other claims competing for the same limited services. As long as the pool of potential claimants remained large and the ability to respond to claims remained limited, the competition persisted. By reducing the expected value of a claim, the direct competition also reduced the number of new claims filed. Some legitimate claims were just not worth filing because their expected values were so low. In effect, the competition among claimants kept the expected value of the special grants below the actual levels set by federal legislation. In direct contrast to Truman's notion of a political interest group, shared attitudes and claims upon government agencies for grants led to competition, not natural group representation. In the absence of group representation, the like-minded welfare recipients were in competition with one another.

The entrepreneurs involved in the creation of WROs were acutely aware of these conditions in the welfare programs. The group entrepreneurs disseminated important information about government services. The welfare rights entrepreneurs explained the problem and offered the solution. The problems were quite easy to explain: only one-half of those individuals eligible for aid actually received it, very few potential recipients knew of the full range of programs, and only one-half of the benefits were actually disbursed. The fundamental building blocks for WROs were the resolution of individual grievances about welfare procedures and the dissemination of grant information to potential recipients of aid under the special-grants programs of the AFDC program. However, to be successful entrepreneurs, the resistance of local officials to expand welfare rolls and the coordination problems among the potential recipients had to be overcome.

Solving the coordination problem required potential members to focus on the same solution. There were few organizations offering support to welfare recipients, so WROs were the natural focal point. Some of the state WROs had the added benefit of having the assistance of Vista workers.[28] Vista workers added visibility and a quasi-official status to WROs. If a potential recipient of AFDC aid were to ask for assistance, he or she would probably seek the assistance of the local WRO. Once the grievances and claims for grants were collected, the WROs combined them. By bundling grievances and requests for assistance and combining direct and indirect lobbying of local welfare agencies, WROs reduced the competition among claimants that was caused by the local resistance problem.

WROs mobilized welfare recipients and their children to pressure the local welfare agencies. Pressure at the local level often meant organizing mass demonstrations and using low-level intimidation. In some circles, low-level intimidation was considered an art form, sometimes known as *mau mauing*. Novelist Tom Wolfe captured both the colorful and the crude aspects of such intimidation in his book *Radical Chic and Mau Mauing the Flak Catchers.*[29] As long as the potential recipients were mobilized and encouraged to sit in at the local agency, the pressure worked. "Mass demonstrations . . . had as their object increasing the bargaining resources of the welfare mothers—a promise to stop the noise, confusion, and shouting could be offered in exchange for special needs grants."[30] Such tactics could "solve hundreds and perhaps thousands of grievances at one time."[31] The combined use of bundling grievances and mobilizing direct pressure reduced the local resistance problem. WROs' success at the agencies made subsequent mobilizations easier, and increased mobilizations enhanced WROs' successes at the agencies. Potential recipients reacted as rational individuals and simply allowed the entrepreneurs to coordinate their concerns. The success of the WROs was a function of their position, which allowed them to be virtually the sole providers of information about government-provided goods and services.

During the early 1970s, the National Welfare Rights Organization (NWRO) commenced traditional lobbying in Washington, but these efforts had little success. After receiving their special grants, most welfare recipients dropped out of their local WRO, so by this time, the base of the WROs was already decreasing rapidly and their flimsy electoral connection soon disappeared. The Democratic Party sought votes from the inner cities of the North, but WROs were not central to the Democratic Party's electoral connections to urban areas.[32] The WROs refused to expand their ranks through liberalized qualifications for aid. In particular, WROs refused to represent the problems of the working poor or the aged poor.[33] To solidify their gains, WROs needed an electoral connection, which could have been achieved through liberalized qualifications for aid and expanded ranks. Without a well-established electoral connection linking voting members and elected officials, the WROs were doomed. The failure of the Washington lobbying was due to the lack of a base to the welfare movement. Welfare recipients responded to the organizers' investments in a rational, self-interested way. Organizers kept dues very low and members were promised increased welfare payments in return for their dues and a couple of afternoons of demonstrating. After they received their special grants, most welfare recipients dropped from the ranks. Increased liberalizations were not likely so there was little incentive to remain. To save themselves money, some states abolished their special grants programs, which further weakened WROs. Given all of their hurdles and limitations, most state-level WROs lasted only about two years.

The WRO entrepreneurs were quintessentially professional entrepreneurs. For George Wiley, longtime leader of the NWRO, working for interest groups and movements was a lifelong career. Wiley worked for the NWRO only after losing a leadership struggle in the Congress of Racial Equality (CORE). Saul Alinsky, an activist in numerous social movements across the country, was a recognized specialist. He wrote a primer for aspiring activists and was often called upon by city leaders to moderate the conflicts between rioters and city governments.[34] Other leaders in the welfare rights movement, such as Richard Cloward and Frances Piven, were social scientists who likely mixed professional curiosity with their desires to reform welfare policies. Alinsky, Cloward, Piven, and Wiley were not unique. From 1965 to 1969, there was a two hundred percent to three hundred percent increase in community organization practitioners.[35] It became "increasingly possible for a committed individual to carve out a career of social issue-related movement leadership without financial sacrifice."[36]

The expanding role for nonprofits and the implications of contracting

On average, one-half of a nonprofit's budget is from the government, and for some nonprofits their entire budget is from the government.[37] A little background may help put these figures in perspective. At the start of the twentieth century, many politicians and social observers argued that the government should dominate the distribution of important social services. Some had noted that many charities avoided the most difficult cases, so there was no real safety net for the most vulnerable and troubled people. Others argued that the government should not allow private charities to dominate such a fundamental policy area as social services. However, only in the area of military pensions did the government develop a clearly dominant position.[38] In all other areas of social relief services, private money and private organizations dominated.

During the Depression of the 1930s, the government's role increased tremendously. However, the government money spent on social relief services tended to crowd out the private money.[39] The government's view toward nonprofits changed dramatically in the 1960s and again in the 1980s, but in each period the move was toward greater and greater involvement of *nongovernmental* organizations. For instance, the 1967 Social Security Act encouraged states to purchase services from private charities. Also during this period, groups and nonprofits benefited from the "maximum feasible participation" rules in federal legislation. Numerous federal policies during the 1960s were designed to enhance the institutions in the local communities. Strengthening the local groups and organizations might provide the best means for reaching the most socially isolated and disenfranchised people. During the 1980s, the federal government renewed its drive to work through private charities and groups. However, by the 1980s, saving money was the primary impetus for working with and through groups. Contracting out or privatizing social services made the government look smaller and more efficient. In other words, for various reasons and for over three decades the federal government forced its own agencies and many affiliated state agencies to work with existing groups at the local levels to facilitate the distribution of social services.

Steven Smith and Michael Lipsky argue that nonprofits became "agents of government in the expansion of the American welfare state."[40] Public policy specialist Donald Kettl notes that "government by proxy" is now quite common in other policy areas, covering everything from the Superfund for environmental clean-ups to federal student loan programs,[41] but only in the area of social services does the government work so closely with groups. Whenever the government chooses to contract out to work through groups, charities, or for-profit firms, the connections between public and private become difficult to untangle entirely. What was public becomes private, and what was private becomes public because government contracts come with strings attached. The ultimate effect of these policies, Kettl argues, is to "govern-mentalize the private sector."[42] That is, the government is not necessarily adopting the ways of private sector firms; rather, it is forcing the private sector organizations receiving government funds to act more as govern-ment agencies. As with any contract, particular guidelines are mandated, causing many nonprofits to lose flexibility in the means of implementing policies and services.

Though they may lose some flexibility, nonprofits with government con-tracts may also develop monopoly power. By contracting, the government recognizes the validity of some, but not all, groups. The contracts force re-cipients of social services to work with the noted groups. Other avenues are not available. Consider the Red Cross, which controls the entire market for blood. It would be difficult for an interest group entrepreneur to enter into the same arena with the Red Cross. The Red Cross is so dominant that many people fail to realize that it is a nongovernmental organization. Contracting may also affect one's sense of citizenship. "From the point of view of welfare state clients, the state has disappeared from view,"[43] and the group's person-nel fill the void. With every new governmental program, new groups emerge to protect and extend the resources mandated for it. The links between some groups and federal programs are relatively straightforward. Consider the Na-tional Association of School Lunch Administrators and the National Associa-tion of School Lunch Officials or the National Association of Community Health Centers, National Association of Community Mental Health Centers, and the National Association of Addiction and Treatment Providers. Prior to the federal school lunch programs, there were no school lunch officials or ad-ministrators, let alone organizations representing them.

The widespread distribution of large government grants leads to other conflicts. Many groups depend on government money through various grants and contracts for their very maintenance and operation. Might a group use government grant money to lobby for more government grant money? Federal law prohibits recipients from using government money to lobby Congress, but from time to time concerns still arise. Representative Ernst Jim Istook Jr. (R-Okla.) remains concerned, and at various times he has attempted to restrict nonprofits from using any of their money, regardless of its source, on lobbying. Money, after all, is fungible. That is, government grants to support one set of group activities allows that group to readjust the distribution of its other funds. Government grants may, therefore, free up ad-ditional funds for lobbying. Representative Istook says "it's a matter of prin-ciple . . . Congress is not required to subsidize lobbying activity for any-body."[44] "It's wrong for people to think that they have the right to get an automatic check from the U.S. Treasury to further their political agenda."[45] Istook often cites the financial situation and political activities of the National Council of Senior Citizens. The 500,000-member group has engaged in numerous battles with Republican legislators over the fate of Medicaid and Medicare. The group also acts as the administrator for the disbursement of millions of dollars. Based on their own reports to the government, Istook estimated that the group secured seventy-three million dollars in government grants, providing ninety-six percent of the group's total revenue.

Istook's arguments may appear sound, but he has numerous opponents. Over 200,000 groups secure government grants. Many firms and foundations secure government research grants. Should the receipt of a grant for services provided lead to a limit on someone's first amendment rights? Most of Istook's opponents see his amendment as an attempt to shackle certain liberal groups, in particular the National Council of Senior Citizens. Representative David E. Skaggs (D-Colo.) stated that "'this has nothing to do with lobbying with Federal taxpayers' dollars. . . . This is . . . legislation having to do with the control of political expression in America.'"[46] Even some of Istook's supporters acknowledge that the groups most affected would be liberally oriented, precisely the sort of groups a conservative Republican might want to constrain.

The point is that the division between government and group is blurred at times. The government's role in the mobilization of groups limits one's ability to think about groups and government as entirely separate. Earl Latham's arguments are most direct.

> Insofar as they are organized . . . groups . . . are structures of power. They are structures of power because they concentrate human wit, energy, and muscle for the achievement of common purposes. *They are of the same genus, although a different species, as the state.*[47]

We live in an interest group society, which behooves us to study government and groups together. That is the best lesson left by the pluralists.

Theory and Practice: Tools for Today's Entrepreneurs[48]

What are the tools for interest group entrepreneurs and how does our academic understanding of entrepreneurship affect how we use these tools?

Direct mail

Many of the basic tools for today's group entrepreneur are readily available. Desktop computers and high-quality printers have become the central tools for all sorts of political activities. Today's entrepreneurs have specialized software that facilitates getting the right message to the right people. When soliciting contributions for a group espousing particular public goals and

offering particular selective, expressive, and solidary benefits, it is essential to
"know your market." Flooding the entire market is seldom a good idea. It is
simply too costly. Fortunately for the entrepreneur, the United States is divided up into many sets and subsets. Depending on the nature of the group,
one can focus organizational efforts in particular states. A successful group in
California may fail in New York. But even within states, there is considerable
diversity, and flooding the market in a large state would still be very costly.
One could focus on particular congressional districts or census tracts as defined by the U.S. Census Bureau. But how does one choose the right districts or the right tracts? As it happens, several software packages link zip
codes to congressional districts; provide aggregate-level information on voter
registration records and voter turnout; and include census data, such as education and income levels and race and ethnicity. All of this information is
generally available to the public, and the software commonly advertised in
newspapers such as *RollCall* allow one to compile lots of information from
diverse sources very quickly.

   The information described so far only facilitates mass mailings to "Resident" or "Addressee." The entrepreneur may have a lot of information about
the *average* income or education level in the said addressee's neighborhood
or congressional district, but so far the entrepreneur knows nothing about
the *individual* addressee. The information is at the aggregate level, not the
individual level. We know a person lives in a wealthy community, but we do
not know whether a particular addressee is wealthy. Entrepreneurs supplement the aggregate-level information that is readily available with individual-
level information drawn from membership lists of various groups and organizations. The prices vary, but typically for less than twenty-five cents per
name, one can buy a list of names from virtually any interest group, association, or firm. These lists contain individual-level information, ranging from
group affiliations, party identification, religious affiliation, family status, income, purchasing patterns, hobbies, education, and age. With individual-
level information, the entrepreneur can personalize the appeal for contributions. Investing time and effort in the selection of appropriate names is
crucial. There is wide agreement that a "poorly prepared mailing to a good
list of names can be profitable, while the best mailing, no matter how well
conceived, to a poor list will lose money."[49] The initial mailing list is referred
to as a *prospecting list*. The typical response rate from prospecting lists is between one and two percent, so most entrepreneurs plan on losing money at
this stage. Those individuals on the prospecting list who do respond com-
prise the *house list*. Responses from the house list range between ten percent
and twenty percent. With a little luck, the house list will turn a profit several
times a year. It is important to note, however, that tools that entrepreneurs
use are not the same as entrepreneurship itself. Strategic concerns remain
crucial.

Step-by-Step Directions

Suppose you want to organize the American Association of Amateur Avian Scientists (AAAAS). How do you start and what are the strategic concerns? First, be aware of the federal and state guidelines affecting nonprofits and mail solicitations. Learning about the legal system firsthand is not always pleasant, and it need not be part of your learning about groups firsthand. Know the law. Second, recognize that the collective-action problem may or may not be surmountable. Money invested in attempts to resolve a collective-action problem may be well spent or lost; that is simply the nature of entrepreneurship. With those cautionary words in mind, the following steps may get you on your way to becoming an interest group entrepreneur.

Step 1 *A: Know the audience that you are seeking to attract. Are they hunters, photographers, or wildlife managers? These categories may not be exclusive, but you should purchase lists of names with some care. Perhaps Bushnell or Nikon would sell a list of binocular buyers in the United States and Canada.*[50] *Consider purchasing membership lists from Audubon and other environmental groups. Think carefully about the nature of the group you want to start. Would the membership lists of Ducks Unlimited or Pheasants Forever help? Depending on the AAAAS's stand on hunting and wildlife management, these lists may or may not be useful.*

   B: Consider piggybacking on other organizations' events for mass appeals. Attend related conventions, fairs, and festivals. Advertise in Audubon *magazine and other appropriate outlets. Seek foundation support and government grants. Professional grants writers may help in this endeavor, but they do charge for their services. Are there patrons or high demanders who might support the group?*

Successful groups raise funds in very diverse ways. Kenneth Godwin reports that the National Organization of Women (NOW) secures about seventy percent of its funds from direct mail. In contrast, about ninety percent of the budget for the Women's Equity Action League (WEAL) comes from grants.[51] Direct mail tends to create larger and more visible groups. WEAL's reliance on grants allows it to remain behind the scenes and work with a very small membership of about two thousand.

Step 2: *Craft a letter of appeal that has a sense of urgency. Emphasize the immediate threats, but be sure to note previous group successes. That is, specify both the problem and the solution. Defining the public good as a step good may enhance the reader's sense of likely efficacy.*

Each of the public goods discussed to this point has been discrete, with all-or-nothing provision. A bridge that goes half way across a river is of little use. Step goods and continuous goods avoid the problems of all-or-nothing provision. Step goods yield benefits with each unit, or step, of the good provided. A narrow wooden bridge is better than no bridge at all. If more money is secured later, the bridge can be enhanced. How should one define the public good? Is it a natural step good or is it a discrete good? If an entrepreneur can credibly claim that the good is not discrete, then contributors secure a better sense of the efficacy of their own small contribution.[52] Step goods reduce the importance of coordinating everyone's efforts.

Mothers Against Drunk Driving (MADD) uses volunteers to provide emotional support to families who have lost loved ones in drunk-driving accidents. These same volunteers counsel families about court proceedings and act as courtroom monitors. For these volunteers, MADD redefines the group goal and clarifies the emotional impact. A contribution to MADD may not end drunk driving, but it can help a family in one's own community. Most appeals to end hunger among children are presented in terms of helping one child at a time. Contributors cannot end world hunger, per se, but they can save one or more individuals. The entrepreneur chooses to define world hunger as a step good because he or she wants the contributors to link their contributions to a particular child's fate, not the elimination of hunger worldwide.[53] In the same fashion, the Nature Conservancy promotes the preservation of environmentally sensitive lands by urging people to adopt a single acre. Knowing the location of the acre, the family of the drunk-driving victim, or the name of the child affects the contributor's sense of efficacy. This strategy also allows the entrepreneur to personalize the follow-up correspondence.

Step 3: *Know the governmental policies and programs that affect the potential members. Are there any government programs to offset the costs of blue-bird boxes or houses for wood ducks? How might wetlands management policies affect potential group members? Where can city wildlife managers secure peregrine falcons to reduce their pigeon population? Be able and willing to act as an ombudsman. Can an electoral connection be established?*

The AMA has a toll-free hotline and an e-mail alert connecting to over seventy thousand members. AMA members get instant information on governmental policies and programs of interest and have ready access to key lawmakers through the same hotline services.[54] The NRA is increasingly working with state game and wildlife agencies to promote youth hunting programs.[55] Both the NRA and the state agencies are sensitive to the declining number of hunters in the United States. With hunting programs designed for youths, the NRA has an opportunity to find young recruits. Many state game and wildlife agencies' budgets are pegged to the sale of hunting and fishing licenses, so the agencies are generally pleased to use NRA funds to increase the pool of hunters.

Step 4: *Establish a set of benefits that allows you to distinguish your group from others. Direct competition with a large, established group such as Audubon may not be wise.*

Think ahead. Many groups provide selective and solidary benefits aimed directly at children. *Ranger Rick* and *Your Big Backyard* are children's magazines published and distributed by the National Wildlife Federation. The NRA has father-son shoots and training programs for young shooters. The NAACP has often viewed its Youth Councils as key components of its long-term success.

Ancillary sources for interest group money

Once a group is up and running, it may secure funds from an increasingly wide array of sources. Numerous groups are well positioned to make money from their magazines' advertising sales. Most magazines make their money through the sale of advertising space rather than through subscriptions, and interest group magazines are no different in this regard. Therefore, one of the most common selective incentives may be a moneymaker rather than a drain on a group's finances. Many large, membership-based groups distribute catalogues filled with a wide assortment of goods. The Nature Conservancy maintains a store in suburban Atlanta. The AMA secures about two-thirds of its revenues from various real estate and business transactions. The AMA recently toyed with the idea of endorsing household products produced by the Sunbeam Corporation.[56] The proposed five-year contract was reported to be worth at least one million dollars a year to the AMA. The Sunbeam Corporation also valued the proposed contract, and they chose to sue the AMA for reneging on the contract.[57] The largest interest group in the United States, the AARP, has worked closely with insurance and mutual fund companies who are anxious to secure access to an important niche market. Of course, some market niches are larger than others. Billions of dollars have been invested in AARP/Scudder mutual funds. Sometimes nonprofits raise money and eyebrows at the same time. Rather than establishing partnerships, some nonprofits maintain for-profit sister organizations. Shifting costs to the for-profit enterprises and profits to the nonprofit enterprises allows an entrepreneur to gain on two fronts at the same time. Tax burdens for the for-profit enterprise are drastically reduced and the nonprofit looks particularly efficient and well run. Some state attorney generals have looked askance at such practices, but such accounting procedures are difficult to monitor and most states do recognize the right of charities and nonprofits to establish for-profit enterprises.[58] The final possible source of revenue harkens back to how it all began, with a group's own house list. If the group is successful over a period of years, then the interest group entrepreneur can sell her own house list.[59]

Conclusion

Sometimes a particularly romantic story of one entrepreneur or another forever clouds our sense of them. Sometimes it appears that interest group entrepreneurs have never worried about any personal hardships and that they nobly pursue the common weal and nothing else. Many interest group entrepreneurs pursue noble goals, but the fact of the matter is that interest group entrepreneurs are first and foremost entrepreneurs with an acute sense of public policy *and* the bottom line. Indeed, for some group entrepreneurs, a group's presence follows upon the heels of other for-profit endeavors. Many of the farm and veteran organizations of the late 1800s and early 1900s were founded by newspaper publishers, suggesting that the quest for group membership might have been a strategy to increase subscription rates.[60] The success of the NAACP during its early years was closely tied to the success of its newspaper, *The Crisis*. For many years the subscriptions to *The Crisis* far exceeded the memberships in the NAACP.[61]

Truman opined that "formal organization is usually a consequence . . . of a fairly high frequency of interaction within a group."[62] The qualifiers are telling. A fairly high frequency of interaction may not lead to formal organization. The storyline for the old *Cheers* television sitcom revolved around a set of regulars who frequented the same neighborhood bar. Though their interactions were frequent, their organization was never evident. Examples from television sitcoms are playful, but whether an interest does or does not become organized is crucial to an interest group society in which the less structured voices with no interest group representation are weaker. Concerns for the unorganized are not new. Writing during the first half of the 1800s, Alexis de Tocqueville noted the weaknesses of the unorganized in the United States.

> Amongst democratic nations, . . . all the citizens are independent and feeble; they can hardly do anything by themselves, and none of them can oblige his fellowman to lend him their assistance. They all, therefore, fall into a state of incapacity, if they do not learn voluntarily to help each other. If men living in democratic countries had no right and no inclination to associate for political purposes, their independence would be in great jeopardy.[63]

In light of our interest group society as well as de Tocqueville's admonitions, our ability to understand the strategies of group entrepreneurs appears more and more important. Entrepreneurs organize the unorganized, the independent and feeble. To accomplish their goals, entrepreneurs must be strategic and calculating, often taking advantage of society's complexity and always being sensitive to social and economic disturbances, which create new opportunities for interest group emergence. Group formation is indeed affected by complexity and disturbances, but only because group entrepreneurs are able to capitalize on them. Truman's proliferation and homeostatic theories are not so much wrong as they are unfocused and incomplete. Entrepreneurship plays a distinct role.

Though easy profits for political entrepreneurs may be rare, as long as individuals' preferences about political action are affected by events around them, the mobilization of interests is never complete and the role for political entrepreneurs never disappears. The astute entrepreneur realizes the connection between disturbances in the interest group environment, latent preferences, and the mobilization of new interests. If entrepreneurs take advantage of fortuitous disturbances, then the distinction between the disturbance and entrepreneurial theories of interest group formation is spurious; indeed the entrepreneur theory subsumes the disturbance theory.[64]

Given the importance of entrepreneurs to interest group formation, one might reasonably wonder what roles group leaders play in structuring and governing their organizations. The next chapter highlights the problems associated with the representation of interests and group governance.

NOTES

1. Carey Goldberg, "Downsizing Activism: Greenpeace is Cutting Back" (*New York Times*, September 16, 1997), A-16.
2. Goldberg (1997), A-16.
3. Keith Schneider, "Selling Out? Pushed and Pulled, Environment Inc. is on the Defensive" (*New York Times,* March 29, 1992), section 4.
4. Goldberg (1997), A-16.
5. Doug McAdam, *Political Process and the Development of Black Insurgency, 1930–1970* (Chicago: University of Chicago Press, 1982), 21.
6. Earl Latham, *The Group Basis of Politics* (New York: Octagon Books, 1965), 31.
7. See, for example, Mark Blaug, *Economic Theory in Retrospect* (Cambridge: Cambridge University Press, 1978), 482–87.
8. In a competitive market wherein everything is in equilibrium and all profits are zero, there is no special role for entrepreneurship.
9. Recall from the first chapter that the criticisms of traditional pluralism by Bachrach and Baratz, Schattschneider, and Walker revolved around the incomplete mobilization of interests.
10. Robert H. Salisbury, "An Exchange Theory of Interest Groups," *Midwest Journal of Political Science* 13 (1969): 1–32, 4.
11. Salisbury (1969), 4.
12. Virginia Gray and David Lowery, *The Population Ecology of Interest Representation: Lobbying Communities in the American States* (Ann Arbor: University of Michigan Press, 1996).
13. Salibury (1969), 11.
14. Some scholars differentiate expressive rewards from purposive benefits. Though distinctions may exist, they are sufficiently close that they are seldom both

included in a brief discussion of interest group benefits. James Q. Wilson states that purposive benefits "derive from the sense of satisfaction of having contributed to the attainment of a worthwhile cause." Wilson (1973), 34.

15. John Mark Hansen, "The Political Economy of Group Membership," *American Political Science Review* 79 (1985), 79–96.

16. It is very hard to secure accurate data to evaluate income and price elasticities. However, work by Christopher Jenck is quite intriguing. Jenck found that contribution levels responded to changes in income levels in a parabolic manner. The poor and the wealthy tend to contribute the most to nonprofits, leaving the vast middle class looking like a bunch of pikers. See Christopher Jenck, "Who Gives to What," in *The Nonprofit Sector: A Research Handbook,* ed. Walter W. Powell (New Haven: Yale University Press, 1987).

17. Daniel Kahneman and Amos Tversky, "Prospect Theory: An Analysis of Decisions under Risk," *Econometrica* 47 (1979): 263–91.

18. Hansen's (1985) work in this area remains somewhat controversial. For more information on these general matters, see Richard Jankowski and Clyde Brown's work entitled "Political Success, Government Subsidization, and the Group Freerider Problem," *Social Science Quarterly* 76 (1995): 853–62. For a very careful specification of individual's demands for group goods, see Paul E. Johnson's "Asymmetries in Political Entry," *European Journal of Political Economy* 6 (1990a): 378–96, and his article, "On the Theory of Political Competition," *Public Choice* 58 (1988): 217–35.

19. Albert O. Hirschman, *Shifting Involvements: Private Interest and Public Action* (Princeton, NJ: Princeton University Press, 1982). Related work by Jonathon Baron is also helpful. See "Political Action versus Voluntarism in Social Dilemmas and Aid for the Needy," *Rationality and Society* 9 (1997): 307–26.

20. This section is based on my collaborative work with Itai Sened. For a more rigorous presentation, see Ainsworth and Sened (1993). Work by Ainsworth entitled "Modeling Efficacy and Interest Group Membership," *Political Behavior* 22 (2000): 89–108 is also relevant.

21. To calculate $\binom{N}{\omega}$ one simply needs to determine all the ways in which one can select ω people out of a larger group of N people. Suppose N is 5 and ω is 2, then $\binom{N}{\omega} = 10$. The general formula is $N!/\omega!(N-\omega)!$, where $N! = N \times (N-1) \times (N-2) \times (N-3) \times \ldots \times 1$.

22. Hansen (1985).

23. Alexis de Tocqueville, *Democracy in America,* Volume Two. (New York: Schocken Books, 1961), 146.

24. Tocqueville (1961), 145–46.

25. Piven and Cloward (1977), 267, 297.

26. Street, Martin, and Gordon (1979), 129.

27. Street, Martin, and Gordon (1979), 129.

28. Wilson (1973), 203. Vista workers were the stateside equivalent of the Peace Corps volunteers.

29. Wolfe (1970).

30. Wilson (1973), 283.

31. Piven and Cloward (1977), 301.

32. Mollenkopf (1983).

33. Piven and Cloward (1977), 316.

34. Alinsky (1971).

35. John D. McCarthy and Mayer N. Zald, *The Trend of Social Movements in America: Professionalization and Resource Mobilization* (Morristown, NJ: General Learning Press, 1973), 16.

36. McCarthy and Zald (1973), 16.

37. Smith and Lipsky (1993), 4.
38. Smith and Lipsky (1993), 16. The role of private organizations in veterans' pensions is carefully detailed in various sources, including Theda Skocpol's *Protecting Soldiers and Mothers* (Cambridge: Harvard University Press, 1992) and Ainsworth's "Electoral Strength and the Emergence of Group Influence in the Late 1800s: The Grand Army of the Republic," *American Politics Quarterly* 23 (1995a): 319–38, and "Lobbyists as Interest Group Entrepreneurs and the Mobilization of Union Veterans," *American Review of Politics* 16 (1995b): 107–29.
39. Russell D. Roberts, "A Positive Model of Private Charity and Public Transfers," *Journal of Political Economy* 92 (1984): 136–48. Note pp. 141–47 in particular.
40. Smith and Lipsky (1993), 71.
41. See two books by Donald F. Kettl: *Government by Proxy: (Mis?) Managing Federal Programs* (Washington, D.C.: CQ Press, 1988), Chapter 5, and *Sharing Power: Public Governance and Private Markets* (Washington, D.C.: Brookings Institution, 1993), Chapter 5.
42. Kettl (1993), 14.
43. Smith and Lipsky (1993), 118.
44. Jerry Gray, "1-Man Crusade over Lobbying Ensnares a Bill," (*New York Times*, November 4, 1995), A-1.
45. Gray (1995), A-1–A-8.
46. Gray (1995), A-8.
47. Latham (1965), 12, emphasis added.
48. R. Kenneth Godwin's *One Billion Dollars of Influence: The Direct Marketing of Politics* (Chatham, NJ: Chatham House Publishers, 1988) is an excellent source for more detailed information. David L. Rados's *Marketing for Nonprofits*, 2nd ed. (Westport, CT: Auborn House, 1996) takes a more traditional marketing approach.
49. Godwin (1988), 11. Nownes (2000) also emphasizes the importance of finding the right prospects.
50. The array of goods popular among avid birders is quite extensive, including spotting scopes, parabolic microphones, and specialized software for recording sightings. Les Line, "Birds in the Bush and Database: The Gadgets Needed to Spot Birds Becomes Ever More Sophisticated," (*New York Times*, June 25, 1998), D-1, D-8.
51. Godwin (1988), 79.
52. This may also affect what James Q. Wilson and others have referred to as the purposive benefits that "derive from the sense of satisfaction of having contributed to the attainment of a worthwhile cause." Wilson (1973), 34.
53. The actual link between a contribution and a particular child's fate may be tenuous. That is, the strategy and the claim may not comport with reality. When reporters from the *Chicago Tribune* adopted twelve children through various relief agencies, they checked up on the agencies' claims about their newly adopted children. Two had been dead for over eighteen months, and "most had received few benefits." The links between a particular child and a particular contribution may enhance fundraising, but they fail to reflect how the agencies actually operate. The four agencies in question ran health clinics and schools, not a matching service. See Jane Fritsch's "Donations from the Heart, Greetings from the Grave" (*New York Times,* April 5, 1998), WK-7.
54. Robert Dreyfuss, "Which Doctors" (*The New Republic,* June 22, 1998), 22–23.
55. Andrew C. Revkin, "Gun Lobby Helps States Train Young Hunters" (*New York Times*, November 17, 1999), A-1, A-27.
56. Dreyfuss (1998), 24.
57. Dreyfuss (1998), 25.

58. Reed Abelson, "At Minnesota Public Radio, A Deal Way Above Average" (*New York Times*, March 27, 1998a), section C, and "Charities Use For-Profit Units to Avoid Disclosing Finances" (*New York Times*, February 2, 1998b), A-1, A-12.
59. Like groups, longtime politicians are often able to sell the list of contributors to their campaigns. Barry Goldwater (the Republican presidential candidate in 1964 and a longtime U.S. Senator from Arizona) sold his contributor list for $300,000 to a political consulting firm. Godwin (1988), 33.
60. Salisbury (1969), 13. Also see Ainsworth (1995a) and (1995b).
61. Wilson (1973), 174–75.
62. Truman (1971), 112.
63. Tocqueville (1961), 129–30.
64. For a different view of these issues, see Jeffrey M. Berry's "On the Origins of Public Interest Groups: A Test of Two Theories," *Polity* 10 (1978): 379–97.

4

Representing Interests

Introduction

Political interests are represented in many ways. Elected officials represent broad political and economic interests in their home states and districts. Those officials who do a poor job of representing such broad interests often fail in their reelection bids. Narrow interests are also represented by elected officials. Citizens seek venues at all levels of government to press their claims. Many individuals contact their representatives directly to seek personal assistance with one matter or another. They may request assistance with the Immigration and Naturalization Service, the Social Security Administration, or the Internal Revenue Service. They may even request information for their latest term paper. Attention to these matters is referred to as constituency service or casework, and representatives spend considerable time and energy on constituency service and casework.[1] In essence, constituency service involves the representation of individuals' narrow concerns, one person at a time.

Of course, elected officials are not alone in their representation of interests. Many interests are represented by some sort of interest group, trade association, or social organization. The array of interests represented in Washington by various groups, organizations, or associations is vast. Directories include hundreds of pages listing thousands of organizations with offices in Washington.[2] These organizations also represent broad and narrow interests, economic and political interests. Given the myriad of interests, finding a position supported by a majority is hardly straightforward. The variety of views represented by interest groups and elected officials complicates any general understanding of the representation of interests, which numerous scholars have sought to clarify.[3]

Identifying Majoritarian Interests

It is commonplace in introductory civics texts to refer to *the* majority or the tyranny of *the* majority. Rather than review the problems associated with a tyranny of the majority, consider a different tack: perhaps more than one majority exists. Suppose, for instance, that there are three groups, Group 1, Group 2, and Group 3, respectively comprising twenty-seven percent, thirty-three percent, and forty percent of a political society. In addition, suppose there are three alternatives under consideration, proposals *A* and *B* and the status quo, *X*. Table 4.1 summarizes this information. Each of the three groups has clear and distinct preferences about these policy alternatives. Group 1 prefers *A* to *B* to *X*; Group 2 prefers *B* to *X* to *A*; and Group 3 prefers *X* to *A* to *B*. Group 1 prefers anything to the status quo, Group 3 prefers nothing to the status quo, and Group 2 likes alternative *B* more than the status quo and alternative *A* less than the status quo.

TABLE 4.1
A Paradox of Majority Rule

Group 1 (27%)	Group 2 (33%)	Group 3 (40%)
A	B	X
B	X	A
X	A	B

Note: Every alternative can be majority rule defeated by some other alternative: *A* is defeated by *X*, *X* is defeated by *B*, and *B* is defeated by *A*.

The largest group prefers *X*, the status quo, over all other alternatives. Group 3 is satisfied, but Groups 1 and 2 suggest alternative *B*. Indeed, using majority rule, alternative *B* defeats *X*. The government responds by beginning a careful analysis of alternative *B*. Alternative *B* is completely undermined when Groups 1 and 3 offer alternative *A*. Alternative *A* is majority preferred to alternative *B*, so the government responds by provisionally adopting alternative *A*. The only problem with alternative *A* is that a majority, Groups 2 and 3, prefer alternative *X*. In this situation, there is no policy that is majority preferred to all other alternatives. Majority rule is inconclusive in this instance. Alternative *X* is the status quo, so one cannot solve this paradox by doing nothing. Perhaps there are reasons for adopting *X* rather than *A* or *B*, but one can adopt *X* only by ignoring the majority that prefers *B* over *X*.

Numerous scholars have analyzed this paradox of majority rule. Kenneth J. Arrow was one of the first scholars to detail carefully some of these aggregation problems and the implications of such problems.[4] Partly for that work, Arrow received the Noble Prize in economics. From time to time, the paradox is dubbed "Arrow's paradox" in his honor. The paradox does not always occur. Sometimes majority rule leads to a clear winner that cannot be undermined, but, as we have seen, majority rule need not produce a clear winner—sometimes a voting cycle does occur. Arrow showed that voting cycles are impossible to guard against without violating some notion of fairness. In the presence of a majority-rule voting cycle, objective public interests are easy to speak of but difficult to point to. If *public* is just another expression for the majority, then we know that the majority-rule paradox may inextricably confuse matters because there is more than one majority and every majority may be readily defeated by some new majority.[5] Suppose *public* implies the entire populace. Demanding unanimity before enacting public policies is a recipe for maintaining the status quo, and even when there is unanimity regarding the need to reform some policy, there is seldom unanimity regarding the best new policy to implement.[6] A voting cycle is most likely to occur when there are numerous alternatives and numerous people involved. A pluralist society with its manifold interests and numerous participants is almost perfectly designed for producing instances of Arrow's paradox.[7]

Principals and Agents

To help tackle the complex issue of representation, many scholars have either implicitly or explicitly employed a principal-agent perspective, wherein a principal is represented by some agent working on his or her behalf. The representation of interests is seldom straightforward, even under the simplest scenario in which one agent is hired by one principal to represent his interests and work on his behalf.

One principal and one agent

A single individual's interests may be represented by someone acting as that individual's agent in the same fashion that a single lawyer acts as an agent for a single client. In essence, the client (principal) hires a lawyer (agent). This form of representation appears most direct, but it is not without complications. Presumably, the lawyer was hired because he or she possesses some expertise that the principal does not. Given the differences in their backgrounds, training, and general areas of expertise, it is difficult for the client to evaluate the lawyer's work. The client knows how to evaluate a courtroom win or loss, but the client may not know how to evaluate the lawyer's work along the way. The lawyer therefore, maintains considerable leeway in the execution of his or her duties. The lawyer's actions and inactions affect the gathering of evidence, the determination of legal strategy, and the presentation of expert testimony. In sum, the lawyer determines his or her own level of effort. The lawyer's heart may or may not be in any particular case. Indeed, to maintain their own sanity, many lawyers try to avoid getting caught up in the numerous cases that land on their desk. Lawyers and other professionals, such as doctors and social workers, work to maintain a professional level of emotional detachment. In the face of all of this, are the client's interests being well represented? Does the client control the lawyer? The area of formal theory related to these issues is called principal-agent theory.[8] The principal-agent problem refers to the inability of the principal to monitor or evaluate all aspects of the agent's work. The principal must rely on the agent's good reputation and on a carefully written contract with appropriate incentive clauses. Even with these safeguards, the principal-agent problem never fully disappears.[9]

Voters and representatives: Many principals and few agents

Most often when one reads of a principal-agent problem, there is one principal represented by one agent. What happens when many people are represented by the same individual? For instance, many individuals are represented by a few elected officials, in which case the standard principal-agent form of representation is less applicable. United States representatives and senators represent interests, but legislators are only loosely controlled by their numerous principals (i.e., constituents).[10] Ostensibly, representatives and senators represent geographic regions, that is, districts and states, but within those geographic constituencies lie additional constituencies. After following a handful of U.S. representatives in their home districts, Richard Fenno noted that representatives develop a very clear sense of who their supporters are.[11] The geographic constituency is the largest and least important to the representative, because it includes all voters, supporters and nonsupporters alike. Within the geographic constituency lies the reelection constituency and within the reelection constituency lies the primary constituency, consisting of the representative's strongest allies. Within the primary constituency lies the personal constituency, made up of close personal friends and the most loyal of supporters. All individuals within the geographic confines of the district are being represented, but not in the same way. Representatives pay more attention to some constituents' concerns than others, so inevitably some voters are more pleased with the representative's job than other voters. The principal-agent problem is different for the personal, primary, reelection, and geographic constituencies.[12]

Group members and leaders: Many principals and few agents

How does group representation affect this increasingly complex picture of representation? All members of a group are represented by just a few group leaders and lobbyists, so the relationship is not one to one. However, if the members are reasonably like-minded, the fact that there are many principals may not affect the applicability of the standard principal-agent model. In other words, although the relationship is not one to one, if the many principals act as one, then the standard form of principal-agent representation may be more applicable than it is with elected representatives. To the extent that the principal-agent relationship holds, representatives of groups are more constrained and have less leeway in their day-to-day activities than elected officials.

The greatest distinctions between representation by group leaders and representation by elected officials derives from the simplest of observations. First, members can readily exit from groups they no longer like. Citizens may vote with their feet by moving to some new district or state, but such moves are rather costly. Second, unlike elected representatives, group leaders need not represent nonsupporters in any way. Legally, elected officials represent *all* citizens within a district, supporters and nonsupporters alike. In contrast, group leaders need only represent their members, who, by the signatures on their checks, indicate their general support. The third major difference between elected representatives and group representatives stems from the differences in the geographic versus the functional bases of representation. As explained in the previous section, elected officials represent geographic areas. Group representatives focus on functional divisions that may be spread across the entire country. Georgia's U.S. representatives represent Georgia farmers, Iowa representatives represent Iowa farmers, and Vermont representatives represent Vermont farmers, but farm groups represent their members from all states and districts.

This discussion only scratches the surface of the nature of representation. Obviously, interests in the United States are represented in many different ways by many different people, including both elected officials and interest group leaders. Not all interests are group related or demand group representation. For instance, in some districts, geographic and functional representation are largely the same. A Kansas district of corn producers will be well represented by its elected officials regardless of the lobbying activities of the Corn Producers Association. However, in most states and districts, functional and geographic representation remain distinct, providing groups an opportunity to complement the geographic representation of interests with a functional representation.

Groups and Democratic Governance

"Let's vote." Virtually everyone has a childhood memory of being with a group of friends and having difficulty coming to a group decision. Someone blurts out, "Let's vote." Instances of democracy at a group level begin very early in our lives and continue throughout our lives. Indeed, some of the most important work on democratic governance views democracy at the group level as essential to democratic governance at the national level. Though barely over one-hundred pages long, Carole Pateman's book on political participation and democratic theory has had a profound and sustained impact on numerous subfields in political science.[13]

Pateman focused on some of the most complex puzzles faced by social scientists. Pateman asked: How do people come to accept democratic governance and how do they learn to participate in democratic politics? Democratic traditions vary tremendously from nation to nation. In the United States, these issues may seem straightforward because democratic traditions appear quite strong.[14] However, some democratic traditions in the United States are stronger than others. Consider, for instance, the simple fact that voter turnout in the United States is generally quite low. Some democratic traditions may be strong, but on average electoral participation is limited. In other countries with long democratic traditions, electoral turnout is often higher, but the allegiance to one form of government or another may be short-lived. France had several different national constitutions during the twentieth century. New Zealand and Italy recently altered their electoral systems in very fundamental ways.[15] Numerous newly independent states in eastern Europe are experimenting with various forms of democratic governance. For the United States as well as other countries, the relevance of Pateman's questions persists: How do people learn about and adjust to democratic governance? What role, if any, do groups play?

At various times, groups have been considered the saving grace of democracy. For instance, during the heyday of corrupt party systems in the late 1800s and early 1900s, various groups fought to instill greater professionalism in government. Put simply, groups led the charge against the spoils system. In the absence of reasonable government standards and regulations for everyone from barristers to builders, associations of engineers, doctors, lawyers, and other professionals regulated themselves by establishing and enforcing their own standards. Such professional associations required the participation of members, and Pateman (as well as the French sociologist Alexis de Tocqueville and others) argued that the very act of participation in groups enhanced democracy by instilling and reinforcing democratic values that were essential to the preservation of the state. For Pateman, the practice of democracy had to be learned, and it was best learned at the local, group level.[16] In the same vein, de Tocqueville had argued that "civil association" in groups and "political association" in the larger state reinforced each other.[17] Perhaps people do learn about large-scale democratic practices through experiments in small-scale group democracies. If there is a congruence of democratic ideals in groups and the state, then group involvement might very well inculcate democratic virtues and enhance democratic participation in the state, which for many commentators would be a good thing. Empirical research indicates that group members are more apt to participate in electoral politics than nongroup members.[18]

Surprisingly, neither Pateman nor de Tocqueville addressed how democracy actually operates at the group level. If decision making in groups does not mirror decision-making processes elsewhere, groups may provide poor training grounds. At the very least, democratic decision making requires that individuals have some input into collective decisions. Typically, such inputs are simply votes. How does voting operate in groups? Are there other means of affecting group policies? How do the institutional structures within groups affect policy choices? How do interest group members react to democratically chosen policy alternatives? These issues and others are explored in considerable detail in this chapter.

Decision Making in Groups

Decision making in groups is quite varied. Some groups engage in direct democracy, allowing members to decide upon everything from dues levels to policy concerns to menus for a holiday party. Some business associations use weighted voting schemes, giving those members who control the most market shares more input. Corporations adopt a similar structure, giving those stockholders with more shares more votes. Most interest groups, however, have limited opportunities for members to express their input; instead, they are governed by a small body of group leaders. Truman stated that "it is virtually impossible for any considerable body of people to solve directly all the problems that may confront it," suggesting that some concentration of decision-making powers in a few group leaders may be both inevitable and perfectly reasonable.[19] Whether members deserve or want increased means of participation may remain a question, but for the vast majority of groups, member input is very limited. Many group members are checkbook members and nothing else. That is, these members decided to send in their dues, but they do not expect or want to participate in the group's decision making. Checkbook members are most common in those groups that rely heavily on direct-mail marketing of the sort discussed in the previous chapter. The members of such groups face a take-it-or-leave-it situation, but their signatures on their membership checks suggest an overall approval. As one group entrepreneur stated,

> the most conclusive vote cast by the individual is his decision to join or resign. His joining is in effect a vote for the movement; his resignation or failure to renew membership is a vote against. Thus, collectively, the members hold life-or-death control over the organization. If enough of them fail to renew their memberships, that will be the end.[20]

Although democracy, as commonly understood, is not practiced by many groups, some of the most important groups in the United States do allow for more traditional forms of democratic input. Many citizen-based public interest groups, occupation-based professional associations (representing doctors, engineers, lawyers, professors, or the like), and labor unions practice democratic governance.

In her work, Pateman focused on unions and direct democracy as practiced on the factory floor. Records of democratic governance in the labor movement dates back to at least 1881, when the Federation of Organized Trades and Labor Unions was created in Pittsburgh, Pennsylvania. More than one hundred representatives of labor organizations from more than a dozen states attended. Although the opportunities for member input into union governance has a long history, member participation was often quite limited by the middle part of the twentieth century.

> One might expect that most groups would exhibit high participation. Yet over-all activity in the locals studied was low. Frequently less than five percent of the total membership attended meetings. . . . Most union leaders admitted frankly that apathy was one of their major problems.[21]

Arguing that unions failed to represent workers and their interests, union opponents pushed hard for federal regulations. The 1947 Taft-Hartley Act mandated regular union elections to be overseen by the federal government's National Labor Relations Board. Supporters of the Taft-Hartley Act viewed the election requirements as a means to check the labor movement. The Taft-Hartley proponents felt that the workers would reject union representation if the ballots were secret and the election monitored. If one thinks of the union as the provider of public goods in the form of safer work conditions and higher union wages, then it is not surprising that, for the four-year period during which elections were mandated, unions won over ninety-five percent of all elections. Indeed, a vast majority of those voting approved of compulsory union membership representation.[22] This may appear ironic: workers agreeing to restrictions on freeriding. However, if a union ensures a coordinated effort to overcome a collective-action problem, then the workers have little reason to seek something different.

Empirical research over the last thirty years has noted the tendency for group members to be more politically active in electoral politics. That is, the civil associations appear to promote broader political involvement. The increased electoral participation is ironic because members of groups are seldom very active in them. It does not appear that members are whetting their appetites for more and more participation, because they are barely participating in the groups. Truman wrote that "no individual is wholly absorbed in any group to which he belongs," suggesting that members may have considerable tolerance of group decisions made by others in the group.[23] Conformity to the group's decisions, Truman argued, is just part of the price of acceptance by the group. However, not all members choose to conform. Some members prefer to leave the group rather than conform. In very different types of work, Larry Rothenberg and Paul Johnson have shown how sensitive groups are to the retention of group members.[24] Indeed, the retention of members is as important as attracting them initially. The remaining sections of this chapter assess the impact of conformity and exit on group decision making and group governance. Although decision making in groups is quite varied, one way or another, groups adopt a particular set of policies. Under what circumstance do members conform to group policies? When do they leave or exit a group? In short, how do members respond to group governance?

Social Choice Theory and Group Decision Making

Social choice theory is a field of study that examines the means by which individuals' preferences can be aggregated into some sort of social or group choice. In the language developed earlier, one might wonder how multiple principals come to agree among themselves. It may seem that this process is fairly straightforward; after all, how difficult is it to structure an election and count hands? But as the earlier discussion of voting cycles showed, many aspects of this aggregation process are not straightforward. An election between more than two alternatives may leave a majority of individuals disgruntled with the results.

Black's theorem

Group members may be called upon to decide any number of important issues, including something as straightforward as membership fees. Though the issue may appear mundane, two points deserve attention. First, membership fees are a common concern across many groups. Second, using a simple, straightforward issue for means of illustration allows one to focus on the primary concern, namely, the effects of democratic governance on groups and group members. So, suppose members of some group needed to determine a level of dues for their organization. Each of the various members might reasonably desire different levels of dues. If some members joined because of social pressure or outright coercion, they might prefer smaller budgets with little money allotted for social activities to larger budgets with money set aside for monthly picnics. In contrast, those people who joined for solidary and expressive benefits might feel that an organization with meager budgets would be of little use. In short, any given member may feel that a particular level of dues is too high or too low. If the dues are too low, the group becomes ineffective and unrewarding for some members. If the dues are set too high, the costs of group involvement sharply constrain other purchases, making group membership unattractive.

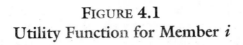

FIGURE **4.1**
Utility Function for Member *i*

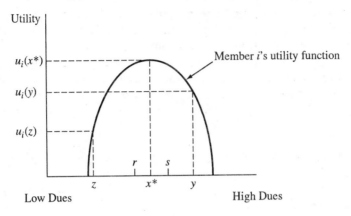

How can one illustrate these diverse preferences for group members? How are these diverse preferences aggregated into some sort of common group voice? In Figure 4.1, the x-axis represents dues, and the y-axis represents utility or benefit. The inverted u in Figure 4.1 displays member i's utility function for dues levels. A utility function provides a graphical representation of someone's preferences. If some alternative y is preferred to another alternative, say z, then the benefit or utility associated with y is greater than that for z. The subscript i is a simple and common label that distinguishes members from one another. Full names might be another reasonable label to use, but they would almost certainly become cumbersome.

Member i's utility is maximized at x^*. That is, the level of dues that i is happiest with is at x^*. As the hypothetical dues level moves further and further away from x* in either direction, i's utility steadily decreases. This feature of the utility function is called single-peakedness. It is easy, for instance, to see that the utility of x^* is greater than the utility of y, which is greater than the utility of z. At this point, we restrict attention to symmetric utility functions so that any two points equidistant from x^* yield the same level of utility for member i. In Figure 4.1, alternatives r and s are equidistant from x^*, so they must yield the same utility to i. With this simplification, the members' ideal points convey all the information that one needs. The closer an alternative is to i's ideal point, the greater the utility or benefit of the alternative to individual i. Distance affects utility in a simple, straightforward fashion, so we no longer have to draw utility functions per se.

The diversity in the members' preferences is indicated by the wide range of members' ideal points. In Figure 4.2, there are five individuals' ideal points displayed. How can these five individuals ($i, j, k, l,$ and n) settle upon an acceptable level of dues? Each individual would most prefer his or her own

FIGURE 4.2
Ideal Points for Members *i, j, k, l,* and *n*

k = median member

x_{ave} = average of members' most preferred levels of dues

ideal point as the chosen alternative. Compromising with some sort of average of all ideal points yields alternative x_{ave}, which is fairly good for member k, but not for i or j. Indeed, individuals i, j, and k could form a coalition to move the outcome from the average to k's ideal point. As drawn in Figure 4.2, k has the same number of people to his left as to his right, which means that k is the median individual. Movements to the left of k's ideal point would be blocked by a coalition of members k, l, and n; and movements to the right would be blocked by a coalition of i, j, and k. If majority rule is used, then regardless of the original level of dues, the unique equilibrium in this setting is the median individual's ideal point. This result is stated most commonly as Black's median voter theorem.

> Black's Median Voter Theorem:[25] If all members of a group have single-peaked preferences, then the median voter's ideal point is the unique equilibrium.

The median voter is the one whose ideal point is middle-most. From Figure 4.2, it is easy to see that the median and the average are different concepts. It is also clear that the median does not leave everyone satisfied. The median is not a compromise position that leaves everyone gaining a bit. If the old level of dues was at x_{ave}, then members l and n lost a bit when the dues shifted to k. However, even member i may feel she gained too little.

As stated here, Black's theorem relies on five assumptions. (1) The policy is unidimensional. Black's theorem will not generally hold in more than one dimension. If a group insists on simultaneously deciding upon a level of dues and a lobbying stand, Black's theorem will not necessarily hold, and the group is more likely to encounter a majority-rule voting cycle. (2) The number of members in the group is odd. This is largely a convenience, but it is worth noting that the uniqueness result depends on it. In even-numbered groups, any alternative between the two middle-most members would be in equilibrium.[26] (3) All individuals participate, so there are no abstentions.

(4) All voting is sincere. If the utility of alternative A is greater than B for some individual, then that individual's vote must correspond to his or her preference for A over B. (5) Lest one forget, the preferences are single-peaked and symmetric. Black's theorem is very powerful. If one can identify the voters and their ideal points, then predicting the winning alternative for any left–right issue is simple. The median voter's ideal point is the unique equilibrium, regardless of the position of the status quo.

To apply Black's result to interest group decision making, the third and fourth assumptions demand careful consideration. On the basis of Black's theorem, members i, j, l, and n will never secure their most preferred outcome. One might counter that in this world no individual ever gets exactly what he or she wants. But in this situation, k does secure his or her ideal point and members i, j, l, and n know that they will never secure any outcome other than k's ideal point. Members i and j have to pay a level of dues they consider too high, and l and n are paying a level of dues they consider too low. How should a member respond to dues levels that are *a little* higher or lower than their ideal points? Most likely, the member would acknowledge that life is not perfect and pay the dues. Now suppose the dues level is appreciably higher or lower than their ideal points. At some point, the member is likely to say, "Life is not perfect, but I can make mine better by quitting this group."

Figure 4.3 reproduces the utility function from Figure 4.1, but this time we have added a tolerance interval marked by x' and x''. Note that the utility levels associated with the dues levels within x' and x'' are all greater than or equal to u^t, where the t indicates the minimum utility for dues levels within the tolerance interval. Any dues level outside the tolerance interval yields a utility less than u^t. To represent a member's conformity to group choices, suppose that members withstand deviations that remain within their tolerance intervals. To help characterize those situations that lead a member to exit a group, suppose that any dues levels that fall beyond the tolerance interval leads the member to leave the group. The precise nature of these utility functions and tolerance intervals will vary by member. Figure 4.4 includes utility functions for two very different kinds of members.

First, their ideal points are very different. These two members seek different outcomes. Second, their tolerance intervals are very different. Member j's narrow and steep utility function necessarily has a very small tolerance interval, (y', y''). Such a member is quick to leave a group when policies diverge from y^*. Member i's broader and flatter utility function portrays an accepting, tolerant, or, perhaps, largely indifferent member. The tolerance interval for member i is relatively large, (x', x''). Such a member is not quick to leave a group. As illustrated in Figure 4.4, member i would tolerate j's ideal level of dues, but member j would not tolerate i's.

The symmetry restriction mandated earlier once again allows for considerable simplification. All necessary information is conveyed by the tolerance in-

FIGURE 4.3
Member *i*'s Utility Function and Tolerance Interval

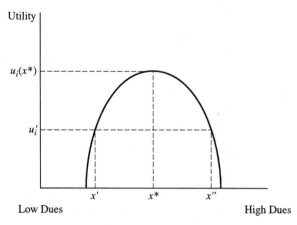

$u_i(x^*)$= Member *i*'s utility derived from her most preferred level of dues

u_i^t = lowest level of utility that member *i* will tolerate

Member *i* stays if a dues level at or between x' and x'' is adopted.

Member *i* leaves if a dues level less than x' or greater than x'' is adopted.

FIGURE 4.4
Two Members' Utility Functions Juxtaposed

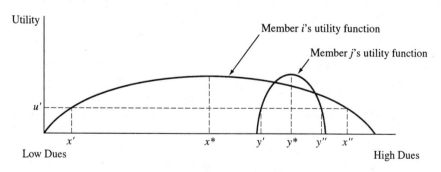

Member *i* stays if a dues level at or between x' and x'' is adopted.

Member *i* leaves if a dues level less than x' or greater than x'' is adopted.

Member *i* stays if a dues level at or between y' and y'' is adopted.

Member *i* leaves if a dues level less than y' or greater than y'' is adopted.

FIGURE 4.5
Ideal Points and Tolerance Intervals
for Members *i*, *j*, *k*, *l*, and *n*

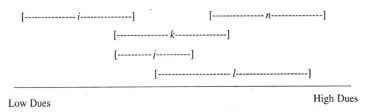

Low Dues   High Dues

$i, j, \ldots, n$ = members' most preferred levels of dues

Brackets indicate the range of members' tolerance intervals.

Results : Dues are set at *k*. Members *i* and *n* leave the group. The group of
j, *k*, *l* maintain the dues at *k*.

tervals and the ideal points of the members. As before, utility decreases as the dues level moves further and further from one's ideal point. Now, however, a member may choose to exit the group. When an outcome falls within a member's tolerance interval, that member will stay and conform to the dictates of the group; but when an outcome falls beyond a member's tolerance interval, that member will leave the group rather than conform. Figure 4.5 portrays the ideal points and tolerance intervals of five individuals. Note that the ideal points are always at the midpoint of the tolerance intervals. This is due to the symmetry condition.

To avoid confusion, different members' tolerance intervals are indicated separately. Those members with large tolerance intervals are more likely to accept group decisions. Those with narrow tolerance intervals are more likely to reject group decisions and exit the organization. Using majority rule, *k*'s ideal point is once again the unique equilibrium. How do the other members react to *k*'s ideal point? Members *i* and *n* exit the group because *k*'s ideal point falls outside their tolerance intervals. What remains of the group? Only members *j*, *k*, and *l* remain, but even in this new, smaller group, *k*'s ideal point remains the equilibrium. The group dwindled in size, but the group's policy stand did not change. One might argue that the milieu of the new group is different because the remaining members are more like-minded and cohesive, as measured by the closeness of their ideal points and the overlap in their tolerance intervals.

FIGURE 4.6
New Ideal Points and Tolerance Intervals
for Members *i, j, k, l,* and *n*

i, j, . . . , n = members' most preferred levels of dues

Brackets indicate the range of members' tolerance intervals.

Results: Dues are set at *k*. Members *i* and *j* leave the group. The group of *k, l, n* adopt a new
level of dues at *l*. Member *k* then leaves the group.

There is nothing general about the manner in which members exited from
the group in Figure 4.5. That is, the extreme members may not always be the
first to exit, and exiting may not occur from both extremes at the same time.
Consider another case in which those members who prefer higher levels of
dues are very tolerant of lower levels whereas those with preferences for very
low levels of dues are very intolerant of higher levels. Figure 4.6 portrays just
such a situation.

The initial equilibrium is once again at *k*'s ideal point, since *k* is the median. This time, however, members *i* and *j* exit the group, leaving only *k, l,*
and *n*. For those remaining, the new median is *l,* not *k*. Member *k* reacts to
the new equilibrium at *l*'s ideal point by exiting the group. Suddenly the
group has unraveled to the point of having only two members, less than half
the number with which it started. Even though the remaining members, *l*
and *n,* would have tolerated lower dues, the organization unraveled anyway.

The impact of unraveling and potential unraveling

Groups do not always completely unravel. But by the same token, members
do not always accept group policies. Paul Johnson, the first person to study
the issue of unraveling formally, has shown that unraveling is always a possibility even though it is not an inevitable result of democratic group governance.[27] At least since the 1950s, when Truman's work was being widely read,

interest group scholars have noted the difficulties of internal group govern-ance. Truman's work was, however, strictly empirical. He observed and documented some groups having difficulties with self-governance, but he never fully explained why. Paul Johnson's social choice theoretic work illus-trated just how sensitive groups are to unraveling. In social choice theory, Black's theorem is a fundamental result; that is, under very general settings, the median voter's ideal point is the unique equilibrium. But whenever exit is an option, the stability of the median individual's ideal point cannot be guar-anteed. Indeed, the adoption of the median voter's ideal point may lead to the complete unraveling of the group. The potential for unraveling forces group leaders to be concerned about both the policy stand of the group and the impact of that stand on membership levels. Traditionally, social choice theorists have focused exclusively on the policy stand a group might make; but for interest groups the effect of a policy stand on membership levels is fundamental to the effective functioning and perhaps even to the very sur-vival of the group.

Solutions to Unraveling

Groups tend to be dominated by entrepreneurs who are flexible. They recog-nize the connections between policy stands, membership levels, and group survival. Those entrepreneurs who are inflexible about group policy risk the possibility of having their groups unravel. Any unraveling weakens a group, but unraveling at the elite level is especially dangerous. When elite members of a group choose to leave, they often encourage others to leave with them to facilitate the formation of a rival splinter organization. The original group thereby loses money and faces greater competition for new members. Not surprisingly, groups adopt various strategies to limit the possibilities of unrav-eling. No one strategy is a panacea, but each tends to dampen the impact of exiting from the organization. The following seven strategies limit either the likelihood or the impact of unraveling.

1: *Selective Incentives and Solidary Rewards:* In the spirit of Olson's by-product theory, groups' leaders increase the emphasis on selective incentives and solidary rewards. By focusing members' attention away from policy con-cerns and toward solidary and selective rewards, groups may survive a less popular policy stand. If one joins a group for its magazine or discounted in-surance, its policy stand may be of little consequence.

2: *Sorting Mechanisms:* Groups sort members by their willingness to pay. Virtually every organization allows members to join at different levels of dues. The less money one has to pay for membership, the less likely one is to become upset about group policies.

3: *Super Majorities:* Requiring supermajorities (e.g., two-thirds or three-quarters) instead of simple majorities (one-half plus one) will also reduce the likelihood of unraveling. Supermajorities make it more difficult to change the status quo. Any procedure that is biased in favor of the status quo limits unraveling. As Johnson states, "present members can be presumed to tolerate the status quo, but they cannot be assumed to tolerate change."[28]

4: *Federal Structures:* Many groups adopt federated structures, that is, they have national, state, and local affiliates. The Chamber of Commerce, labor unions, and many environmental groups maintain a federal structure, with affiliated organizations existing at the national, state, and local levels. At least since the time of Truman's *Governmental Process,* interest group scholars have recognized that federations have less internal cohesion because the national concerns and the state or local concerns are seldom the same. Federations do, however, ensure a certain amount of autonomy at the local level. Although the state and local affiliates typically pay dues to the national organization, the locals and the national generally agree not to meddle in each other's affairs. Although there is less cohesion within the entire federated structure, the larger, national group may avoid the unraveling problem by allowing the locals to determine some policies while reserving other policies for the national organization.

5: *Foresight:* Johnson showed that members' own foresight may limit unraveling. Members who recognize that their support for a policy may lead to the unraveling of the group are in a position to alter their votes. Of course, the fourth assumption related to Black's median voter theorem requires that all voting be sincere. If the utility of alternative A is greater than the utility for alternative B for some member, then that member must support or vote for A over B. Foresight may require a different action. Foresight demands that if the utility of alternative A is greater than B for some individual, then that individual's vote must correspond to his or her preference for A over B *as long as A does not lead to the unraveling of the group.* If all members of a group use foresight, their induced preferences over dues levels are no longer single-peaked. Recall that one of the assumptions related to Black's median voter theorem is that all individuals' preferences are single-peaked. Without single-peaked preferences, Black's median voter theorem no longer holds, so predicting which level of dues will actually be obtained is more difficult.

6: *Internal Propaganda:* Truman argued that "internal propaganda" was key to maintaining cohesion in groups.[29] That is, group leaders must constantly lobby the members to maintain support for the group. Often internal propaganda efforts are referred to as "farming the membership."[30] Group leaders engage in such efforts to ensure that members accept the group line. The direction of influence, from leader to member, is clear. Truman, however, also included group referenda as propaganda tools. With referenda, members may influence group leaders. Referenda are commonly used in Common Cause and Sierra Club to determine which issues should be pursued by group lobbyists. Common Cause, a prominent public interest group active in Washington lobbying since its founding in 1970, dropped some of its lobbying campaigns because of members' opposition. The members registered their opposition in various ways, including the group's own referenda.[31] Whether the focus is on leaders' attempts to keep members in line or on referenda that allow members to influence leaders, once again the limits to Truman's notions of "shared attitudes" and "like-mindedness" become clear.

7: *Sanctions and Coercion:* One should not overlook the role of sanctions or coercion. In the same fashion that sanctions or coercion may induce individuals to join a group, they can also be used to prevent individuals from exiting. For instance, various scholars have wondered why workers typically retain their union memberships even during costly strikes. To be certain, strike funds, which pay partial salaries during the work stoppage, are very important. However, strike funds only go so far, and union dues can be substantial. Unions, it seems, should be particularly vulnerable to members choosing to exit during rough times, only to rejoin later if things look better. As it happens, key benefits are tied to one's seniority or length of continuous current membership in unions. If one leaves the group, even temporarily, one risks losing all the benefits tied to seniority. Therefore, the youngest workers with little seniority have little to lose by quitting the union during the strike. If need be, these younger workers can rejoin after the strike is over. Very senior members, who are close to retirement, might view the chances of a strike resolution to be too slim to make union retention worthwhile. The vast numbers of workers with moderate amounts of seniority are those who would be most apt to stay. A seniority system establishes penalties for those who exit. Though vulnerable to unraveling, unions, like other voluntary associations, adopt procedures to limit such unraveling.[32]

Obviously, there are ways to limit unraveling, but it is impossible to prevent an individual's exit. Even in those groups that are not democratically governed, members can still vote with their feet and their wallets and pocketbooks.

Examples of Group Governance

There is no reason to consider the issue of unraveling narrowly. Whether democratically governed or not, exit from a group is always an option. Unraveling, therefore, is a concern of all groups and not just those that are democratically governed. The illustrations developed so far dealt with a group's level of dues, but any policy decision that allows for a simply left–right portrayal can be analyzed in the same fashion. In the rest of this section, the potential of the unraveling problem is used to highlight the difficulties of group governance. The groups discussed, the NAACP, the Sierra Club, and the NRA, each have formal channels for members' input into group governance. Each group has elected board members, and the Sierra Club allows ballot initiatives from members. Because these groups have formal means for members' inputs, their empirical record is easier to follow. The recorded votes and referenda tell the tale. Brief histories of some of the key concerns for these groups help to highlight the problem of unraveling.

The National Association for the Advancement of Colored People[33]

The history of the The National Association for the Advancement of Colored People (NAACP) is intertwined with the increased sensitivity to civil rights and liberties and the economic and social conditions of black Americans after the Civil War. What is less well known about the late 1800s and early to mid-1900s is how many different organizations were involved with these issues. What happened to the Committee of Twelve, the Niagra Movement, the Constitution League, and others? Many groups concerned about the fate of black Americans emerged during this period of time, and most of them failed. If one lives in an interest group society, it is especially important to remember that sometimes groups fail. The dominance of *groups* or the *group system* does not imply any individual group's omnipotence. The collective-action problem and the unraveling problem illustrate how easy it is for groups to fail. Internal policy disputes led to the failure of several of the earliest groups addressing the concerns of black Americans. That is, internal governance could not overcome policy differences among members.

Some black interests were represented prior to the Civil War by groups organized and maintained by whites. These organizations had various motivations. The American Anti-Slavery Society pursued abolitionism with a genuine religious fervor. It considered slaveholding a sin that jeopardized the souls of both the slave and the owner. The Freedman's Bureau focused on the means to ease the economic hardships created by emancipation. Urban League Clubs were created under the leadership of the Republican Party. These clubs existed prior to the end of the Civil War, let alone the Fifteenth Amendment (which gave blacks the right to vote in all states and regions) or Reconstruction in the South.[34] Urban clubs were vote mobilizers for the Republican Party during a period of considerable partisan jostling.

Though still aligned with white supporters, a black movement emerged around the turn of the twentieth century. Two very different black American intellectuals, Booker T. Washington and W. E. B. DuBois, dominated the debates in the emerging black movement. Washington stressed the need for technical training to promote self-sufficiency and economic vitality in the black community. Throughout much of the late 1800s, Washington's emphasis on economic conditions held sway. The Constitution League and Afro-American Councils embodied many of Washington's arguments. DuBois was considered more radical. Quoting the English poet Lord Byron, DuBois's call to arms did sound literal: "Hereditary bondsmen! Know ye not Who would be free themselves must strike the blow?"[35] In Chapter 3 of *The Souls of Black Folk*, DuBois's assessment of Washington is equally sharp and direct.

It has been claimed that the Negro can survive only through submission. Mr. Washington distinctly asks that black people give up, at least for the present, three things,—

First, political power,
Second, insistence on civil rights,
Third, higher education of Negro youth,

and concentrate all their energies on industrial education, the accumulation of wealth, and the conciliation of the South. This policy has been courageously and insistently advocated for over fifteen years, and has been triumphant for perhaps ten years. As a result of this tender of the palm-branch, what has been the return? In these years there have occurred:

1. The disfranchisement of the Negro.
2. The legal creation of a distinct status of civil inferiority for the Negro.
3. The steady withdrawal of aid from institutions for the higher training of the Negro.[36]

In DuBois's view, blacks' conditions would never improve until their political rights were guaranteed. Despite the passage of the Fourteenth and Fifteenth Amendments, few blacks had access to the ballot at this time, many were vulnerable to physical violence, and all faced discrimination. The end of Reconstruction allowed the southern states once again to govern themselves completely without interference from the North. Various laws or procedures were used to limit blacks' access to the ballot. Collectively referred to as Jim Crow laws, poll taxes, literacy tests, and grandfather clauses limited black participation. With the end of Reconstruction, Jim Crow governed with a harsh hand. Economic advancement meant little if personal safety and economic property rights were not recognized and guaranteed.

Of course, black leaders, including Washington and DuBois, recognized that they would be stronger if they could bridge their differences and combine forces. The Committee of Twelve for the Advancement of the Interests of the Negro Race was formed in 1904 in New York City. Given the composition of the group, the Committee of Twelve was dominated by Washington, and given the lessons of this chapter it should not be surprising that Washington and DuBois were unable to bridge their differences. The Committee of Twelve disintegrated after DuBois's exit. That is, the group unraveled. DuBois started the Niagra movement the next year, 1905.

In 1908, race riots throughout much of the United States proved especially vicious.[37] Blacks had always feared unequal treatment under the law, but riotous white mobs brought lynchings, looting, and the destruction of homes and property. Many noted with tragic irony that the Springfield, Illinois, riot in the "Land of Lincoln" was among the deadliest. Though not formally incorporated until 1910, a small handful of white leaders started to meet on a regular basis, after the worst of the riots, to assess the ways to advance the concerns of black Americans. By 1909, the NAACP formed, and the DuBois movement quickly merged with it. Like the earliest black organizations, the NAACP was initially formed by whites. DuBois merged his forces with it because he needed a larger membership pool and the resources of the wealthier white community. DuBois soon emerged as a leader within the NAACP, leading more conservative members to form a spin-off organization. In the tradition of Washington, the National Urban League focused almost exclusively on economic rather than civil issues. Once again, divisions led to a large exodus and the formation of a splinter group.

Unraveling problems are not just a concern for history. Unraveling problems are never solved once and for all. Fast-forward to the 1990s. During the early 1990s, the NAACP experienced losses in membership and patronage support, increasing debts, and an internal struggle for power.[38] The NAACP is headed by an elected chair, who is then responsible for hiring an executive director to run the day-to-day operations. Dr. William F. Gibson, as chair, and Benjamin Chavis Jr., as executive director, led the organization during the particularly turbulent and scandal-ridden period. By the middle of the 1990s, intense competition for numerous leadership positions emerged. Chavis quit the organization entirely, and Myrlie Evers-Williams defeated Gibson by a single vote to gain the chair position. Evers-Williams then managed to attract former U.S. House Representative Kweisi Mfume to guide the organization as executive director. Mfume's rise from destitution and life as a petty criminal to become a highly respected member of Congress is difficult to parallel. Mfume's image of success against all odds and his proven track record were irresistible. Soon after attracting Mfume, Myrlie Evers-Williams resigned her position to devote full time to the organization of a memorial foundation in honor of her first husband, the slain civil rights leader Medgar Evers. Evers-Williams was replaced by a another long- standing leader in the Civil Rights movement, Julian Bond. In his first major address, Bond spoke of the recent in-fighting: "I promise that you will read about the NAACP because we are fighting for civil rights and not because we are fighting with each other."[39] Though on a firmer footing, securing new leadership seldom provides a quick fix. Some patronage support has returned, but debt remains, and the staff continues to be a fraction of its former size. In 1995, the staff numbered about sixty-five, down from 240 just a couple of years earlier.[40] Obviously, unraveling can be attenuated or addressed with the careful selection of leaders, but sometimes genuine policy differences are insurmountable, as seen in the debates between Washington and DuBois.

The Sierra Club

Unlike most broad-based groups, the Sierra Club's board is elected by the membership. Campaigns for seats on the Sierra Club's board of directors are often rancorous, but during the spring of 1998 the elections were particularly volatile. Sierra Club members were asked to decide the group's stand on immigration and population control. For some members, these issues are central to the preservation of the environment because with any population increase, there is an inexorable pressure to develop more and more of the country's natural resources. For others in the group, immigration and population control are too far afield of the group's initial goals and concerns. A coordinator for those members seeking a moratorium on immigration as a means to control the U.S. population called the dispute a "part of a larger struggle for the soul of the environmental movement."[41] Other members pleaded that the club should not "commit suicide over the immigration issue."[42] Each side expended considerable resources to present their concerns to the entire membership. Each side maintained its own extensive web site, and numerous state and local chapters were involved on one side of the issue or another. Although the anti-immigration side lost, it secured almost thirty-nine percent of the votes cast.

What makes good environmental sense? What makes good politics? One side of the population- and immigration-control issue argues that environments have a carrying capacity that cannot be overloaded without dire consequences. Population control, therefore, becomes an environmental issue. The other side of the issue is straightforward as well. Controls on *global* population control, rather than U.S. immigration restrictions, are best suited to control the environmental hazards of unabated population growth. Furthermore, over one-third of the Sierra Club's 550,000 membership lives in California, where immigration issues are particularly volatile. About twenty-five percent of the foreign-born U.S. citizens counted in the most recent census live in California. The concerns on each side were genuine, but the impact of the debate was not only over group policy. In 1969, David R. Brower resigned from the Sierra Club board of directors to start the Friends of the Earth. Brower felt that the Sierra Club had become too complacent politically. He wanted to promote both the enjoyment of the environment and the protection of the environment through political action. Under Brower's leadership, Friends of the Earth would be much more aggressive politically. With the debates over immigration policy, another splinter may be in the offing.

The National Rifle Association

The National Rifle Association (NRA) has had various incarnations throughout its long history. Like so many groups in the United States, it has at times relied heavily on government support. The roots of the NRA go back to the late 1800s. The founding members of the NRA, chagrined by the poor shooting skills of Union soldiers, sought surplus government guns and ammunition for organizations devoted to the improvement of marksmanship. The NRA, therefore, started as a sports organization. As hunting became more popular, the NRA stressed both marksmanship and hunting. There were no major strains in the group, which remained primarily fraternal and sports oriented. Not until the mid-1960s did the NRA begin to take a law-and-order stand. The 1960s were a tumultuous period for the United States, particularly in its inner cities and on some college campuses. During those years, there were assassinations of three prominent political figures: one president, one civil rights leader, and one former cabinet official and presidential aspirant. Riots in the inner cities and on one college campus were quelled with deadly force. Also during this period, the Supreme Court handed down two unpopular decisions: Escobedo and Miranda.[43] Many individuals assailed the Court, accusing it of preserving suspects' rights at the cost of victims' rights and the preservation of an orderly society. Police organizations were particularly upset by the Escobedo and Miranda decisions because they allowed courts to ignore evidence and signed confessions if police failed to protect a suspect's rights to due process. Procedures trumped evidence. During much of this time, the NRA worked closely with police organizations on law and order issues.

The 1960s also brought the first major piece of federal gun control legislation. The NRA and law enforcement officials initially viewed the 1968 Gun Control Act in very similar ways. However, the NRA's official support for the 1968 act led to dissensions within the group. A growing number of NRA members feared that their Second Amendment rights were jeopardized. Internal NRA disputes culminated at the 1977 Cincinnati convention in a wholesale change in the NRA leadership. The new NRA de-emphasized hunting and sport and target shooting. The new leadership focused more narrowly on Second Amendment rights, and they actively opposed legislation limiting the sale or distribution of guns or ammunition. Federal legislation—affecting everything from hollow-pointed or Teflon-coated ammunition, to automatic and semi-automatic weapons, to waiting periods before one can purchase a gun—has strained the NRA's relations with law-enforcement officials. Reference to federal agents as "jack-booted government thugs" ready to steal weapons pushed many members beyond the pale. In a very public show of disapproval, verging on outright disgust, former President George H. W. Bush, a lifetime member of the NRA, quit.[44]

The persistent divisions between the conservative and the very conservative members of the NRA remain significant. In 1982, the very conservative

Neal Knox was unceremoniously fired as the NRA's chief lobbyist and was dropped from the board in 1984.[45] Knox, however, remained involved with the NRA and has long led a dissident faction within the ranks, seeking to oust people from various positions and seeking a firmer stand on gun control issues from the NRA. Marion Hammer, the NRA's president in 1997, stated the following: "In terms of whether or not there is a crisis, or whether or not there is just an internal struggle, it is both. You can destroy an organization from within, just as effectively as your external enemies can destroy you."[46] The NRA has reason to be concerned. Its membership dropped from a high of 3.5 million in 1995 to about 2.8 million. Wayne R. LaPierre Jr., the executive vice president in charge of the day-to-day operations of the NRA, refers to Knox and those he represents as part of the fringe. "We don't want to be about training for war in the woods or extremism of rhetoric. They represent the fringe."[47] To get money from the fringe is not so bad, but if the fringe influence leads to the unraveling of the organization, that becomes another story. The governing structures within the NRA are well suited for maintaining the status quo. To dismiss an officer requires fifty-seven votes on the governing board, which has only seventy-six members. LaPierre has worked within the NRA since 1977, during which time he has weathered as much criticism from NRA members as from nonmembers. Within the NRA, LaPierre has learned to "always watch his back."[48]

Conclusion

Regardless of the merits of democracy, it does not always operate smoothly in groups. Group members may reject positions arrived at through democratic means by quitting the organization. Because of the opportunities to exit and the varied nature of group governance, "the most baffling problems of democratic government are to be found not in legislatures or executives . . . but in the internal politics of the . . . groups upon which the whole system has turned out in large measure to rest."[49]

Groups deal with their self-governance in many ways. That few groups are completely open and democratic does not mean that members do not have powerful means to affect a group's course. Leaders try very hard to anticipate members' reactions to policy stands, and the member's checkbook is a very powerful tool to express loyalty and support. Indeed, large donations from a faction within a group may help to steer the course of a group toward that faction. More democratically governed groups allow members to voice their concerns through formal channels, such as elections and referenda. Even if one is on the winning side of an internal group struggle, changes may be necessary to prevent unraveling. Recall from Chapter 3 that the AMA canceled its contract with the Sunbeam Corporation. For a fee, the AMA had agreed to endorse household Sunbeam products. Within the AMA, the criticism of the deal with Sunbeam was widespread. The critics argued that they would be viewed as cheap hucksters rather than as professional physicians if the Sunbeam agreement was maintained. The AMA holds regular elections to determine its leaders, and a strong challenge to the AMA leadership was based almost entirely on the Sunbeam issue. The head of the old leadership, Dr. Thomas R. Reardon, won a very narrow reelection.[50] Upon reelection, Reardon stated, "We have learned that we need to be more what is it they say at Nordstrom's?—more responsive to our customers, our members."[51] Reardon got the message, and he was fully aware of the AMA's declining membership. As many as four thousand doctors chose not to renew their AMA memberships during the turmoil.[52] Reardon's reelection was not the end of the story and his conciliatory tone may or may not have assuaged his opposition and stemmed the resignations.

Obviously, shared attitudes have their limits in organizations. Struggle for control of the group is interesting not only from a policy perspective but also from an organizational perspective, that is, from the perspective of how the organization survives, establishes and promotes its agenda, and retains its members. De Tocqueville stated that one cannot belong to associations "for any length of time without finding out how order is maintained amongst a large number of men, and by *what contrivance* they are made to advance, harmoniously and methodically to the same object."[53] In other words, carefully structured group procedures may provide a contrivance that maintains the group and keeps unraveling at bay. For Truman, organization is simply a set of regular interactions among people. At times Truman even viewed freeriders as members.[54] After all, freeriders may share some like-mindedness and moral support with the group. Considering both dues-paying members and freeriders as members of a group makes the whole group concept very nebulous and less meaningful. Furthermore, it is difficult to imagine dues-paying group members and group leaders being very sympathetic toward freeriders. Though never fully detailed, for de Tocqueville, organization is understood as a contrivance that maintains group harmony. Finally, Johnson's work on unraveling indicates why such contrivances are necessary. With apologies to Truman, like-mindedness once again fails to yield a viable group.

NOTES

1. See Morris Fiorina's *Congress: Keystone of the Washington Establishment,* 2nd ed. (New Haven: Yale University Press, 1989), for a nice overview of the role and impact of constituency service.
2. Standard references include *Washington Representatives, 1999,* ed. J. Valerie Steele (Washington, D.C.: Columbia Books, 1999), and *The Encyclopedia of Washington Representatives,* 35th ed., ed. Tara E. Sheets (Farmington Hills, MI: The Gale Group, 1999).
3. A good starting point for additional reading is Hanna Pitkin's *The Concept of Representation* (Berkeley: University of California Press, 1967).

4. Other names for Arrow's paradox include *Condorcet's paradox, the voting paradox,* and *the voting-cycle paradox.* See Kenneth J. Arrow's *Social Choice and Individual Values* (New Haven: Yale University Press, 1963). For an introduction to Arrow's reasoning and for a careful presentation of the political implications of Arrow's work, see Shepsle and Bonchek (1997). Riker (1982) remains quite insightful. Social choice theory has become a vast field with practitioners in sociology, philosophy, economics, and political science.

5. Riker (1982) remains one of the best statements about the limits of concepts such as *public interest* or *general will.*

6. Unanimity does have certain virtues, and it is required in many political and social settings. Most marriages are conducted with the unanimous consent of all involved. The U.S. Senate uses unanimous consent agreements to structure debate and amending activity on the floor. James M. Buchanan and Gordon Tullock are perhaps most eloquent in the defense of unanimous consent. See their *Calculus of Consent* (Ann Arbor: University of Michigan Press, 1967).

7. Miller (1983) provides an excellent analysis of these issues.

8. Terry Moe provides a good overview of this material in "The New Economics of Organization," *American Journal of Political Science* 28 (1984): 739–77.

9. Incentive clauses have limitations. Although it is beyond the scope of this book, it has been shown that incentive mechanisms can never fully solve the problems associated with principal-agent relationships. Chapter 6 of Eric Rasmusen's *Games and Information* (Oxford: Basil Blackwell, 1990) is a good starting point for more information.

10. Some scholars have adopted a principal-agent perspective to analyze voter control of elected officials, but they often focus on the relationship between a single elected official and the median voter of the district or state. That is, they simplify matters by positing one agent—the median voter—and one principal—the elected official.

11. Richard Fenno, *Home Style: House Members in Their Districts* (Boston: Little, Brown, 1978).

12. William T. Bianco's *Trust: Representatives and Constituents* (Ann Arbor: University of Michigan Press, 1995) explores this issue in greater detail.

13. Carole Pateman, *Participation and Democratic Theory* (Cambridge: Cambridge University Press, 1970).

14. Robert Putnam suggests that some democratic institutions are indeed weakening. See his "Bowling Alone: America's Declining Social Capital," *Journal of Democracy* (1995a): 63–78; "Tuning in, Tuning out—The Strange Disappearance of Social Capital in America," *PS-Political Science & Politics* 28 (1995b): 664–83; and *Bowling Alone: The Collapse and Revival of American Community* (New York: Simon & Schuster, 2000).

15. Although Italy and New Zealand each maintained systems of proportional representation, their party thresholds differed. Before a party secures seats in the national assembly, it must garner a certain percentage (or threshold) of votes in the national election. If the threshold is high, few parties gain seats in the assembly. If the threshold is low, many parties flourish. Ironically, the two boot-shaped countries all but swapped electoral systems. New Zealand lowered its threshold for party representation whereas Italy raised its threshold.

16. In particular, see her discussion of John Stuart Mill, Pateman (1970), 30–31.

17. Tocqueville (1961), 138.

18. Any list of relevant sources on these issues would be woefully inadequate, but one can get started with Steven J. Rosenstone and John Mark Hansen's *Mobilization, Participation, and Democracy in America* (New York: Macmillan Publishing, 1993); Jan Leighley's "Group Membership and the Mobilization of Political Par-

ticipation," *Journal of Politics* 58 (1996): 447–63; and Sidney Verba and Norman H. Nie's *Participation in America* (New York: Harper & Row, 1972).

19. Truman (1971), 140.
20. John Gardner, founder of the public interest group Common Cause, is quoted from Andrew S. McFarland's *Common Cause: Lobbying the Public Interest* (Chatham, NJ: Chatham House Publishers, 1984), 97.
21. Olson (1965), 85.
22. Olson (1965), 85.
23. Truman (1971), 157.
24. Rothenberg (1988). Three articles by Paul E. Johnson are relevant: "Unraveling in Democratically Governed Groups," *Rationality and Society* 2 (1990b): 4–34; "Foresight and Myopia in Organizational Membership," *Journal of Politics* 49 (1987): 678–703; and "Unraveling in a Variety of Institutional Settings," *Journal of Theoretical Politics* 8 (1996): 299–329. Albert O. Hirschman's *Exit, Voice and Loyalty: Responses to Decline in Firms, Organizations and States* (Cambridge: Harvard University Press, 1970) also addresses some of these issues.
25. Duncan Black's median voter theorem is so widely referred to that there are seldom any citations to his original work. His *Theory of Committees and Elections* (Cambridge: Cambridge University Press, 1958) is quite readable and remains valuable.
26. Suppose there are n members, where n is even. If each member is numbered from 1 to n, then the two middle-most members would be $n/2$ and $n/2 + 1$. If n is odd, the median is $(n+1)/2$.
27. See Johnson (1987), (1990b), and (1996). Hirschman (1970) raised similar concerns, but his arguments were never formally developed.
28. Johnson (1990b), 15.
29. Truman (1971), 116.
30. It is not clear to me who first coined the expression "farming the membership," but Lester W. Milbrath used it in *The Washington Lobbyists* (Chicago: Rand McNally, 1963), and it has been in regular use since then.
31. McFarland (1984), 95–99.
32. The arguments in this section are based on Johnson (1987).
33. There are numerous sources for more information on the NAACP and related organizations. Warren D. St. James's book *The National Association for the Advancement of Colored People* (New York: Exposition Press, 1958) is a glowing portrayal of the organization and its leaders, including W. E. B. DuBois. McAdam (1982) takes a broader view of black insurgency, assessing the political opportunities for the success of the black movement. Finally, the ninth chapter of Wilson (1973) is a valuable reference.
34. Electoral procedures were (and still are) largely determined by state and local governments. The opportunities for black participation, therefore, varied by state and region. The Fifteenth Amendment simply made it illegal to prevent blacks access to the ballot.
35. Lord Byron, *Childe Harold's Pilgrimage*, Canto II, Stanza 76. See Volume II of Lord Byron, *The Complete Poetical Works*, edited by Jerome J. McGann (Oxford: Clarendon Press, 1980).
36. W. E. B. DuBois, *The Souls of Black Folk* (New York: Knopf, Random House, 1993), Chapter 3.
37. During the last couple of decades, the term *race riot* has been used to refer to black insurgencies and associated random violence. During the early 1900s, race riots consisted of mobs of whites attacking blacks.
38. Paul Delaney, "A Purge at the Top: Confusion in the Ranks" (*New York Times*, March 29, 1992).

39. "NAACP's Julian Bond Sees a New Civil Rights Era Ahead" (*New York Times*, July 13, 1998), A-12.
40. Steven A. Holmes, "Despite New Top, An Impatient NAACP" (*New York Times*, May 19, 1995), A-6.
41. John H. Cushman Jr., "An Uncomfortable Debate for Sierra Club: Competing Views on Immigration Divide an Environmental Group" (*New York Times*, April 5, 1998), 12.
42. Cushman (1998), 12.
43. *Escobedo v. Illinois*, 378 U.S. 478 (1964), and *Miranda v. Arizona*, 384 U.S. 436 (1966).
44. Osha Gray Davidson's *Under Fire: The NRA and the Battle for Gun Control* (New York: Henry Holt and Company, 1993) is an excellent source for information on the NRA. Davidson's book highlights the internal disputes that have riven the NRA. Also see Michael Powell's "The Revival of the NRA" (*The Washington Post Weekly Edition*, August 28, 2000), 6–9.
45. Kathleen Q. Seelye, "An Ailing Gun Lobby Faces a Bitter Struggle for Power," (*New York Times*, January 1, 1997), A-1, A-9.
46. Seelye (1997), A-9.
47. Wayne R. LaPierre Jr. quoted in Seelye (1997), A-9.
48. Marc Lacey, "NRA Stands by Criticism of President" (*New York Times*, March 20, 2000), A-15.
49. Oliver Garceau quoted in Truman (1971), 168.
50. Bill Dedman, "AMA Retains Chief Despite Sunbeam Furor" (*New York Times*, June 18, 1998), A-24.
51. Dedman (1998), A-24.
52. Dreyfuss (1998), 24.
53. Tocqueville (1961), 140, emphasis added.
54. Truman (1971), 114. See his discussion of the American Association of University Professors.

Summary of Part I

It is important to consider groups from many perspectives—as organizations in and of themselves and as actors in the larger political community. The remaining chapters analyze the activities of groups and lobbyists in Washington, D.C., but there are a few key highlights from the first four chapters that are worth repeating at this point.

First, in many ways Truman was correct when he argued that groups of all sorts define many aspects of our day-to-day existence. Consider a college or university setting. There are groups of faculty, students, staff members, and administrators. The scholars may conduct research in the sciences, social sciences, or humanities. The students (and sometimes faculty and administrators) may live on or off campus. At the workplace, even the simplest items, such as parking permits, divide people into groups. Not everyone is allowed to park in central campus. At restaurants, one chooses to sit with smokers or nonsmokers. Most of these groups are simply categories that one does not join in the usual sense. For instance, joining the junior class or the football team is not the same as joining the campus affiliate of the Democratic or Republican Party. It is important, however, to remember that individuals define and make up groups. The character and nature of a junior class or football team are defined by the individuals in them. In those groups that people join in the traditional sense, individuals have even greater impact. To lose sight of

individual input in traditional groups is to ignore all of the problems associated with collective action, entrepreneurship, and unraveling.

An understanding of the problems associated with collective action, entrepreneurship, and unraveling allow one to question the accepted wisdom
that groups are omnipotent. Groups have difficulty forming, securing financial support, maintaining their membership levels, and governing themselves.
These problems highlight just how difficult it is to organize individuals with
similar interests. Even after many successful years, a group may still fail.
Robert H. Salisbury used a particularly poignant pun to portray the demise
of farm groups during the early part of the twentieth century: the "empirical
landscape is cluttered with abandoned farm group vehicles."[1] Not all groups
survive. The Farmers Union, the Farmers Alliance, the Grange, and the
Brothers of Freedom are all gone. The entrepreneurial efforts of leaders constantly change the interest group environment. Salisbury noted that farm organizers working with the Grange branched out on their own to form
groups differentiated by crop and region. Both the Southern Cotton Growers Association and the Brothers of Freedom were headed by former Grange
leaders.

To read some newspaper headlines, groups are all-powerful within the
Washington, D.C., beltway. Such views do not necessarily comport with the
previous discussions of collective-action problems and unraveling. The internal structures of groups are crucial to understand for several reasons. First,
the best represented groups in Washington are those that are well organized.
Typically, when one hears complaints about the dominance of groups in
Washington, the real concern is centered around the composition, not the
existence, of the group environment. If the composition of the group environment is the real concern, then a thorough understanding of collective action, entrepreneurial strategies, and unraveling is crucial, because only by
overcoming those problems does the makeup of the group environment in
Washington begin to change.

Second, it is worth remembering that many groups secure support from
the government through direct grants, contracts, fees for service, and recognition of licensing and accreditation boards. At one time or another, the
American Farm Bureau Federation, the Chamber of Commerce, and the
NRA have received government support. Groups of artists and scientists and
groups engaged in the delivery of social services receive government support.
Simply put, government actions affect the makeup of the group environment. Is Washington being held hostage by groups? There may be undue
group influence in Washington, but the government is hardly an innocent
bystander.

The final reason to study the internal dynamics of groups also relates to
the Washington lobbying scene. Group voices are deemed worthy because
they aggregate and amplify many individuals' concerns. Groups may
strengthen the voice of lone individuals, who would otherwise have little in-

dependent influence, but some caveats are necessary. Which interests are being communicated? What is the level of member involvement? Group voices in Washington are difficult to interpret. Interest groups are seldom democratically governed, and many members are generally unaware of group activities. How are group interests communicated in Washington? This is a concern for Chapters 6 and 7. Increasingly lobbyists try to augment direct lobbying of legislators with extensive grassroots and advertising campaigns. Grassroots lobbying strategies are analyzed in Chapter 8. Even if members are generally unaware of group policies, they may still be well represented by groups. Recall the discussion of a principal-agent relationship—some delegation of authority is inevitable. In essence, members delegate authority to groups that generally support their concerns. Chapter 8 assesses the ability of individuals with limited information to use group positions as cues for other political activity. For instance, even if one does not know a lot about the NRA, one still might glean important political information from NRA positions. Finally, Chapter 9 focuses on money—PAC money, soft money, party funds, and even individual contributions.

NOTE

1. Salisbury (1969), 7.

～ II ～

Groups and Government

5

The Lobbying Environment in Washington

Introduction

"Naomi says, 'There are too many lobbyists in Washington and as far as I am concerned they should be outlawed because they are not representing the entire country.'" Who is Naomi? Naomi is simply a member of a focus group brought together by political scientists John Hibbing and Elizabeth Theiss-Morse to discuss the U.S. government.[1] Naomi's feelings are fairly common, but are they balanced, justified, or even reasonable? The previous chapter illustrated some of the complex issues surrounding the idea of representation. In this chapter, we begin to explore in greater depth how interests have been represented in the United States. In particular, we examine the historical basis for the representation of narrow interests in Washington.

Most individuals either overreact or underreact to group activities in Washington. The overreactors are keen to discuss the latest outrageous example of undue group influence. The overreactors love the anecdote that supports their point, but they generally have little information about typical group activity in Washington. Their reaction to the individual case clouds their judgment about the interest group environment as a whole. The underreactors ignore group influence entirely. For them, organized interests are so commonplace in politics that they are often overlooked. The underreactors are not blind, but they are not particularly observant either. Just as one might ignore the readers in a library because they are so prevalent, underreactors overlook groups in politics. Groups in Washington are simply anticipated, much as one might expect readers in libraries. Neither the overreactor nor the underreactor helps us to understand groups or group influence better, but when an unpopular group secures a policy success, one is reminded of how powerful groups can be. What does the lobbying environment in Washington look like? Who do the lobbyists in Washington represent? How much policy influence do lobbyists generally have? In short, how do lobbyists communicate with legislators and other government officials, and how do government officials respond to lobbying?

Three themes are woven throughout the next four chapters. The first theme highlights the interest environment. What are the most important characteristics of the interest group society? Who is represented? The second theme highlights the structures of Washington institutions and electoral procedures that affect lobbying strategies and lobbying influence. The final theme evaluates interest group influence and the means of influence. These three themes are related. Discussion of them is begun in this chapter and returned to from time to time throughout the following chapters.

Interests and the Government

Why do we want to represent our claims before government bodies? We lobby our friends and neighbors, parents and siblings, teachers, co-workers and bosses, spouses, girlfriends, boyfriends, and lovers. Must issues be dragged into the open and aired before a governmental body? How does one move from lobbying her neighbor to lobbying her local government? In short, why is there a gravitation toward government?

Truman and the inevitable gravitation toward government[2]

Recall that Truman argued that interest groups make "claims upon others" and that political interest groups make claims upon others through government. Truman's simple point is rather powerful: one need not mediate claims through governing bodies. If a neighbor is playing music loudly, one might simply ask her to turn down the volume. The mediation is direct. If the neighbor smiles and turns the volume up, one might consider calling the police for assistance. Suppose, however, that the police officer explains that there are no local noise ordinances in effect until after 11:00 P.M. If one truly wants to adhere to Benjamin Franklin's admonition ("early to bed early to rise"), then it may be time to lobby the local city council for a general noise ordinance. The most important point from this little tale is that many issues are mediated without government involvement. People resolve many minor and some major disputes without any government involvement. Why then did Truman argue that interest groups inevitably gravitate toward government?

Consider another example. Suppose one suffered some sort of injury related to a product. If the injury was minor and there was no major nuisance, one might simply ignore the whole matter or perhaps ask the manufacturer about its money-back guarantee. Now suppose the injury was major. In addition to medical treatment, one might pursue legal remedies. Of course, suing for damages requires leaving what Albert O. Hirschman called the private sphere and working in the public sphere, because a governmental body (a court) must now adjudicate.[3] Courts' juries have determined liability in cases ranging from the absurd to the sublime and heart-wrenching. If the manufacturer is found to be at fault, jury settlements are often generous. Not surprisingly, manufacturers have often complained about their vulnerability to the least worthy of these lawsuits, and for almost twenty years they have sought federal legislation to protect themselves from product liability lawsuits. Whenever one loses a high-stakes dispute, the gravitation to a more inclusive arena is inevitable. One enters the court only if the private negotiations between the manufacturer and the injured party break down. The court decisions can almost always be appealed to a higher, more inclusive court. Following a series of courtroom losses, one party or another may seek new legislation to limit future liability. Because courts interpret the laws, new legislation in Congress is equivalent to making an appeal to a more inclusive body. The only way to trump one's opponent is to seek redress from the most powerful, fully institutionalized, and inclusive bodies. In some countries, religious officials adjudicate most social and economic problems. During the colonial period of the United States, churches and their clergy were especially dominant in the affairs of colonists. For many decades, the national government has been the most inclusive and powerful body that might adjudicate claims. It was true in the 1950s when Truman wrote, and it is still true today. Hence, the gravitation toward government is inevitable if one party or another is dissatisfied with the prevailing decisions.

The gravitation toward government is facilitated by two additional factors. First, the U.S. government's federal structure increases the points of access. Groups and individuals can seek to affect local, state, or national legislation; local, state, or national bureaucratic agencies; and local, state, or national courts. Indeed, the choice of venue becomes a strategic concern in and of itself.[4] In countries with a unitary structure, there are fewer opportunities to affect local or state policies—all policies are national in scope. Second, the state and federal governments are becoming increasingly important. There is more legislation affecting more aspects of more and more people's day-to-day lives. The expansion of the state and federal governments into more and more policy areas is not necessarily a bad thing. It does, however, affect the incentives of groups and individuals to lobby government officials.

Madison's view of narrow self-interests and government

In "Federalist #10," James Madison warned of the dangers of faction. By faction, Madison meant

> a number of citizens, whether amounting to a majority or minority of the whole, who are united and actuated by some common impulse of passion, or of interest,

adverse to the rights of other citizens, or to the permanent aggregate interests of the community.[5]

The analogy between Madison's notion of faction and today's interest groups can be found in almost every book on interest groups. Aside from noting the parallels, there are other important points to keep in mind. First, although Madison clearly understood the potentially fractious nature of interests, he did not ask people to forgo their own self-interest. Madison recognized that the "causes of faction are sown in the nature of man."[6] One may preach about the evils of faction, but the impulse to promote and protect one's own interests is inherent in people. Indeed, Madison himself engaged in interest group activity throughout his adult life, including student demonstrations on the College of New Jersey campus (now better known as Princeton University).[7]

Madison did not rail against individuals' fractious self-interests. Self-interests were simply accepted by Madison, much in the manner in which we earlier posited goal-oriented behavior. Further, Madison did not recommend the destruction of the causes of faction. Rather than destroying the liberty that gave breath to self-interest, Madison recommended that the new government be structured to minimize the impact of factions. That is, elected officials should *expect* to be pressured by narrow, fractious interests because such narrow interests are simply part of human nature. The lessons of Madison and Truman are twofold. First, both Madison and Truman anticipated the presence of narrow self-interests in public settings. Second, Madison argued that the government could be structured to minimize the effects of factions. That is, since the founding of this country, elected officials have been encouraged to structure (and restructure) governmental bodies in anticipation of group pressures. If everyone recognizes the inevitable gravitation toward government, then no doubt government officials will steel themselves to the onslaught.

A Brief History of Interest Representation in Washington

A thorough history of lobbying is certainly beyond the scope and aims of this book, but some background on early lobbying activities might be helpful for understanding the current lobbying environment in Washington. In the earliest colonial and state assemblies, petitions from individuals often dominated legislative action.[8] These early state assemblies typically had some sort of committee on grievances, propositions, or petitions. Regardless of the precise name, the purpose of these committees was always the same: to redress the narrow concerns of individual constituents. Indeed, in some states, representatives traveled the state seeking grievances to address. These early practices suggest that there is nothing novel about narrow, private interests being represented in public bodies.

Private interests and elected representatives

Given the experience of the colonial assemblies, it is not surprising that citizens of the newly formed United States frequently sought assistance from their elected representatives through the use of claims and petitions. In these instances, claims and petitions were, quite simply, individual demands or claims against a government. Early petitions seldom sought redress of general policy failures. The most well-known use of petitions to redress a general policy did not occur until the 1820s, when abolitionists used claims and petitions to seek an end to slavery. Most often the policy focus remained narrow. The Committee on Claims was made the second standing congressional committee during the Third Congress (1794).[9] Standing committees serve from one congress to the next, so by designating the Committee on Claims as standing, members were recognizing the crucial nature of constituents' claims and petitions.[10] The committee proved to be a mixed blessing. Legislators established the committee to expedite constituents' claims, but the committee was constantly overrun with demands. Legislators were loath to refuse constituents' demands outright, but their attempts to facilitate the processing of claims made more and more constituents interested in filing their own new claims. The Committee on Claims was not the only standing committee created during the early congresses to address predominantly narrow or parochial concerns. Public Lands (1805), Post Office and Post Roads (1808), Pensions and Revolutionary Claims (1813), Private Land Claims (1816), Military Pensions (1825), Railways and Canals (1831), and Invalid Pensions (1831) were also made standing. Many of these committees were designed to reduce the workload of the original Committee on Claims, and all but the last three predated such venerable, broad-based policy committees as Manufactures (1819), Agriculture (1820), and Military Affairs (1822).

The committee structures in Congress appeared well designed to address the narrow issues that interest groups so often pursue. In his administrative history of the Jacksonian era, Leonard White wrote that "members were devoted to the needs of their constituents and to their own fence-building for reelection rather than to developing a competent and trustworthy administrative organization."[11] At this time, elected officials often acted as paid agents representing individual clients. Senators frequently were on retainer with major banks and corporations. Throughout the first half of the nineteenth century, representatives and senators commonly represented clients (who were often their constituents) before federal agencies and federal courts. Though Senator Daniel Webster (Whig-Mass.) is best remembered for representing the United States Bank before the Supreme Court more than forty times, he represented numerous clients before various federal agencies and on the floor of the Senate. Webster's efforts were not *pro bono publico,* and he was not reluctant to remind his clients to send along their retainers. Of course, claims that received unfavorable adjudication before an agency or court could always be addressed with special legislation. To be assured that his clients were aware of the full extent of his efforts, Webster frequently dragged his clients to the Senate to let them hear his grandiloquence.[12]

The historical emergence of lobbyists in Washington

The earliest lobbyists active in the United States were generally called lobby-agents. Their name was derived from the fact that they acted as agents for others and they plied their trade in the halls and lobbies of Congress and executive branch agencies. More often than not, the earliest lobby-agents represented individual rather than group concerns. The relationship was largely one to one—one principal (the client) and one agent (the lobbyist). Unfortunately, little work has analyzed the changing roles for lobbyists here in the United States, and there has been a much greater emphasis on the personal attributes of famous lobbyists and the scandalous activities of some lobby-agents. For instance, we know much about Sam Ward. After the Civil War, Ward emerged as one of the most powerful lobbyists in Washington. Ward, known as the "King of the Lobby," amazed everyone in his company with his incredible facility with languages and poetry, his colorful stories of worldwide travel and of fortunes made and lost, and his avuncular warmth. The important thing to note about the lobbyists in Washington during the nineteenth century is that they seldom (if ever) represented organized groups. The lobbyists of this period were primarily old style lobbyists with individuals, not groups, for clients. Even Ward is best remembered for representing single, albeit wealthy, interests.[13] In sum, the earliest lobbyists were not group phenomena.

The mid- and late 1800s was a period of intense social and political upheaval. Few political issues could avoid being affected by the divisiveness of the Civil War or Reconstruction. After the war, reconciliation came very slowly. Politicians either waved the "bloody shirt," or accused their opponents of waving the bloody shirt. Party competition in Washington was intense. All politics was suspect and intensely partisan. Against this tumultuous backdrop, lobbyists were portrayed by numerous popular authors as the lowest creatures in the political environment—portraits of evil incarnate. Lobbyists were slick, wheeler-dealers who knew how to read political winds and who would adopt any stratagem to secure their goal. J. W. DeForest was probably most successful within this genre, but many authors touched on political issues and lobbyists' activities, including Mark Twain.[14]

Although lobbyists solidified their questionable reputations in the late 1800s, that period was important for lobbyists in another, more fundamental way. The movement away from the old style of lobbying with one principal and one agent representing very narrow interests began in the late 1800s. The most prominent example of early group lobbying occurred in the area of veterans' benefits. In the 1870s, 1880s, and 1890s, Union veterans often hired lobbyists to present their claims for pensions related to their service in the Civil War. These lobbyists were called claims agents, and federal laws stipulated that they could charge as much as ten dollars for a successfully prosecuted claim.

Claims agents soon found that unprocessed claims for pensions were valuable, worth as much as ten dollars, which was no small sum in the late 1800s. Indeed, claims agents bought and sold unprocessed claims. Claims agents also found that pushing single claims through the Pension Bureau or the U.S. Congress was particularly time consuming. A small handful of claims agents recognized the inefficiencies of processing claims individually. These same agents reinvigorated a newly politicized Grand Army of the Republic (G.A.R.). The G.A.R. had never really been an army, rather it was a benevolent association with a declining membership during the 1870s. The repoliticized G.A.R. sought general legislation, such as the Arrears Act of 1879, providing veterans' pension benefits. The early group entrepreneurs in the G.A.R. found that they could represent thousands of veterans at once more efficiently than thousands of veterans one at a time. There were what economists commonly refer to as efficiencies in scale. Natural monopolies have gains to scale. When natural monopolies exist, smaller firms (i.e., those agents processing few claims) are bought out by larger firms (i.e., those agents processing many claims). In the Civil War pension–claims business, larger operations were more efficient than smaller operations. When such efficiencies exist, economic theory says that the number of claims agents should decrease and prominent agents should buy unprocessed claims from less prominent agents. This is indeed what happened. The lobby-agents acting as group entrepreneurs collected similar demands for pensions from individual Union veterans, physically bundled them together, and presented them en masse. These Civil War claims agents were among the earliest interest group lobbyists as we think of them today.[15]

When it came to claims for Civil War pensions, group representation was more efficient for the lobbyists than individual one-to-one representation. Processing many claims at once and successfully lobbying for legislation that led to even more claims being processed certainly enriched the claims business. What about the claimants themselves? Or the legislators? One might imagine that one-to-one representation, with one principal and one agent, would be better for the claimant than the situation where there are many principals and only one agent. Can a single agent represent all individuals effectively? The effectiveness of such representation is partly a function of the extent to which the principals have common interests. The claimants had shared interests in Civil War pensions, but they competed with each other over the scarce resources of the Pension Bureau.[16] Claimants were better off with group representation because the flood of unprocessed claims had created huge backlogs at the Pension Bureau. With only the proverbial twenty-four hours in a day, the Pension Bureau—then the largest U.S. agency—

could not reduce the backlog. The individual claimants were actually competing with one another for the attention of the Pension Bureau or some other helpful figure. Claimants, in short, were better served by group representation because they, too, gained from the improved efficiency.

What about the legislators? When the Pension Bureau became overloaded with unprocessed claims, the demand for private legislation rose tremendously. Indeed, the congressional calendars were so clogged with requests for private legislation to secure pensions that other legislative activity ground to a virtual halt. The improved efficiency of group representation allowed legislators to improve the overall efficiency of their chamber. Harvard University political scientist John Mark Hansen argues that group representation solidified when groups developed certain comparative advantages over other political actors, and especially over political parties.[17] Hansen highlights the importance of the information that groups can provide to legislators. Lobbyists emerged, he argues, because they served the informational demands of legislators better than traditional political entities. Group lobbyists can and do provide valuable information to legislators, but in the instance of the G.A.R., lobbyists also improved the efficiency of the chamber. Parties were not able to reduce the backlog of unprocessed claims in the Pension Bureau, nor were they able to protect the congressional calendars from intrusive demands for private legislation. Lobbyists for the G.A.R. did. Group representation also facilitated candidates' desires to talk to organized groups of electorally active individuals. Many politicians sought to address the Annual Encampments (conventions) of the G.A.R.

Did group representation come at no cost? Certainly not. The U.S. Treasury was opened wide to accommodate the demand for Civil War pensions. Group representation reduced certain inefficiencies, but that is not the same as saying that the G.A.R. only sought to promote the common good. The G.A.R.'s demands were very narrowly focused. They reduced some inefficiencies in the representation of interests, but one may or may not approve of the policy outcomes associated with those interests.

Changes in Congress: Leadership and Committees

Given that lobbyists must work in and around the U.S. Congress, they are very sensitive to changes in Congress. In this section, changes within the U.S. Congress are linked to changing lobbying strategies. Formal and informal structures inside of Congress channel lobbying efforts and thereby affect lobbyists' influence. Understanding how legislators structure their environment clarifies the role of lobbyists and lobbying strategies. Recognizing the changing nature of the leadership and committee systems can help us to understand the changing nature of lobbying and interest group access to Congress. Three episodes in the history of the U.S. Congress are particularly good for illustrating how legislative structures affect lobbying strategies and group access. Prior to the political attacks on Speaker of the House Joe Cannon (R-Ill.) in the early 1900s, Speakers ruled the House with considerable authority. The U.S. House of Representatives was indeed the Speaker's House. If he so desired, the Speaker was able to determine virtually all committee assignments and committee agendas. By stacking committees properly, a Speaker could set up the House and affect the policy process for each and every issue that might arise. Legislators and lobbyists alike recognized the influence of Speakers during the late 1800s and early 1900s.

Kerr-Cannon

The 1875 competition between Michael C. Kerr (D-Ind.) and Samuel J. Randall (D-Penn.) for the position as Speaker of the House pivoted around proposed subsidies for the Texas & Pacific railroad and the composition of the Pacific Railroads Committee. Kerr prevailed, and he acknowledged his debts to his most ardent supporter *outside* of Congress, Manton Marble, editor of the New York *World* and part-time lobbyist. Marble stood to gain $350,000 if Texas & Pacific received its subsidy, and his support for Kerr was based on the assumption that Kerr would befriend Texas & Pacific.[18] Kerr not only favorably disposed the Pacific Railroads Committee, he sought advice about the composition of other committees, too. In a fawning letter to Marble, Kerr wrote

> now, and specially, I want your advice about the fittest person for chairman of Ways & Means. . . . What do you advise? . . . Can't you . . . write me many suggestions touching [on] matters here? I will most gladly and thankfully receive any such suggestions. . . . A thousand thanks for the kindness of the World and for your personal kindnesses toward me.[19]

Other members of the House also understood the pivotal role that lobbyists filled. Members often expressed their preferences for committee memberships to powerful lobbyists, not congressional leaders, and sought their assistance in gaining those memberships.[20] When the Speaker is strong, the U.S. House is the Speaker's House. Lobbyists' successes during strong speakerships depend on their relations with those speakers. If a lobbyist could persuade the Speaker, the Speaker would ensure that the other members toed the line.

The attack on leadership: The 1910 rules

Not surprisingly, rank-and-file members of the House sometimes chafe under the harsh leadership of strong speakers. Sometimes, the members even depose one leader for another. Joe Cannon's term as Speaker was ended by just such a revolt. The attacks on Speaker Cannon in 1910 and 1911 left rule changes that distributed power throughout the House and away from the Speaker. Most importantly, Speaker Cannon lost his ability to determine committee memberships. Prior to his being voted out of the position, Cannon could alter committee memberships at will, and he dominated the ever-important Rules Committee. In 1910, Cannon was removed from the expanded Rules Committee, and by 1911 he lost the ability to affect the composition of all House committees. Of course, committees are central to the legislative process and the development of public policy. By losing control over committees, the Speaker lost control over the legislative and policy processes. Members secured greater control of their professional futures when Cannon's stronghold was broken. After the attacks on Cannon, members lobbied for committee memberships with one another, rather than with powerful figures outside Congress, and their committee positions were generally maintained from one congress to the next. Such an ability to retain their seats encouraged members to gain considerable policy expertise and to seek committee assignments in policy areas of genuine interest to them. Committees became stronger, more independent centers for influence. These changes in leadership and committee structures also affected lobbyists. By weakening the Speaker's position, members forced lobbyists to expand the scope of their lobbying. No longer was influence over the Speaker sufficient to ensure influence over the House. Lobbyists could no longer concentrate their efforts on the Speaker and a select few members. Lobbyists would have to work with numerous committee chairs. In this sense, dispersed power led to more widespread lobbying activity.

The freshmen onslaught of 1974: Liberal Democrats revolt

After the revolt against Cannon, it was more difficult to violate the norm of seniority when making committee assignments. The more senior members, as determined by length of time in office, were able to choose their committee assignments before the more junior members. Seniority on the committee was generally used to determine committee chairs. For established legislators, seniority was a valuable norm. For more junior members, seniority was a norm that over time one got used to. Throughout the period of growing committee strength, the Democratic Party was securing an absolute stranglehold on southern politics. For the large incoming Democratic class of 1974, seniority was not easy to accept. The seniority system in Congress coupled with the Democratic Party's stranglehold on electoral politics in the South created an awkward situation.[21] The committee chairs were chosen by seniority, but those members most able to retain their House memberships came from noncompetitive southern districts. The freshmen of 1974 were predominantly northern, liberal, and Democratic. Their own party brethren from the South were staunchly conservative. Such differences might have been manageable for some issues, but the seniority system combined with the Democratic Party dominance in the South meant that many of the most important committees were chaired by conservative southern Democrats. These southern chairs were more conservative than the Democratic Party in general. The new liberal Democrats felt that the southern chairs failed to represent their party. Liberal Democrats felt that the Southern Democrats' dominance of the legislative and policy processes had no connection to the party's desires; rather it was an artifact of one-party rule in the South. The northern liberals revolted.

Seniority, once thought of as a means to subvert Joe Cannon, a willful and too powerful Speaker, was now protecting powerful committee chairs who were too conservative for the majority of Democrats. The reforms in the 1970s decentralized power throughout the House. First, seniority was weakened substantially. Committee seniority no longer guaranteed the committee chair. Second, committee chairs themselves were weakened. Prior to the reforms of the 1970s, committee chairs dominated their committee's subcommittees. Some committees had no subcommittees; some had subcommittees only in name. A weak subcommittee with limited or no staff and little control over its own agenda was an extension of the chair rather than a sovereign entity. The reforms of the 1970s insured that every committee would have subcommittees with their own resources and control over their own agenda. These subcommittee reforms were dubbed the Subcommittee Bill of Rights. In addition, every member of the Democratic Caucus would have the opportunity to chair a subcommittee.

Two prominent interest group scholars, Kay Schlozman and John Tierney, noted that the congressional reforms of the 1970s coincided with a massive increase in interest group activity in Washington, D.C., in the 1970s and 1980s.[22] Seventy percent of all groups with Washington offices had opened them since the 1960s. Schlozman and Tierney suggested that the increase of group activity was linked to various changes in the political environment. The importance of the federal government was growing. More and more people and groups were affected by government action. During the 1970s communication technologies dramatically improved, which made the coordination of lobbying campaigns cheaper and easier. "Sunshine" procedures mandated open legislative hearings that lobbyists could bypass only at the risk of appearing uninterested in the policy changes at stake. All these changes were important, but Schlozman and Tierney also noted that changes within Congress itself increased points of access and the volume of lobbying activity. Committee dominance was eclipsed by subcommittee dominance. In a period of about one hundred years, lobbyists had moved their attention from the Speaker alone to include committee chairs and then to include subcommittee chairs, which ensured that every member of the majority party was a potential lobbying target.

Lobbying Enterprises and Reverse Lobbying

The congressional reforms in the 1970s increased members' access to committee and subcommittee staff and staff resources. In addition, members had more personal staff members in their own offices. Of course, members must work with each other, but they must also guide and coordinate the work of a large number of staff members. In essence, members have two jobs inside Congress: working with each other and working with their own staffs.[23] To be certain, members of Congress play a complicated inside game with their staff members, party leaders, committee chairs, and other congressional members. The inside game entails arm twisting, cajoling, and negotiating with members. Coalition building and careful nose counting are important . skills. However, members of Congress also play an outside game. The outside game focuses on interest groups that can help with lobbying activity, coalition building, and with grassroots campaigns. Working with groups to coordinate the lobbying of constituents, the media, party officials outside of Congress, and other groups constitutes the bulk of the outside game. To help with the outside game and to coordinate their inside and outside games, individual legislators may establish their own lobbying enterprise.[24]

Though centered around individual legislators and their staff, lobbying enterprises include groups of like-minded lobbyists and interest group and industry personnel. The individuals in lobbying enterprises are united by their common policy goals. Lobbying enterprises develop for some of the same reasons that interest group lobbying itself developed. Lobbying enterprises regularize the interactions between one or more legislators and a small group of lobbyists. If, as some scholars have argued, repeated interactions are necessary for groups to gain access to Congress, it is not surprising that some legislators and lobbyists create and promote lobbying enterprises to formalize their interactions.[25] Such regularized interactions reduce the uncertainty and costliness associated with intricate negotiations. Legislators and lobbyists have mixed motives in the sense that sometimes they want to help one another and sometimes they want to undermine one another. Just as principals try to monitor their agents, legislators and lobbyists monitor one another. If legislators have regularized interactions with a small group of lobbyists, then for at least some issues the monitoring costs are reduced. Legislators can also reduce the search costs associated with finding groups and individuals willing to sway public opinion through grassroots campaigns. In short, lobbying enterprises develop when they improve the efficiency of the legislator–lobbyist interactions. By the same token, they fade away as the motives and goals of the members and lobbyists conflict and as the efficiency gains disappear.[26]

Lobbying enterprises are easy to find throughout the last one hundred years of the U.S. Congress. Writing in the early part of the twentieth century, Matthew Josephson noted that lobbyists in the late 1800s often maintained their own desks in important committee rooms.[27] Lobbyists were not guaranteed such access to committee rooms, but some legislators chose to grant it. Members of the U.S. Congress have sat on the boards or been members of special legislative committees of such influential groups as the G.A.R., the National Grange, and the NRA. Coordinating activities between legislators and lobbyists is hardly novel, but, not surprisingly, most information about lobbying enterprises comes from recent congresses.

Members of Congress use both legislative and nonlegislative committee hearings to provide forums for lobbyists expressing particular views.[28] In addition to these more traditional committee venues, Congress has many less formal work groups and caucuses representing interests from A to Z. Although these caucuses and work groups are less permanent than standing committees, some have established histories. Caucuses related to agricultural issues have been in continual existence for more than fifteen years. Caucuses play no formal role in the legislative process, but they are sources of information for members and they often play a part in a lobbying enterprise.[29] In the 1980s, Congress made a crucial distinction between caucuses and legislative service organizations (LSOs). These LSOs were identical to caucuses except for the fact that they received funds from the U.S. Congress. Some LSOs combined their public funding from the Congress with private funding from groups and trade associations, and LSO personnel were often on the private payrolls of these outside groups. Typically, LSOs were housed in federal office buildings near the Capitol. Housing LSOs in the same buildings that held members' personal offices and mingling taxpayer money with private money to support LSOs struck some legislators as inappropriate. Although caucuses are still operating, congressional support for LSOs ended in the 104th Congress, the first congress of Republican control after several decades of Democratic dominance. The funding and hiring practices of the now-defunct LSOs intertwined LSO members with their supporters from outside Congress. Caucuses (and in the past LSOs) allow legislators and lobbyists to coordinate their efforts, operating in effect as lobbying enterprises.[30]

Although funding for LSOs was canceled in the 104th Congress, legislators were still working assertively to establish lobbying enterprises. Though LSOs were often dominated by Democrats rather than Republicans, the interest in lobbying enterprises crosses party lines. Representative Jerry Weller (R-Ill.) recently created a trade association called the New Economy Republicans, Inc. to bring together elected officials and lobbyists from high-tech industries. Though the tax-exempt status of the group raised concerns, the idea of bringing together a set of lobbyists and legislators for regular interactions is not novel.[31] Representative Tom DeLay (R-Tex.) maintains an informal kitchen cabinet to bolster closer ties to outside interests.[32]

Some scholars have referred to the activities related to these newer lobbying enterprises as reverse lobbying. There is nothing new about reverse lobbying, it is a simple extension of lobbying enterprises. Lobbyists may have regular channels of influence, but those channels allow influence to flow both ways. Groups may very well find themselves lobbied. Perhaps the most prominent examples of reverse lobbying occurred during the 104th Congress.[33] Representative Newt Gingrich (R-Ga.) coordinated a common electoral platform for those Republicans running for the House in 1994. The platform, entitled Contract with America, spelled out ten issues that the Republicans would pursue if they were in the majority. The Contract served as both the platform and later the agenda for the Republicans. Developing the Contract took months of planning, during which time Republican pollsters conducted focus groups to help fine tune the language.[34] More than three hundred Republican candidates signed on to the Contract in a public ceremony in Washington, D.C., on September 27, 1994.

Each plank of the Contract was associated with a working group consisting of members and senators and lobbyists from supportive groups and trade associations. John Boehner (R-Ohio) and the late Senator Paul Coverdell (R-Ga.) met weekly with the Thursday Group to coordinate grassroots and legislative support for the Contract with America tax cutting pledge. The Thursday Group was one of the most publicized lobbying enterprises in the 104th Congress. Those groups involved in the Contract's working groups funded the grassroots efforts. Indeed, DeLay reminded many groups that the Democrats had lost control of the House. With the new boys in town, support and contributions should move toward the Republicans. DeLay courted "special interests with undisguised ardor, . . . loaning his favorite lobbyists space in House committee rooms."[35] Indeed, DeLay is known as "'the Hammer' for his skill at pounding lobbyists for cash," and a friendly lobbyist credits him for being particularly "'good at putting together the inside and outside operation.'"[36] In the rush to reorganize Washington politics, some Republicans asked groups and lobbying firms to fire some of their lobbyists if they were known Democrats. The replacements, obviously, should be Republican. Bill Paxon (R-N.Y.) distributed a list to all Republican members detailing how four hundred electorally active groups had distributed their money to Democrats and Republicans. The contribution patterns of the groups led Paxon to label them as friendly, unfriendly, or neutral. With this information, Republicans would know how to respond to the pleas of lobbyists.[37]

Not all reverse lobbying is linked to the Contract for America. Boehner pressured the Chamber of Commerce to reject President Clinton's 1994 health care proposal. The success of Boehner's efforts was particularly dramatic because the Chamber had been supportive of aspects of the plan and had even submitted congressional testimony to that effect. Boehner had dozens of Republican members contact their local chambers to secure the reversal.[38] Representative Bud Shuster (R-Penn.) chaired the House Transportation Committee after the Republican takeover. While all other committees were searching for ways to cut spending, Shuster insisted on preserving transportation money. To coordinate his efforts, Schuster held numerous gatherings with groups of transportation lobbyists that sometimes had the aura of pep rallies. According to some accounts, Schuster designated certain representatives as lobbying targets and virtually dictated the lobbying assignments for the transportation lobbyists. Being the Transportation Committee chair may seem rather blasé, but Shuster controlled the largest domestic discretionary funding programs. To deny Schuster the money risked losing transportation dollars for one's own district, so even as other Republicans strove to hold back spending, Shuster fought successfully to expand spending in those areas affected by his committee. Of course, Shuster did not fight alone; he was aided by numerous lobbyists who also benefited from the transportation programs.

Who's Represented in Washington

Washington, D.C., is the headquarters for all sorts of political activities. Who is represented by all this activity? As it turns out, member-based interest groups do not dominate the Washington lobbying environment, institutions do. Institutions, such as corporations, universities, think tanks, state and local governments, churches, and so forth, are much more prevalent than member-based groups.[39] By contrast, one cannot belong to or join an institution in the usual sense. One does not belong to a corporation or university. State and local governments are active in Washington, but one's state citizenship is not equivalent to one's group memberships. Many of us are affiliated with institutions that regularly engage in politics, maintain a lobbying presence in Washington, and overtly pursue political goals.

In what sense do colleges and churches pursue political goals? Colleges and universities are affected by federal tuition grants and work study and loan programs. In 1999, the federal government spent more than $15 billion on university-based research. Though it is tied to research, colleges and universities use some of that grant money for indirect costs or overhead. Of course, universities and colleges pay most of their overhead costs through other means, but grants do help. Those universities spending more than a quarter of a million dollars on Washington lobbying in 1999 included Harvard, Yale, University of Miami, Tufts, Northwestern, New York University, and Columbia. The top spender was Boston University—$760,000. University lobbying is not limited to a small handful of prominent schools. One lobbying firm alone had thirty colleges and universities as clients.[40] Work by Alan Hertzke indicates why churches are institutions with manifold interests in political affairs. "Churches own property, employ people, enjoy tax exemptions, operate schools, colleges, hospitals, nursing homes, large charitable groups, and even life insurance companies. Some churches receive government grants."[41] Institutions, such as churches and universities, with manifold interests cannot easily avoid political affairs.

Among the institutions active in Washington, business corporations are most dominant. Corporations are very sensitive to public policies for the simple reason that those policies affect profits. Corporations are not simply concerned about major policy initiatives; indeed, more often than not, corporate lobbyists are concerned about what might seem like minor issues. For example, the possessions tax break was a little-known IRS provision for those firms working in U.S. possessions or territories. As it was written, firms operating in Puerto Rico had the most to gain. Until its repeal, few people (other than those directly affected) knew anything of the tax break. Not everyone has read Section 936 of the Internal Revenue Code. Political scientist Sandra Suarez noted that pharmaceutical companies benefited the most from the possessions tax break because of their operations in Puerto Rico, so they also stood to lose the most if it were repealed. Suarez found that several firms were able to reduce their tax liabilities by over fifty percent.[42] Johnson & Johnson reduced its tax burden by more than $1 billion in a five-year period from 1989–1994.[43] Merely the hint of a change in the tax break in 1993 led the *Wall Street Journal* to run a headline reading, "Drug Stocks Take a Hit Over Loss of Much Coveted Puerto Rican Tax Break." With this sort of potential financial impact, it is difficult to imagine corporations not following political affairs very closely. Simply put, the line between economics and politics is hardly distinguishable.

Do corporations lobby just for tax breaks? Which companies are most active? Well aside from tax breaks, companies are also affected by government regulations and government contracts. Few corporate giants sell their wares only to individuals. Local, state, and federal governments buy goods and services from the private sector as well. A firm's abilities to sell goods overseas is affected by government policy. Finally, all corporations are regulated, but some industry sectors are more highly regulated than others. Those corporations most directly affected by trade policies and government regulations and contracts are most apt to maintain a political presence in Washington.

Why do institutions dominate the lobbying scene in Washington? Institutions enjoy advantages that groups do not. Within institutions, there is no overarching concern about finding and retaining members. Unlike groups, institutions have no collective-action problem. Resolving leadership disputes within institutions is often easier than within groups because institutions seldom allow for democratic governance. Institutions are not tightly bound by their "members" because they have no members in the traditional sense. Universities' concerns are not always directly tied to students, and corporations' concerns are not always tied to employees or even stockholders. People associated with institutions are only tangentially affected by institutions' interests. Stockholders may sell their shares in a company or students may transfer from one school to another, but there can be substantial transaction costs associated with such changes. Divesting from a company is particularly costly if the value of one's stock has gone down, and divesting when a stock is appreciating forgoes profits. Students may transfer between schools, but they are likely to lose some credits. Though dropping one's membership to an interest group has virtually no costs, ending an affiliation with an institution often leads to considerable transaction costs. In short, institutions do not unravel as member-based groups do. Institutions seldom need to worry about whether they are legitimate members of the political community. The financial support for institutions is more stable when compared to that for groups. In sum, institutions are more stable organizations than interest groups, so their presence in Washington is more dominant and more lasting. By their very nature, broad-based movements and groups are not well positioned to compete in Washington.

The dominance of institutions is certainly affected by the collective-action and unraveling problems, but it is also affected by the nature of representation, namely, the principal-agent problem. Consider the decision facing a corporation. It can rely on its membership in a large trade association for Washington representation or it can rely on its own lobbyists. Trade associations with numerous corporations as members might focus on some members more than others. This unequal representation would be most apt to occur when dues to the association are a function of firm size, which is often the case. With a trade association, there are multiple principals seeking representation from, at most, a small handful of agents. The presence of multiple principals may create additional representation problems if the principals must compete for the agent's attention. If the corporation uses its own lobbyists, there is only one principal and one agent, which keeps the representation problem more manageable. For all the growth in lobbying activity in the 1960–1980s, the number of active trade associations appears to have been relatively steady.[44]

Conclusion

There is nothing novel about private influence in public legislatures, especially if one accepts that private interest embodies more than crude vote buying. Long before votes become an issue, legislators structure their environment to channel interest group influence and facilitate access for particular interests. Why is the channeling of interests so important? Simply put, the channeling of interests affects the representation of interests. Recall that the pluralists were criticized on the grounds that unequal mobilization and unequal participation might skew policy outcomes. Rather than concentrate on the mobilization of interests and the organization of interest groups, this chapter focused more narrowly on the structures within Congress that affect the representation of interests. Altering either the mobilization or the representation of interests could affect the course of policy debates and help to ensure certain policy outcomes. Legislators may only indirectly affect the mobilization of interests, but there is no denying that they affect the representation of interests. Legislators facilitate the representation of some interests and provide no more than benign neglect to others. Legislators affect the scope of the policy conflicts within their chambers.[45] The ability of legislators and other government officials to affect the scope and nature of policy conflicts led E. E. Schattschneider to conclude that *"government is about the least neutral thing in the world."*[46]

Although it is important to recognize that there have always been narrow interests represented in the public domain, one may still be unsettled by the dominance of institutional representation.[47] The Washington lobbying environment does not simply reflect a popular groundswell of citizen-based group activity; rather it primarily represents long-established institutions. Though the representation of narrow interests has a long history in Washington, one might still contend that there has been an increase in lobbying activity and influence. There is no lack of people willing to represent interests in Washington. Elected officials are eager to represent some interests. When it comes to the nonelected representatives of interests (that is, the lobbyists), there is no shortage. The makeup of the Washington environment is always changing, but there are no shortages of lobbyists. By some counts, lobbyists outnumber members and senators by about forty to one,[48] and the size of the Washington bar continues to grow steadily.[49] Clearly, there is evidence of increased lobbying activity in Washington. There appear to be more interests in Washington today than ever before, but do these interests have more influence? Answering the question of influence is not easy, but an attempt is made in Chapters 6, 7, and 8.

NOTES

1. John Hibbing, "Do Americans Care about and Trust Their Government? A Congressional Briefing," Consortium of Social Science Associations (1999), 5.
2. The title of this section is borrowed directly from Truman (1971), 104.
3. Hirschman (1982).
4. The strategic concerns related to the choice of venue were a primary interest of Schattschneider (1960). The venue affected the scope of the conflict and the likely participants.
5. Madison (1961), 78.
6. Madison (1961), 79.
7. See James Yoho's "Madison on the Beneficial Effects of Interest Groups," *Polity* 27 (1995): 587–605.
8. Early colonialists also petitioned government officials in England. See Alison Gilbert Olson's *Making the Empire Work: London and American Interest Groups, 1690–1790* (Cambridge: Harvard University Press, 1992).
9. The Committee on Elections was the first standing congressional committee (1789).
10. See, for example, Noble Cunningham's *Circular Letters of Congressmen to Their Constituents, 1789–1829* (Chapel Hill: University of North Carolina Press, 1978), and Leonard D. White's *The Federalists: A Study in Administrative History* (New York: Macmillan Company, 1956), 355.
11. Leonard D. White, *The Jacksonians: A Study in Administrative History, 1829–1861* (New York: Macmillan Company, 1954), 161.
12. See Richard Allan Baker's "The History of Congressional Ethics" in *Representation and Responsibility: Exploring Legislative Ethics* (New York: Plenum Press, 1985).

13. For more information on Ward's life, see Lately Thomas's *Sam Ward: King of the Lobby* (Boston: Houghton-Mifflin, 1965). For more information on lobbying in the late 1800s, see Margaret Susan Thompson's *The "Spider Web": Congress and Lobbying in the Age of Grant* (Ithaca: Cornell University Press, 1986).

14. J. W. DeForest's works include *Playing the Mischief* (State College, PA: Bald Eagle Press, 1961, originally published 1875) and *Honest John Vane* (State College, PA: Bald Eagle Press, 1960, originally published 1875). Mark Twain's foray into this genre was entitled *The American Claimant* (New York: C. L. Webster & Co., 1892).

15. For more information on the entrepreneurial activities of the G.A.R., see two of my articles: Ainsworth (1995a), 319–38, and (1995b), 107–29. Additional information is available in my dissertation, *The Evolution of Interest Representation and the Emergence of Lobbyists* (Unpublished Ph.D. dissertation, Washington University, St. Louis, 1989). Skocpol (1992) is the best recent resource investigating how pension policies affected the development of social policies in the United States.

16. This point is made most clearly in an excellent book by Thompson (1986).

17. For Hansen's discussions of this issue, see "Choosing Sides: The Creation of an Agricultural Policy Network in Congress, 1919–1932," *Studies in American Political Development* 2 (1987): 183–229, and *Gaining Access* (Chicago: University of Chicago Press, 1991).

18. Thompson (1986), 194.

19. Thompson (1986), 199.

20. Thompson (1986), 169.

21. During much of the 1900s, there simply was no Republican Party presence in the South. In the 1990s, the Republican Party revived in many southern states.

22. See Schlozman and Tierney (1986) and "More of the Same: Pressure Group Activity in a Decade of Change," *Journal of Politics* 45 (1983): 351–75. Also see Valerie Heitshusen's "Interest Group Lobbying and U.S. House Decentralization," *Political Research Quarterly* 53 (2000): 151–76, and John R. Wright's "Interest Groups, Congressional Reform, and Party Government in the United States," *Legislative Studies Quarterly* 25 (2000): 217–35.

23. See, for example, Robert H. Salisbury and Kenneth A. Shepsle, "U.S. Congressman as Enterprise," *Legislative Studies Quarterly* 6 (1981): 559–76.

24. See Scott Ainsworth, "The Role of Legislators in the Determination of Interest Group Influence in Legislatures," *Legislative Studies Quarterly* 22 (1997): 517–34.

25. See, for example, Hansen (1991).

26. An analogy to the economics literature on the organization of the firm is straightforward. Firms organize themselves to reduce transaction costs. If negotiations for firms' inputs become problematic, firms may integrate vertically. That is, they may buy up the suppliers of the inputs. Vertical integration can reduce transaction costs by regularizing the interactions between the input supplier and the input purchaser.

27. Matthew Josephson, *The Politicos: 1865–1896* (New York: Harcourt, Brace, 1938), 450.

28. Ken Kollman, "Inviting Friends to Lobby: Interest Groups, Ideological Bias, and Congressional Committees," *American Journal of Political Science* (1997): 519–44. Jeffrey C. Talbert, Bryan D. Jones, and Frank R. Baumgartner, "Nonlegislative Hearings and Policy Change in Congress," *American Journal of Political Science* 39 (1995): 383–406.

29. Caucuses generally provide information that is not available from committees. See Scott Ainsworth and Fran Akins, "The Informational Role of Caucuses in the U.S. Congress," *American Politics Quarterly* 25 (1997): 407–30.

30. For more information on caucuses see Susan W. Hammond, Arthur G. Stevens, and D. P. Mulhollan's "Congressional Caucuses: Legislators as Lobbyists," in *Interest Group Politics*, eds. Allan J. Cigler and Burdett J. Loomis (Washington, D.C.: CQ Press, 1983), and Hammond's *Congressional Caucuses in National Policy Making* (Baltimore: Johns Hopkins University Press, 1998).
31. John Bresnahan and Damon Chappie, "Members Quit Weller Tech Group: Tax Structure Would Allow Companies to Write Off Membership Dues in Full" (*Roll Call Monthly*, December 3, 2001).
32. Alison Mitchell, "Enron's Ties to the Leader of House Republicans Went Beyond Contributions to His Campaign" (*New York Times*, January 16, 2002), C-1.
33. See Ronald G. Shaiko's "Reverse Lobbying: Interest Group Mobilization from the White House and the Hill," in *Interest Group Politics*, eds. Allan J. Cigler and Burdett A. Loomis (Washington, D.C.: CQ Press, 1998).
34. One of the best resources for information on the Contract with America is found in Darrel M. West and Burdett Loomis's *The Sound of Money: How Political Interests Get What They Want* (New York: W. W. Norton, 1999).
35. Hanna Rosin, "Whiplash" (*The New Republic*, February 16, 1996), 18.
36. Rosin (1996), 20. Also see Mitchell (2002).
37. Paxon's role is nicely detailed in David Grann's "Comeback Kid: Bill Paxon's Triumphant Return to Capitol Hill"(*The New Republic*, November 1, 1999), 24–27.
38. Michael Weisskopf, "Lobbyists Shift into Reverse" (*Washington Post*, May 13, 1994), A-3.
39. Robert H. Salisbury, "Interest Representation: The Dominance of Institutions," *American Political Science Review* 78 (1984): 64–76.
40. Tim Weiner, "Lobbying for Research Money" (*New York Times*, August 24, 1999), A-1. William H. Honan, "With Money Threatened, Colleges are Moving on all Lobbying Fronts" (*New York Times*, June 28, 1995), B-11.
41. See Alan Hertzke's *Representing God in Washington* (Knoxville: University of Tennessee Press, 1988), 101.
42. Sandra L. Suarez, "Explaining the Political Behavior of Business," paper presented at the 1997 American Political Science Association Meeting in Washington, D.C., p. 3. Also see Larry Rohter's article "Puerto Rico Fighting to Keep Its Tax Breaks for Business" (*New York Times*, May 10, 1993), A-1, C-5.
43. Suarez (1997), 3.
44. Berry (1997), 22.
45. Numerous interest group scholars have adopted the expression "scope of conflict," which is due to Schattschneider (1960). Congressional scholars have applied some of the same language in discussions of interest representation in Congress. See, for example, Richard L. Hall and Frank W. Wayman's "Buying Time: Moneyed Interests and the Mobilization of Bias in Congressional Committees," *American Political Science Review* 84 (1990): 797–820.
46. Schattschneider (1958), 10.
47. A critic with a darker rhetorical touch might make the analogy that cancer has a long history, and it brings no benefits.
48. David Stout, "Tab for Washington Lobbying" (*New York Times*, July 29, 1999), A-14.
49. Berry (1997), 24, 25.

—6—

Lobbying

Introduction

What sort of interests predominate in Washington, D.C.? Part I of this book suggested that collective-action problems would limit the abilities of broad-based groups to organize as readily as smaller and wealthier groups. Three points deserve repetition. First, private interests of individuals have often been represented in public legislatures. Second, institutions rather than groups dominate the K Street corridor in Washington, the favored spot for lobbyists, organized interests, and institutions maintaining a home in the nation's capital. Third, there is indeed an upper-class bias in representation in Washington. However, upper-class dominance is not due to some elitist-conspired plan to dominate politics. If politics were that simple, one might imagine that uncovering the conspiracy would solve many people's problems. As it happens, the upper-class bias is more endemic, and, therefore, more lasting. Simply put, human nature makes overcoming the collective-action problem difficult. The fight to organize will always be more difficult for the larger, widely dispersed groups than for the smaller, more concentrated groups.[1]

What about the lobbyists themselves? Tufts University political scientist Jeffrey Berry calls lobbyists "the nerve endings of an interest group."[2] Lobbyists are paid agents with very clear incentives to behave strategically. What strategies are available to lobbyists? What structures their interactions? This chapter focuses on the nerve endings of organized interests to explore how lobbyists fit into the day-to-day world of Washington politics.

The Day-to-Day Context of Lobbying

The previous chapter took a long-range view of lobbying in Washington; here the focus is on day-to-day interactions. From moment to moment and day to day, Washington is a city run on and driven by information. Indeed, Washington has among the highest per capita consumption rates of newspapers. The more information someone has, the more valuable that individual is. The information can take many forms. Sometimes the information is about people and events back home. Sometimes the information is very technical and highly specialized.[3] If, for instance, legislators want to regulate genetic engineering, they need some rather technical information. Sometimes the information is all about who's hot and who's not. Players in Washington's organized interest community are only as valuable as the information they possess. Minimally, lobbyists need information about the immediate personal and institutional context of Washington politics.

The personal context

Washington lobbyists often consider personal communications the most efficacious of their tactics, ahead of grassroots or indirect methods and ahead of partisan or electoral methods.[4] For lobbyists to understand a legislator's personal context, information about the legislator's home state or district is crucial. Legislators are always looking toward the next election. They recognize that they may need to explain their Washington activity to their constituents. Elections structure much of their existence. Disregarding such an important aspect of a legislator's life ultimately hurts a lobbyist. Lobbyists can be most helpful when they provide information that is tailored to the personal context of the legislator. Suppose, for instance, a lobbyist is promoting the continued support for gasohol—a gas blend with corn by-products. Should the lobbyist speak about its impact on air quality, its impact on corn producers, the United States's overreliance on foreign gas and oil, or some other related issue? The most important information to the legislator will depend on that particular legislator's personal context. The representative from Atlanta or Los Angeles might be most interested in the air-quality issues. The representative from Houston will consider the gas and oil industry. The midwestern representative is most likely to want information about the impact of the program on corn growers. Lobbyists need to know representatives' personal contexts.

The institutional context

In addition to the personal context, lobbyists need to know the institutional context in which they are working. For congressional lobbying, that means they must know the legislative process forward and backward. Lobbyists spend considerable time keeping track of who key policy leaders are. To be certain, the usual suspects emerge, committee and subcommittee chairs, party leaders, and so on. In addition to knowing these leaders, lobbyists must know what the flow of events is already, which legislation of interest is pending in committees or on the floor, when recesses are planned, how far off the next election is. Typically, lobbyists work with existing legislation, looking for ways to amend or kill aspects of it. If one needs to start from scratch, then bill introduction and committee referral become important, and connections to the right subcommittees and committees are crucial.[5] If the issue at hand has no established connections to a particular committee, then the lobbyist needs to find a legislator who, regardless of his or her committee positions, is willing to help. Consider the various issues related to global warming. There is no global warming committee in the House or the Senate, and numerous committees could lay claim to the issue. In such situations, knowledge of the personal context may help one navigate the unclear institutional context. Senator Charles Hagel (R-Neb.) has developed a keen interest in global warming, and he may use his parliamentary skills to negotiate the intricate legislative process. If the fight is drawn out on the floor, then a different skill is required. As Christine DeGregorio succinctly stated, "different talents are needed along the way. Advocates recognize this and look for individuals [such as committee and subcommittee chairs] with agenda-setting privileges early and eloquence late in the lawmaking cycle."[6]

In 1994, the Republicans gained a majority of seats in the House for the first time in decades. With the takeover came massive changes to the institutional context that lobbyists thought they knew. First, with any change in party control, there is a one-hundred-percent turnover in positions related to agenda setting. There is a new speaker and there are new committee and subcommittee chairs. All the information gathered about Democratic chairs' personal contexts is of little use when the Republicans take over. In addition to the new personal contexts, the Republicans altered key aspects of the institutional context. With the ascendance of Speaker Newt Gingrich (R-Ga.) in 1994, committee chairs were considerably weakened, and semiformal working groups dominated by party leaders were strengthened.[7] Three committees and twenty-five subcommittees were completely abolished. Lobbyists scrambled to figure things out as the personal and institutional contexts were both changing. The era of unchallenged committees was over, but no one was exactly sure what defined the new institutional context. When the leadership was in turmoil after Gingrich's abrupt resignation as Speaker, everyone wondered who had the ear of the Speaker-select Bob Livingston (R-La.). When Livingston abruptly resigned his House seat, Dennis Hastert (R-Ill.) was elected Speaker. Hastert was not a household name, even among some House members and Washington insiders. Insider newspapers ran numerous articles on the new Speaker and those people who were close to him.[8] With the changing leadership, the personal context was again changing.

Legislator–Lobbyist Interactions

Many civics texts portray Washington politics as the balancing of competing interests. In what sense is such a view justified? How are these interests actually balanced? In "Federalist #10," Madison wrote that it is in vain to say that enlightened statesmen will be able to adjust these clashing interests and render them all subservient to the public good. Enlightened states-man will not always be at the helm. Nor, in many cases, can such an adjustment be made at all without taking into view remote and indirect considerations, which rarely prevail over the immediate interest which one party may find in disregarding the rights of another or the good of the whole.[9]

That is, elected officials may not be impartial referees. Organized interests themselves must try to counter the activities of their opponents. Earl Latham in an oft-quoted passage wrote that a "legislative vote on any issue tends to represent the composition of strength, i.e., the balance of power, among the contending groups at the moment of voting."[10]

Latham himself defined groups very broadly. Groups were not simply in-terest groups operating beyond the traditional confines of the U.S. Capitol. Any collection of people constituted a group. Within the legislature itself, there were numerous groups, including Democrats and Republicans, junior and senior members, large- and small-state senators, northerners, southern-ers, midwesterners, southwesterners, northwesterners, House and Senate members, and House members from urban districts and House members from rural districts. There is no reason to define the groups interested in a policy struggle too narrowly. The legislators themselves are key players, not impartial referees. As key players with interests of their own, legislators have the incentives to establish various formal and informal regulations in antici-pation of the lobbying onslaught. Understanding the problems associated with the representation of interests and the varied means of regulating lobby-ist communication are central to this chapter.

The Representation Problem

Legislators frequently claim that it is impossible to determine precisely whom a group's lobbyist represents. Former Senator William Brock (R-Tenn.) questioned whether "as individuals entrusted with decision-making powers, [we can] accurately assess the goals and needs for legislation without know-ing the source of the information and the opinions we receive."[11] Without knowing the composition of the group's membership, the members' loyalty to the group, and the salience of the members' concerns about the group's lobbyist's stand, it is impossible to ascertain to what extent a lobbyist's claims are representative of the group. Writing about this problem during the first decades of the twentieth century, E. Pendleton Herring noted that

> A representative from Texas likened some of the national associations to the coy-ote, an animal that has the ability to howl in divers keys and discords so that the listener is unable to tell whether it is one coyote or a dozen.[12]

In his work on state-level lobbying, Alan Rosenthal interviewed lobbyists who had represented as many as four different clients by midday. Rosenthal notes that "in a single conversation with a legislator, a lobbyist may deal with different issues, and on behalf of different clients."[13] Such lobbying practices make it difficult to evaluate a lobbyist's message, thereby keeping the connection between the lobbyist's message and the impact on legislator's constituents rather murky. Writing about this same general problem, Frank Baumgartner and the late Jack Walker concluded,

> Before we can fully understand the complex linkages between the public and the government in democratic societies, we must make an accurate assessment of the depth of citizen involvement in the interest groups that press their claims upon the government.[14]

Whether a lobbyist is representing a longtime ally or a traditional opponent, a legislator is never certain about how representative a lobbyist's claims are. Although lobbyists represent groups, lobbyists' claims need not be representative of the groups' members' concerns. The representation problem stems from four related and commonplace sources.

Salience

Lobbyists may exaggerate the salience of an issue in a technical, policy-oriented way or in a more overtly political fashion. Often, but not always, these two types of exaggerations operate hand in hand. For instance, one might misrepresent a technical issue to create the impression of greater political support. This tendency has been noted for decades. In his discussion of the Smoot-Hawley tariff legislation, E. E. Schattschneider introduced the "first law of behavior . . . [arguing that] groups seek to exaggerate their importance, to identify themselves with larger interests, and to speak for whole categories of loose aggregates."[15] Jack Wright details several recent examples of the same phenomenon, including one involving the Student Loan Funding Corporation (SLFC).[16] The SLFC has no dues-paying members, but it is connected to such loose aggregates as university and college students and banks. The SLFC spent $25,000 on an Ohio campaign to convince college students to use a toll-free number to contact their U.S. senators and express displeasure with proposed changes in the loan program. How salient is the SLFC to students? Students seeking loans never interact with the SLFC. The SLFC simply manages the buying and selling of established loans on a secondary market. The SLFC sought to connect its interests with a broader community.

Group preferences

Numerous political scientists have noted that the preferences of a group's leaders, who guide the group's political action, do not always correspond with the preferences of members who may not be fully informed about the group's lobbying activity.[17] Certainly, the behavior of lobbyists and group leaders is circumscribed to some extent by the group's membership; but the member's goals, the leader's goals, and the lobbyist's goals are not equivalent. Legislators recognize this fact. For instance, Bill Browne, a close and careful observer of the agriculture policy community, records a member of Congress stating, "The Farm Bureau . . . is a vague collection of unrelated sentiments."[18]

Trade-association lobbyists are of special interest in this instance because they may be presenting the concerns of their entire membership, or they may be presenting the concerns of an individual firm that has funded a particular lobbying effort.[19] Misrepresentation can occur because a legislator never knows whether the trade-association lobbyist represents all association members or only one or two firms that are temporarily funding the association's effort. E. E. Schattschneider called this sort of representation problem the "representation of the one by the many."[20] That is, what appears to be the lobbying campaign of a large association is actually the effort of a very small subset of the entire membership. The representation problem is further exacerbated by multiple affiliations. Large corporations typically belong to dozens of trade associations, which allows them to choose the most effective association for particular lobbying efforts.

Group composition

Many groups exist on paper only and have no actual membership or even a desire to establish a membership base. Indeed, there are "groups" "to which no one belongs and which do not even provide for the possibility of membership." Other groups "are little more than institutionalized personalities."[21] With a laser printer and a little imagination, anyone can create a letterhead organization. There are no laws limiting the number or type of RESCIND chapters. (RESCIND is the acronym for Real Emergency: Self-Centered Individual Needs Dollars.) From time to time trade associations create affiliated groups to air certain issues or ideas. The drug industry's trade association, Pharmaceutical Research and Manufacturers of America, provided seed money, research support, and funds to cover day-to-day operating costs to Citizens for the Right to Know. Citizens for the Right to Know argued before Congress that the high price of drugs was due to drug stores overcharging rather than to the pharmaceutical industry itself. The membership base for the Pharmaceutical Research and Manufacturers of America is readily known; the membership base for Citizens for the Right to Know is less transparent.

Temporary coalitions of several groups or corporations often emerge for specific short-term purposes. It is very difficult to ascertain the genuine composition of such coalitions, let alone the depth of involvement of the various groups. Ironically, just such a coalition formed to oppose the 1995 Lobbying Disclosure Act. The Free Speech Coalition was comprised of "over fifty disparate special interests," including Washington lobbyists, fundamental Christian groups, and advocates from both sides of the abortion and gun control issues.[22] The depth of citizen involvement in such temporary, issues-based coalitions is particularly difficult to evaluate.

Crossover effects

Most firms like to diversify. Lobbying firms diversify by developing a broad pool of clients. Prominent Washington lobbyists and large lobbying firms are only as valuable as their client list. If a lobbyist maintains an impressive client list, he or she may be able to lend considerable influence to less celebrated clients, thereby creating a crossover effect. That is, legislators may be responsive to the impressive client list, even if the particular client at hand is not noteworthy. Robert Gray was one of the most powerful lobbyists of the 1980s and early 1990s, with a most impressive client list. In addition, Gray managed Hill and Knowlton, one of the most powerful public relations (lobbying) firms in Washington. Hill and Knowlton had represented everyone from the Teamsters to the Citizens for a Free Kuwait. Hill and Knowlton traded so frequently on the crossover effect that there was a direct backlash. In the early 1990s, Hill and Knowlton "lost a flood of clients and staff" and fell down "a notch on the rung of prestige." Hill and Knowlton muddied their reputation by carelessly trading on crossover effects. Confusion and frustration ensued when Gray "mounted an anti-pornography campaign for one client, while simultaneously promoting Playboy and Penthouse for another."[23]

Without an accurate assessment of lobbyists' representativeness, legislators are unsure of the interests that they balance. If legislators do not know what they are balancing, legislative tradeoffs and compromises may be haphazard and lack meaning. The next two sections characterize the legislator–lobbyist interaction, discuss formal and informal means of regulating lobbyists, and examine how legislators are able to structure their interaction with lobbyists to limit their vulnerability to the representation problem.

Characterizing the Legislator–Lobbyist Interaction

It is commonly accepted that lobbyists provide valuable information to legislators—information that legislators might otherwise not have.[24] Legislators readily acknowledge that lobbyists fulfill "extremely useful functions in the national interest. They can be tapped for expert information on problems, [and] they can analyze the impact of proposed legislation on their areas of concern."[25] Legislator's personal confidants and constituents are more influential, but legislators frequently contact lobbyists for advice.[26] Congressional staff members admit that "drafting complex language [for a bill] means I need a lobbyist."[27] During the summer of 2001 when Congress debated President Bush's tax-cut proposal, many senators relied on the analysis of Robert S. McIntyre, the director of Citizens for Tax Justice. One senator stated that the "agencies of government that are supposed to provide this information don't, and the only way we can get it is from Bob [McIntyre]."[28] Although a lobbyist's technical expertise may allow him or her to instruct and inform rather than pressure, no legislator or lobbyist is blind to the electoral implications of legislative decisions.

Of course, the unequal distribution of information that makes a lobbyist valuable also makes a lobbyist potentially dangerous, because incentives for the truthful revelation of information may not exist. Indeed, if Schattschneider's "first law of behavior" holds, lobbyists have an incentive to exaggerate both the electoral benefits of assisting them and the costs of ignoring them, which is at the root of the representation problem. In the last decade, game theorists have developed intricate signaling models in which valuable information is unequally distributed among the players. The better-informed players communicate (i.e., signal) to the less well-informed players. Signals have been especially important for the analysis of reputations, beliefs, threats, bluffs, and deception—partly because signals need not truly reflect underlying intentions or attributes. Ideally, a player who receives a signal can learn about the structures of the game if certain signals are most likely to be sent under certain conditions.

Signaling games can be used to highlight many of the concerns related to legislator–lobbyist interactions. To keep the present game as simple as possible, there are just two players, a lobbyist and a legislator. Each of the two players has just two strategies. The lobbyist can make a typical claim or a grand claim, choosing one of the two matrices in Table 6.1. These claims are the signals to the legislator. Some grand claims are pure exaggeration, but others can indeed be substantiated. The legislator responds by complying with or ignoring the lobbyist's claim, as noted in the columns in Table 6.1.

Although there is only one lobbyist, the game in Table 6.1 is set up as if there were two, those who can substantiate grand claims and those who cannot. The first type of lobbyist, t_1, can substantiate only typical claims, but the second type, t_2, can substantiate grand claims. The legislator has incomplete information, limiting his or her ability to determine a priori what type the lobbyist is. The legislator may have beliefs about the lobbyist's type but does not have incontrovertible information.

The payoffs for the game in Table 6.1 are easier to untangle if two things are kept in mind. First, regardless of the lobbyist's type and regardless of the signal sent, the lobbyist would rather the legislator choose to comply. A t_1 lobbyist would secure either b or $b - k$ if the legislator chose to comply. A t_2 lobbyist would secure either a or $a - k$ if the legislator chose to comply. The differences in the b and $b - k$ and the a and $a - k$ payoffs are due to the additional costs, k, associated with making a grand claim. Second, regardless

TABLE 6.1
A Signaling Game between a Lobbyist and Legislator

Game Sequence:
    The lobbyist chooses a matrix by stating a *Typical Claim* or a *Grand Claim*.
    The legislator responds, choosing to *Comply* with or *Ignore* the lobbyist's claim.

Typical Claim	Comply	Ignore
t_1	$b, 0$	$0, 1$
t_2	$a, 1$	$0, 0$

Grand Claim	Comply	Ignore
t_1	$b-k, 0$	$0-k, 1$
t_2	$a-k, 1$	$0-k, 0$

Note: The lobbyist's payoffs are to the left, the legislator's to the right, and $a > b$.
$k > 0$ represents the cost of making a grand claim.

of the signal sent, the legislator would rather ignore a t_1 lobbyist and comply with a t_2 lobbyist. Indeed, the legislator worries about signals only to the extent that they can help him or her determine what type the lobbyist is. Some grand claims are true and well founded, others are not. If the lobbyist is of type t_2, meaning that he or she can substantiate grand claims, then the legislator would rather comply than ignore what may become tremendous policy consequences. However, either type of lobbyist can make a grand claim. Misrepresentation occurs whenever a t_1 lobbyist makes a grand claim or a t_2 lobbyist makes a typical claim. Though we would not expect a t_2 lobbyist to make a typical claim, it is clear that t_1 lobbyists, from time to time, make unwarranted grand claims.

Two kinds of equilibria in this signaling game deserve special attention. Recall that equilibria are simply outcomes in which no player has any incentive to alter his or her strategy. In one equilibrium, the lobbyists' messages precisely correspond with their types. In essence, lobbyists send honest messages, t_1 types make only typical claims, and t_2 types make only grand claims. In game theoretic parlance, these are called separating equilibria because lobbyists representing different types of clients or issues send different messages. For instance, a lobbyist's signals are often claims about the electoral strength of a client or the electoral salience of an issue.[29] In a separating equilibrium, each lobbyist sends a unique signal that reflects the true electoral implications. The lobbyist's message is readily connected to the lobbyist's type, and all information is disclosed.[30]

In contrast, lobbyists' messages in pooling equilibria are of no value to legislators. In a pooling equilibrium, all lobbyists, regardless of their type, send the same message. In essence, no information is disclosed, because all lobbyists make the same grand claim, whether it is merited or not. Recalling

Schattschneider's "first law of behavior" that lobbyists exaggerate the electoral benefits of assisting them, pooling equilibria nicely illustrate a crucial aspect of the representation problem. In separating equilibria, lobbyists are honest with legislators and legislators can learn from lobbyists' communication; whereas, in pooling equilibria, some lobbyists are obviously exaggerating their claims and legislators gain no information from any of the lobbyists' messages.

In light of this characterization of the interaction between lobbyists and legislators, separating equilibria have attractive features for legislators. If legislators can induce a separating equilibrium, then politically relevant information is disclosed and the representation problem is lessened. The crux of the representation problem remains unresolved as long as the only equilibria are pooling equilibria. Legislators would like lobbyists "to separate" to ensure that lobbyists' signals contain useful information. If lobbyists have informational advantages and have an incentive to exaggerate their claims, how can legislators structure the interaction so that lobbyists' signals are informative and trustworthy? The trick for legislators is to structure the legislator–lobbyist interaction so as to minimize the representation problem without inhibiting lobbyists' incentives or abilities to disseminate valuable information. Legislators use both formal statutes and informal means to regulate lobbyists. These formal and informal means affect legislators' incomplete information about a lobbyist's type and the costs associated with lobbying strategies.

Statutory Regulations of Lobbyists

Statutory regulations focus on various ethical standards as well as the unequal distribution of politically relevant information.[31] Legislators design disclosure requirements so that they can secure politically relevant information about whom a lobbyist represents. In the parlance of a signaling game with incomplete information, legislators seek to learn the lobbyists' type.

Regulations for specific lobby agents

Lobbyists for foreign clients, utility companies, and federal agencies or firms that receive government money have been more closely scrutinized and regulated than other lobbyists. The Merchant Marine Act of 1936 required those individuals wishing to alter shipping regulations to register with the Commerce Department prior to lobbying members of Congress or federal agencies. In the late 1930s, members of Congress took umbrage when they learned that certain utility companies were having thousands of postcards sent to them by high school students who were paid to sign names taken randomly from phone books. Some members of Congress immediately pushed for a comprehensive lobbying regulation bill, but in the end only lobbying by utility companies was regulated. Lobbyists representing the interests of utility companies have to provide a list of their clients to the Securities Exchange Commission and an account of the sources and amounts of their funds. By forcing utility company lobbyists to list their clients and their sources of funds, the representation problem was lessened because the lobbyists' true clients could be identified. Since 1938, lobbyists for foreign clients have had to register with the Attorney Generals' office, and they must file extensive accounts of their activities and expenditures every six months. Revisions in 1966 mandated that lobbyists must inform their interlocutors of the foreign principal. More recently, lobbying activity by the Legal Services Corporation has been proscribed (PL 98-166, 1983), and lobbyists for recipients of federal grants, loans, or contracts are required to file extensive accounts of their lobbying expenditures (PL 101–121, 1989). Each of these statutes was designed to force lobbyists to reveal politically relevant information about their clients. However effective these laws might be, they are narrowly focused and cover relatively few lobbying campaigns.

Attempts to create comprehensive lobbying regulations

The first comprehensive lobbying regulation dates back to 1946. Title III of the 1946 Legislative Reorganization Act mandated that lobbyists register their affiliations and record their finances to "enable Congress . . . to evaluate . . . evidence, data, or communications from organized groups seeking to influence legislative action."[32] Although there was an immediate increase in the number of registered lobbyists, it was well known that few lobbyists covered by the 1946 legislation ever registered. A lack of enforcement and legal challenges weakened the law. In 1954, the Supreme Court limited the law's purview by defining lobbying in the most narrow of ways.[33] Only the most direct communications with members and senators were considered to be lobbying. Interactions with congressional staff members, congressional testimony, and grassroots activity was either exempted or largely ignored. Many lobbyists could avoid registering because lobbying was not, strictly speaking, part of their job description. In 1994, former Senator William Cohen (R-Me.) lamented that

> We have thousands of lobbyists in this town. Only a small percentage actually register according to the existing law. Of those who do, the information they provide [through registration] is meaningless, it is useless.[34]

In light of the shortcomings in the 1946 legislation, stricter regulations were frequently proposed, but never passed until 1995. The 1995 Lobbying Disclosure Act requires lobbyists and lobbying firms to file twice yearly reports for each of their separate clients. The reports include information on the amount of money spent and the issues being followed. Interestingly, one important set of lobbyists were exempted from the act. Individuals and groups associated with intergovernmental lobbying are not covered by the 1995 act. Unfortunately, the registration data, maintained by the Clerk of the House and the Secretary of the Senate, is collected and stored in a very cumbersome manner. The data are simply scanned versions of the hard copy reports that lobbyists and groups provide. There are no neat and tidy spreadsheets to facilitate study by social scientists.[35]

Even stricter guidelines have been proposed. Years ago, George Galloway, a prominent political scientist, recommended that lobbyists be required "to certify that they are advocating only measures that have been specifically approved by a majority of the membership of the organization which they claim to represent."[36] Indeed, proposals to require the disclosure of group members and a record of the amount of money each member contributed to the group were made in the two Congresses prior to the 104th when the 1995 Act was passed. Such disclosures would aid control to the extent that politically relevant information held privately by lobbyists would have to be revealed to legislators, thereby lessening the representation problem; however, the legality of such regulations is suspect.[37] Freedom of association means little if it is too closely monitored by government agencies. Even if the strictest of disclosure requirements could be employed, they would address only three of the causes of the representation problem. Legislators would have politically relevant information about group composition. The disclosure of how much money each member contributed would provide an indication of group preferences and overall issue salience. However, crossover effects would continue to create a representation problem. Even after recognizing a lobbyist's immediate client, a legislator may be most attentive to the lobbyist because of his or her *other*, more powerful clients.

The reluctance to pass stricter regulations stems from three sources. First, revising lobbying regulations without violating the Constitution's First Amendment "requires artful draftsmanship" because U.S. citizens enjoy the right to petition the government for the redress of grievances.[38] Second, legislators and lobbyists have been generally wary of altering their status quo. Third, legislators have other informal means to regulate lobbying activities. It is worth noting that legislators themselves have not made a mad-dash for the lobbying registration data collected since the passage of the 1995 Lobbying Disclosure Act. Perhaps legislators have nonstatutory means to secure politically relevant information from lobbyists to thereby lessen the representation problem. In the next section, informal means of regulating lobbyists are examined.

Informal Means of Regulating Lobbyists

Formal, statutory regulations are distinct from informal means of regulation in crucial ways. Formal controls are designed to have a global effect on lobbying practices throughout the chamber(s). Informal means of control work on an office-by-office or legislator-by-legislator basis. Thus, the aims as well as the effects of the two controls are very different. The two different means of regulation are not, therefore, perfect substitutes for one another. However, scholars need to explore the day-to-day legislator–lobbyist interactions to discover how informal means of regulation might work. Regardless of the formal regulations in place, legislators still possess the incentives and abilities to protect themselves from undue lobbying influence.

Controlling access

Legislators cannot be forced to visit with a lobbyist. The legislator must grant access to the lobbyist. Many interest group scholars have written about the importance of having access. At times, David B. Truman argued that access, taken literally, is the most fundamental objective for interest group leaders and lobbyists. Interest groups cannot be successful in their endeavors if they lack "access to one or more of the key points of decision in the government."[39] Lobbyists fear that without access legislators will simply balance the interests immediately before them. Without access, all interests are not considered and decisions are biased against the absent parties.[40] Lobbyists themselves repeatedly state the importance of access and have an intense fear of the loss of access.[41]

If lobbyists fear the loss of access, then controlling access provides one means of checking the undue influence of lobbyists when the same legislators and lobbyists interact on a fairly regular basis. By credibly stating that future access will be denied to any lobbyist who has been less than frank, a legislator favorably affects a lobbyist's current behavior. Clearly, the viability of controlling access as a means of regulating lobbyists depends crucially on repeated interactions and a fear of losing future access. Hence, controlled access works best with established lobbying concerns interacting with established legislators. Fear of losing access carries little punch if one interacts with lobbyists who represent coalitions that will soon disappear into the political ether. Unfortunately, those coalitions have become increasingly common.[42] Finally, the notion of controlling future access has little impact for lame duck legislators. If for whatever reason the likelihood or value of future interactions is too small, then controlling access has little or no effect on regulating lobbyists, and other means of controlling lobbyists should be considered.

Audits

David Austen-Smith and John Wright have shown how simple audits of a lobbyist's claims and counteractive lobbying by opposing groups can limit the ability of lobbyists to pressure legislators unduly.[43] Legislators need not double-check or audit every bit of information that they get from lobbyists. A deterrence effect exists as long as there is the possibility of an audit. When auditing is difficult for legislators, one is most apt to see counteractive lobbying by opposition groups. That is, groups jostle back and forth and compete for legislators' support whenever it is particularly difficult for legislators themselves to audit lobbyists' claims.

Reputations

Lobbyists repeatedly state how important their reputations for honesty and forthrightness are. Lobbyists do not maintain such standards of honesty because they are naturally of a higher moral order; rather, lobbyists refrain from dissembling because of the consequences of dishonesty. Reputations by themselves mean little if legislators fail to control access. "Once a lobbyist 'doubles' [i.e., dissembles to] a senator, he is through."[44] A member of Congress stated that "If anyone ever gives me false or misleading information, that's it—I'll never see him again."[45] These legislators described (and claimed that they used) the strategy of controlling access. Clearly, legislators are aware of their ability to control access. If controlling access is effective, then lobbyists develop reputations for truthfulness fortuitously.

Lobbyists view aspects of the situation similarly. A lobbyist and ex-member of Congress opined that "You can't ever afford to lie to a member of Congress because if you lose access to him, you've had it." He continued by stating "that the mark of a good lobbyist is someone who will tell the representative the truth, even if the truth hurts him in particular."[46] The lobbyist who stated that "it's all built on confidence. It really is, it's just amazing, it's credibility and confidence" was generally correct; but the relationship remains delicate.[47] Repeated legislator–lobbyist interactions create an environment in which cooperation may flourish, but it requires that both individuals value future interactions and that legislators punish uncooperative behavior.[48] Alan Rosenthal reports a lobbyist stating that "you get credibility in teaspoonsful and lose it in gallons." Rosenthal concludes that any "lobbyist can deceive a legislator, but only once."[49] By denying all future access in response to a lobbyist's uncooperative behavior, a legislator is employing a strategy frequently labeled *permanent retaliation*. The threat of permanent retaliation maintains cooperation whenever the better-known tit-for-tat strategy is able to maintain cooperation. Credibility and confidence in the lobbying environment stem from legislators' abilities to control access and lobbyists' fear of the loss of access.

Costly signals

In the signaling game in Table 6.1, k, the costliness of making the grand claim, affects the existence of separating and pooling equilibria. If a legislator is unable a priori to make a lobbyist's signal costly, then the lobbyist has both the motive and ability to misrepresent. In other words, if k is too small, then both types of lobbyists can make grand claims. If a legislator makes signals too costly, then neither type can afford to make a grand claim, even when it is warranted. Given that separating equilibria have appealing properties for legislators and that pooling equilibria do not, it behooves legislators to adjust the costliness of lobbyists' signals to effect a favorable outcome. That is, by adjusting the costs of the signals, legislators can lessen the representation problem by ensuring that only separating equilibria exist.[50]

Legislators do have the ability to structure the environment in which they interact with lobbyists, affecting who can testify and directly and indirectly affecting lobbying costs. For instance, the general costliness of business-related lobbying was increased when Congress determined that the costs of lobbying would no longer be a tax deductible business expense. In addition, lobbyists on the Hill spend much of their time making the rounds through the Capitol. One lobbyist lamented that "if I don't see ___ at least once a week, he'll say, 'Where the hell have you been? You only stop around when you want something from us.'"[51] Though continued interaction creates an important personal rapport, such maintenance functions are also costly.[52]

Specific lobbying campaigns must frequently rely on additional costly signals:

1. It is crucial for a lobbyist to connect or associate his or her client with the legislator's constituents.[53] To accomplish this task, lobbyists frequently fly high-ranking corporate executives, whose time is very valuable, to Washington to assist in a lobbying effort. Important individuals from a legislator's constituency can be very persuasive.[54] Of course, there is no reason the professional lobbyist could not say everything the constituent or executive from home might say. The only difference between the lobbyist working alone and the lobbyist bringing along an executive or important constituent is that the latter tactic is more costly. One might argue that the uninitiated enjoy flying to Washington to meet with their legislators. There are, however, limits. At some point, these requests are costly to the executive and his or her employer. Using the more expensive tactic provides information about the salience of the issue and group composition.

2. Lobbyists often encourage group members to contact their representatives and senators. Of course, legislators are known to discount inspired mail, but well-executed mail campaigns are costly signals and, therefore, appear more genuine. Jack Wright likens grassroots mobilization to "field experiments in electoral mobilization."[55] Legislators monitor grassroots activity carefully because it provides an indication of issue salience, group composition, and group preferences.[56]

3. Though legislators sometimes seem to pay little attention to them, those committee hearings that resemble a parade of witnesses are actually quite helpful because a witness's presence is a costly signal. By

opening most congressional hearings to the public, sunshine legislation increased both lobbyists' access to the policy process and lobbyists' costs. More and more groups have responded to the increased opportunity to debate legislative decisions.[57] Whenever a lobbyist chooses not to attend a public hearing, he or she signals a lack of interest to legislators. Of course, one might argue that testifying before Congress is exciting for the uninitiated witness, but two points should be kept in mind. First, the professional lobbyist receives little enjoyment from testifying himself. If the lobbyist must find some average group member to testify, there is no reason to suspect that the lobbyist receives vicarious enjoyment from the process. Second, members of Congress can make testifying a grueling experience. Presence in Washington is costly, so once again, legislators learn about the issue's salience for the group.

Personal testimonies were important for some legislators wondering how to vote during the summer of 2000 on permanent trade status for China. Farm organizations flew farmers to Washington to testify about the importance of permanent trade relations with China. The presence of these farmers was crucial for some wavering legislators. Their presence was aimed at legislators like Richard Pombo (R-Calif.), who stated that "I think any of the big [agricultural] corporations" favor permanent trade relations with China, but "I think if you get a real family farmer, you'd get a different story."[58] The representation problem for Pombo was clear. Are the agricultural interests large corporate concerns or family farmer concerns?

Simply by evaluating lobbyists' signals and controlling access, legislators can protect themselves against three of the four causes of the representation problem. Legislators can learn about issue salience, group composition, and group preferences. However, as with formal, statutory regulations, undue influence due to crossover effects may still exist. Legislators may respond favorably to a lobbyist with an impressive list of clients, regardless of whom the immediate client is. In sum, disclosure laws are just one means of regulating lobbyists and controlling the representation problem. Legislators can also control the representation problem by controlling access, auditing lobbyists' information, being sensitive to lobbyists' reputations, and affecting lobbying costs. By controlling access and structuring the interaction in order to ensure that there are only separating equilibria, legislators show that they can influence lobbyists and limit undue pressure. Stricter lobbying regulations are not the only means of solving the representation problem. Too often legislators are presumed to be constrained to reactive or defensive actions. Indeed, legislators have a distinct advantage over lobbyists: legislators design the rules governing their interactions with lobbyists. In the end, lobbyists must "meet the professional standards that *legislators* have established for them."[59] Those standards may or may not ensure good lawmaking.

Does the System Work?

The system failed in 1999 in New York State at the county level of government. Although smoking bans have been addressed by the national government and numerous state governments, in New York, county governments effected smoking bans in public places. Given their prominent policy role, county governments were lobbied more heavily than they were accustomed to. Lobbyists worked the entire state, moving from county to county. At least one lobbyist for the Empire State Restaurant and Tavern Association was, as it happens, also on retainer with Philip Morris. The lobbyist worked in various counties contemplating a ban on smoking in restaurants. Smoking bans, he argued, might drive away tavern and restaurant patrons. What he did not disclose is that he was paid primarily by Philip Morris, not the Empire State Restaurant and Tavern Association.[60] Indeed, Philip Morris had been spending about $40,000 a month lobbying in New York State. Officials in Duchess County were particularly incensed. Why did such deception work? State-level lobbying tends to be less developed and less professionalized than lobbying in Washington. At the county level, lobbying is very rare. Repeated interactions are unlikely, so there is little concern about reputations or the loss of access. Access and reputation mean little if the lobbyists know they are leaving town. Such deception works from time to time, but it is unlikely that the offending lobbyists will be of much use in Duchess County for the foreseeable future. For that very reason, lobbyists who go bad are sometimes ousted by their own organizations.[61]

On October 10, 1990, the representation problem affected the course of events at the national level in a most dramatic fashion. The backdrop for the story includes Iraq's invasion of Kuwait and the close links between a congressional caucus and Hill and Knowlton, one of the most powerful lobbying/public relations firms in Washington. On October 10, 1990, the Human Rights Caucus asked a fifteen-year-old Kuwaiti girl to testify about the Iraqi disregard for basic human rights. Nayirah, the young girl's name, testified that babies were taken from incubators by Iraqi soldiers who then "left the babies on the cold floor to die." Such gripping eyewitness testimony received much coverage in the days leading up to the Persian Gulf War. After all, legislators and the U.S. public needed considerable justification for engaging in such a dangerous, expensive, and risky endeavor as freeing Kuwait might have been.

Hill and Knowlton had been hired by the Kuwaiti government to mount a public relations campaign to support the freeing of Kuwait. As it happened, Hill and Knowlton employees had earlier helped to organize the Congressional Human Rights Caucus; the caucus was even housed at Hill and Knowlton's Washington headquarters. The Human Rights Caucus was the center of a lobbying enterprise that linked the leaders of the caucus, Tom

Lantos (D-Calif.) and John Edward Porter (R-Ill.), with Hill and Knowlton and, indirectly, with the Hill and Knowlton client list, which included nations such as China, Indonesia, Turkey, and Kuwait. Securing information in the midst of a military conflict is always difficult, which is perhaps why senators and members were so taken by the eyewitness testimony of Nayirah. What was the representation problem and why did Hill and Knowlton receive such bad press related to Nayirah's testimony? Susanne Roschwalb argues that Hill and Knowlton received bad press for two related reasons:[62] First, Nayirah was never fully identified as the daughter of the Kuwaiti Ambassador to the United States. Was Nayirah whisked away to safety, saved from a war-torn country, or was she driven into the Capitol from the Washington suburbs? Whose interests was she representing? Second, Nayirah and Hill and Knowlton provided information that could not be verified or audited in any meaningful fashion until after the war. Regardless of the veracity of her statements, Roschwalb questioned the reasonableness of communicating information that could not be verified.

The incubator story was everywhere, and seven senators cited it when explaining their Gulf War vote. The actual truthfulness of the incubator story is still debated, though many commentators are comfortable with the notion that it was at the very least exaggerated.[63] Did the exaggeration lead to miscalculations in votes? The fog of war or impending conflict has often led to political miscalculations. As long as legislators remained unaware of who was behind the Free Kuwait group, misrepresentation could, and did, occur. Who and what caused this particular debacle? Hill and Knowlton? The Kuwaiti government? Nayirah? The legislators who had associated with Hill and Knowlton? Both the formal and informal means of regulating lobbyists failed to prevent the embarrassment. The regulations affecting lobbyists representing foreign entities did not protect against misrepresentation. Informal means failed or were impossible to employ. Auditing was impossible. There were no costly signals. Nayirah was not concerned about losing access to Congress or a loss of reputation on the Hill. She was a young fifteen-year-old, not a professional lobbyist. Finally, there was little direct, counteractive lobbying. To be certain, some opposed the effort to free Kuwait, but no one questioned Saddam Hussein's proclivities for human rights violations; his track record was consistent. Who paid the costs for the misrepresentation? Many people were embarrassed, but it was Hill and Knowlton's revenues that declined ten to twenty percent each year in the early 1990s.

Theory and Practice:
Interpreting Rules and Guidelines for Lobbying

There are numerous authors who offer guidelines for effective lobbying. Sometimes lobbyists themselves write such work, explaining their day to day activities. These works will emphasize the importance of only telling the truth and always protecting your reputation. Of course, that is sound advice for a vast array of occupations. Such guidelines do not define the essence of lobbyists or lobbying. Many lobbyists follow these guidelines, some do not. Those guidelines also fail to distinguish successful lobbyists from unsuccessful ones.

Christine DeGregorio offers four rules for lobbying that come much closer to defining successful lobbying.[64] She refers to these rules as the ABC and D's of lobbying. First, **Assess** the situation. That is, think about the personal and institutional contexts that you are entering. Consider how the personal and institutional contexts can be used to further your cause. Identify potential pitfalls. **Be** patient and persistent. Recognize that legislators and bureaucratic officials are busy people. Present your information in a helpful format. Follow up on initial meetings. Lobbying is a process, not a one-time event. **Conform** to the flow of events. Recognize that your pet project may or may not be prominent in the minds of congressional leaders. However, as the flow of events changes, the prominence of issues in legislators' minds also changes. For instance, legislators may reconsider farm policy after a long period of poor commodity prices. Trigger locks or owner-recognition technology for handguns may get a more favorable hearing after a widely publicized gun-related incident. Legislators adjust to the flow of events; lobbyists should as well. **Don't** put all your eggs in one basket. Developing a working relationship with a small set of legislators is very important, but ignoring the possibility of a change in partisan control is risky. On big issues, consider coordinating a broad-based team effort. What about truthfulness? Does DeGregorio view truthfulness as unimportant? Of course, not. Truthfulness is important for any social interaction among people.

There are over one hundred former representatives or senators who now lobby in Washington.[65] What makes some former legislators such good lobbyists? As former members, they have greater access to the floor and certain areas such as the House gym and cafeteria, but most former members avoid lobbying in those areas. A vice president for congressional communications at Blue Cross/Blue Shield stated that "what a former member brings to the table is an understanding of the process, what it is like to be a member; they know the personalities, the hot buttons." Another official working for the Independent Insurance Agents of America stated that former members know "all those arcane parliamentary procedures . . . and can serve as guides to the committees."[66] In short, former members and senators know the personal and institutional contexts of lobbying and lawmaking. Indeed for some former members turned lobbyist, there is little difference between lawmaking and lobbying. Former Representative Robert Livingston (R-La.) says "The only thing I can't do is . . . vote."

What makes a lousy lobbyist? How are the real clunkers defined? "They're lead-footed [as in slow and plodding, not fast driving], they're predictable, they're incompetent, they're bland, they're handcuffed, *they don't under-*

stand how Washington works."[67] They have "a difficult time bringing an issue to a close."[68] That is, they do not understand the personal and institutional contexts and they fail to respond to changes in those contexts. Even former legislators fail as lobbyists if they neglect to keep up with institutional and personnel changes.[69]

Conclusion

For many years, pluralists and interest group scholars focused their studies on group pressures and expressed little concern for the individual lobbyist's role in the aggregation, articulation, or communication of those pressures to legislators. Though some writers have acknowledged that group concerns and lobbying efforts are not equivalent, they typically pay little attention to lobbyists when they describe interest group pressure. Indeed, lobbying and lobbyists seemed especially unimportant after three prominent scholars working together found that lobbyists were underfunded and that they communicated primarily with legislators already prone to support their lobbying stand.[70]

More recently, various writers have portrayed the full array of feelings in a love-hate relationship. Lobbyists either buy and sell Washington votes at will or are central to the preservation of informed legislative decisions. If one is concerned with interest group influence, then those individuals most integrally involved in the articulation and communication of group concerns cannot be ignored. Interest groups, per se, do not lobby or communicate with members of Congress; lobbyists do. Even those scholars who have focused on lobbyists' roles as communicators have generally overlooked the problems associated with the aggregation and articulation of group concerns. Therefore, they failed to recognize the representation problem. What does it mean to argue that lobbyists communicate helpful information if they are integrally involved in the representation problem and the misrepresentation that stems from it? One cannot understand group pressures without understanding the aggregation, articulation, and communication of those pressures (whatever they might be) by lobbyists.

Concern about lobbying influence will not and should not go away. However, there are collective benefits derived from lobbyists' presence in the legislative process, and there are means for individual legislators to limit their own vulnerability to undue influence of lobbyists. A lobbyist relays both technical information about issues and politically relevant information about the electoral consequences associated with particular actions. Their technical expertise on issues allows lobbyists to involve themselves in the legislative process—often instructing and informing more than pressuring or persuading. Lobbyists also communicate issue saliency. Saliency is important in a pluralist society because it affects the balance of opposing preferences. Recognizing what an interest group wants is relatively easy, but measuring the importance or saliency of a particular desire is much more difficult. Though measuring saliency is difficult, some information about the saliency of an issue to an interest group can be gleaned from the group's lobbyist's signals.

As voters become increasingly cynical about politics in Washington, the fear of lobbyists becomes stronger and the calls for increased lobbying regulations become louder. In this political climate, most legislators publicly endorse the need for increased regulations. Concerns are prompted by lobbying scandals and general mistrust; but such concerns seldom result in careful, analytical studies of lobbyists' interactions with legislators. Too often political scientists are more interested in prescribing reforms of lobbying laws than they are in studying the legislator–lobbyist interaction or the role of lobbyists in the articulation and communication of group pressures. Lobbyists' effects on group pressures and group influence and their adaptation to changing institutional structures are usually ignored. Regulating lobbyists either formally or informally has become increasingly complicated. The regulation of campaign contributions or gifts from lobbyists may be a relatively simple matter, but the regulation of the lobbying communication, per se, is much more complicated. For instance, how should one write lobbying regulations to convince lobbyists to present their cases in a fair, straightforward manner? What can be done to prevent lobbyists from exaggerating their claims? Need a lobbyist disclose his or her client?

In conclusion, five points must be stressed. (1) It has long been recognized that lobbying is a two-way street. Legislators often contact lobbyists because they can often provide helpful information to legislators. (2) Lobbyists are not harmless; but they can be controlled through formal and informal means. (3) Lobbyists are not extraordinarily magnanimous; but they do recognize the value of mutual gains as well as legislators' abilities to control those gains. (4) Lobbyists attain credibility because legislators structure their interactions so as to limit lobbyists' incentives to misrepresent themselves. (5) Although there may be no single best method of controlling lobbyists— either formal or informal—the informal means of controlling lobbyists are not weaker than the formal, statutory means. Stricter disclosure requirements, such as those in the recently proposed statutory regulations, have a definite weakness; they may violate constitutional rights to free association. Informal means of regulating lobbyists require legislators to remain vigilant. Legislators must control access, remain sensitive to lobbyists' reputations, regulate lobbying costs, and audit lobbyists' claims from time to time.

NOTES

1. Jeffrey Berry's *The New Liberalism* (Washington, D.C.: Brookings Institution, 1999) argues that there has been a recent resurgence in citizen-based groups.
2. Berry (1997), 98.
3. See Kevin Esterling's work for a nice analysis of this issue. "Modeling Lobbyist Access: Ideology, Political Participation, and Specialized Policy Knowledge," pa-

per presented at the 2001 Southern Political Science Association Meeting, Atlanta, Georgia.

4. Milbrath (1963) was among the first to report this finding.

5. See Kollman (1997) for a careful look at group-committee relations.

6. Christine DeGregorio, *Networks of Champions: Leadership, Access, and Advocacy in the U.S. House of Representatives* (Ann Arbor: University of Michigan Press, 1997), 123. For a formal characterization of the impact of lobbying at the agenda-setting and floor-voting stages, see David Austen-Smith's "Information and Influence: Lobbying for Agendas and Votes," *American Journal of Political Science* 37 (1993): 799–833.

7. John H. Aldrich and David W. Rohde detail some of these reforms. "The Transition to Republican Rule in the House," *Political Science Quarterly* (1997–98) 112: 541–67. Also see Christine DeGregorio and Kevin Conway, "Some Consequences of Changing Majorities in the U.S. House of Representatives (1991–1996): Leaders and Advocates in Pursuit of Policy," paper presented at the 1999 Southern Political Science Association Meeting, Savannah, Georgia.

8. See for instance, Jim VandeHei, "Speaker Hastert's Inner Circle: Meet the Key Members, Staffers and Lobbyists Who Have the Boss's Ear" (*Roll Call Monthly*, February 1999), 6.

9. Madison (1961), 80.

10. Latham (1965), 36.

11. Hope Eastman, *Lobbying:A Constitutionally Protected Right* (Washington, D.C.: American Enterprise Institute, 1977), 17.

12. Herring (1929).

13. Alan Rosenthal, *The Third House: Lobbyists and Lobbying in the States* (Washington, D.C.: CQ Press, 1993), 39.

14. Baumgartner and Walker (1988).

15. E. E. Schattschneider, *Politics, Pressures and the Tariff* (Englewood Cliffs, NJ: Prentice Hall, 1935), 225.

16. John R. Wright, *Interest Groups and Congress* (Boston: Allyn & Bacon, 1996), 106–09.

17. See, for instance, Godwin (1988); Grant McConnell, *Private Power and American Democracy* (New York: Alfred A. Knopf, 1966); Salisbury (1984), 66; Frank J. Sorauf, "Who's in Charge: Accountability in Political Action Committees," *Political Science Quarterly* (1984–85) 99: 591–614.

18. William P. Browne, *Cultivating Congress: Constituents, Issues, and Interests in Agriculture Policy Making* (Lawrence: University of Kansas Press, 1995), 15.

19. Raymond A. Bauer, Ithiel de Sola Pool, and Lewis Dexter noted this tendency in *American Business and Public Policy* (New York: Atherton, 1963), 372. Also see Schattschneider (1935).

20. Schattschneider (1935), 271. Also see Wright (1996), 106–07.

21. Salisbury (1984), 67.

22. Katherine Q. Seelye, "Conservatives Hobble Lobbying Bill" (*New York Times*, October 7, 1994), A-13.

23. Gary Lee, "Robert Gray, 'Master of the Universe'" (*The Washington Post National Weekly Edition*, September 28–October 4, 1992a), 36.

24. Truman and Milbrath were among the first to make this argument. The list of works that have sought to formalize this argument is quite long, but it would certainly include my own: Scott H. Ainsworth, "Regulating Lobbyists and Interest Group Influence," *Journal of Politics* 55 (1993): 41–56; David Austen-Smith and John R. Wright's "Competitive Lobbying for a Legislator's Vote," *Social Choice and Welfare* 9 (1992): 229–57; Jan Potters's *Lobbying and Pressure*

(Amsterdam: Tinbergen Institute, 1992); Randolph Sloof's *Game-theoretic Models of the Political Influence of Interest Groups* (Boston: Kluwer, 1998); and Eric Rasmusen, "Lobbying When the Decision Maker Can Acquire Independent Information," *Public Choice* 77 (1993): 899–913.

25. Eastman (1977), 18.

26. Anthony Nownes investigated the "advice advantages" of lobbyists at the state level. What type of lobbyist is most frequently contacted for advice? Full-time lobbyists with many years of experience are more likely to be contacted than their younger part-time associates. In addition, lobbyists connected to government agencies and female lobbyists are more apt to be solicited for advice. Though it is not clear why, in the world of state-level lobbyists women are contacted more often than men. Nownes, "Solicited Advice and Lobbyist Power: Evidence from Three American States," *Legislative Studies Quarterly* 24 (1999): 113–23.

27. Browne (1995), 112. Also see William P. Browne and Won K. Paik, "Beyond the Domain: Recasting Network Politics in the Postreform Congress," *American Journal of Political Science* 37 (1993): 1054–78.

28. David E. Rosenbaum, "Little Known Crusader Plays a Big Role in Tax Debate" (*New York Times,* May 21, 2001), A-12.

29. See, for example, Ross K. Baker's *House and Senate* (New York: W. W. Norton, 1989), 155; Hedrick Smith's *The Power Game* (New York: Random House, 1988), 236–40; and Wright (1996).

30. There is a second separating equilibrium in which the t_1 lobbyist sends a grand claim and the t_2 lobbyist sends a typical claim. Numerous equilibrium refinements eliminate such backward equilibria. Such refinements are beyond the scope of present work. For more information, see Jeffrey S. Banks and Joel Sobel, "Equilibrium Selection in Signaling Games," *Econometrica* 55 (1987): 647–62.

31. For more information about ethical standards in Congress, see Dennis F. Thompson's *Ethics in Congress* (Washington, D.C.: Brookings Institution, 1995).

32. Quoted from page 65 of George B. Galloway's "The Operation of the Legislative Reorganization Act of 1946," *American Political Science Review* 45 (1951): 41–68.

33. *United States v. Harriss,* 347 U.S. 612 (1954). See *United States v. Rumely,* 345 U.S. 41 (1953) for an important precedent.

34. Adam Clymer, "GOP Filibuster Deals a Setback to Lobbying Bill" (*New York Times,* October 7, 1994), A-1, A-13.

35. Fortunately, there are scholars looking at each scanned sheet to create meaningful databases. See Scott Furlong's, "The Lobbying Disclosure Act and Interest Group Lobbying Data," *VOXPOP: Newsletter of the Political Organizations and Parties Section of the American Political Science Association* 17 (1998): 4–6, and Frank R. Baumgartner and Beth L. Leech's "Studying Interest Groups Using Lobbying Disclosure Reports," *VOXPOP: Newsletter of the Political Organizations and Parties Section of the American Political Science Association* 18 (1999): 1–3.

36. George B. Galloway, *Congress at the Crossroads* (New York: Thomas Y. Crowell, 1946), 308.

37. *National Association for the Advancement of Colored People v. Alabama,* 357 U.S. 449 (1958).

38. Stanley M. Brand, Stephen M. Ryan, and Margit H. Nahra, "Disclosing Lobbying Activities," *Administrative Law Review* Fall (1993): 343–65, 347.

39. Truman (1971) 264.

40. Truman (1971), 266–70.

41. Donald R. Mathews's *U.S. Senators and Their World* (Chapel Hill: University of North Carolina Press, 1960) is perhaps clearest on this issue, but Mathews is by no means the only scholar to note the importance of access.

42. For work on the prevalence of interest group coalitions, see Kevin W. Hula's *Lobbying Together: Interest Group Coalitions in Legislative Politics* (Washington, D.C.: Georgetown University Press, 1999). Also see Marie Hojnacki's "Interest Groups' Decisions to Join Alliances or Work Alone," *American Journal of Political Science* 41 (1997): 61–87.

43. Wright (1996), 112, and Austen-Smith and Wright (1992).

44. Mathews (1960), 184.

45. Norman J. Ornstein and Shirley Elder, *Interest Groups, Lobbying, and Policymaking* (Washington, D.C.: CQ Press, 1978), 77.

46. Ornstein and Elder (1978), 77.

47. Ornstein and Elder (1978), 77.

48. The classic reference on this issue is Robert Axelrod's *The Evolution of Cooperation* (New York: Basic Books, 1984).

49. Rosenthal (1993), 121.

50. Elsewhere I show that if $a > k > b$, then a unique separating equilibrium exists. Ainsworth (1993).

51. Mathews (1960), 181.

52. See, for example, Lewis Anthony Dexter's *How Organizations Are Represented in Washington* (Indianapolis: Bobbs-Merrill, 1969), 59.

53. Browne (1995); John R. Wright, "PAC Contributions, Lobbying, and Representation," *Journal of Politics* 51 (1989): 713–29; Wright (1996), 157–64.

54. Browne (1995), 110; Baker (1989), 160.

55. Wright (1996), 90.

56. See, for example, Ken Kollman's *Outside Lobbying: Public Opinion and Interest Group Strategies* (Princeton, NJ: Princeton University Press, 1998).

57. Although they explored different legislative arenas, both Browne (1995) and John Anthony Maltese, *The Selling of Supreme Court Decisions* (Baltimore: Johns Hopkins University Press, 1998) recorded such increases.

58. Lori Nitschke, "Agriculture Has Muscle in Free-Trade Fight," *CQ Weekly* 58 (March 2000): 444–48.

59. Rosenthal (1993), 121, emphasis added.

60. Clifford J. Levy, "Quietly, Tobacco Giant Philip Morris Lobbies against Local Efforts to Curb Smoking" (*New York Times*, December 7, 1999), A-23.

61. Ainsworth (1993).

62. Susanne Roschwalb, "The Hill & Knowlton Cases," *Public Relations Review* 20 (1994): 267–75.

63. See, for instance, John R. MacArthur's "Remember Nayirah, Witness for Kuwait?" (*New York Times*, January 6, 1992), A-11, and Cornelius Pratt's "Hill and Knowlton's Two Ethical Dilemmas," *Public Relations Review* 20 (1994): 277–93.

64. DeGregorio (1997), xx.

65. It is generally safe to say that fifty percent of all lobbyists have either elected or nonelected government experience. (See Robert H. Salisbury's "Washington Lobbyists: A Collective Portrait," *Interest Group Politics*, 2nd ed. (Washington, D.C.: Congressional Quarterly, 1986). Nonelected government officials have some of the same advantages as elected ones. They know the institutional and personal context of Washington policy making.

66. Karen Foerstel, "Grass Greener after Congress" (*CQ Weekly*, March 11, 2000), 515, 519.

67. Burt Solomon "Groups That Don't Cut the Mustard" *National Journal* (July 4, 1987), 1710, emphasis added.

68. Gary Lee, "Ex-Lawmaker w/Hill Contacts Seeks Jobs w/Big Bucks, Prestige: Washington Headhunters' Advice: Get Real" (*The Washington Post Weekly Edition*, October 5–11, 1992b), 32.

69. Lee notes that the law firm that hired former Senators Paul Laxalt (R-Nev.) and Russell Long (D-La.) went out of business. It was simply unable to attract enough clients.

70. Bauer, Pool, and Dexter (1963).

~7~

Organized Interests and the Executive and Judicial Branches

Introduction

When the media report on lobbying activities, they focus almost exclusively on the U.S. Congress. Congressional lobbying is very important both for organized interests and for legislators themselves, but organized interests are very active throughout the realm of Washington politics. After all, organized interests are affected by each branch of government, so it is not surprising that they lobby the executive and judicial branches as best they can. Lobbying before these branches is no less important to organized interests than is congressional lobbying. Indeed, there are some types of organized interests that are most affected by regulatory decisions of the executive branch or by judicial decisions. For those interests, congressional lobbying plays second fiddle. What sort of actions do executive agencies take that warrant lobbying by outside interests? To understand the interactions between organized interests and executive agencies, one must appreciate the role of agencies in the implementation of congressional statutes. How do access and information operate at the agency level? Certainly, courts are more impervious to outside influence than are the other branches of government. How then can organized interests affect the courts?

Historical and institutional context was important for congressional lobbying, and it remains important for the analysis of lobbying before the executive and judicial branches of government. The key features of the institutional context for this chapter are the relations between the branches of government. To appreciate the role of organized interests and lobbying in the executive and judicial branches, one must have a thorough understanding of the relations between the Congress and executive agencies and between Congress, the courts, and executive agencies.

Executive Branch Lobbying

The following analogy may help explain some of the key aspects of the institutional context for executive branch lobbying.

Dent's dilemma

In the mid-1960s Douglas Adams wrote a science-fiction adventure novel that soon became a pop classic. In the first few pages of *The Hitchhiker's Guide to the Galaxy,* the hapless Arthur Dent lies in front of a bulldozer poised to destroy his house to make room for a highway. A government representative and Dent have the following exchange:

> "But Mr. Dent, the plans have been available in the local planning office for the last nine months."
>
> "Oh yes, well . . . you hadn't exactly gone out of your way to call attention to them, had you?"
>
> "But the plans were on display . . .
>
> "On display? I eventually had to go to the cellar to find them."
>
> "That's the display department."
>
> "With a flashlight."
>
> . . .
>
> "But look, you found the notice, didn't you?"
>
> " . . . yes I did. It was on display in the bottom of a locked filing cabinet in a disused lavatory. . . . "[1]

The science fiction angle in Adams's book comes a few pages later when Dent learns that the earth is about to be destroyed by aliens making room for some sort of "hyperspatial express route." Once again, Dent learns that the plans were available and on display for about fifty earth years in the "local planning department in Alpha Centauri." Those destroying the earth express surprise and annoyance at the lack of interest among earthlings in "local affairs."[2]

The Washington equivalent of these displays is a posting in the Federal Register. Of course, few people wake up each day to peruse the latest listings in the Register, but some do. Lobbyists read the Register, looking for announcements related to upcoming hearings or recently adopted regulations. Lobbyists recognize that their clients will want to know how and when to participate in bureaucratic decision making and how the latest bureaucratic decisions will affect them. Perhaps what Dent needed was a good lobbyist.

Participation and accountable bureaucracies

Increasingly, Congress has addressed complicated issues involving the most technical aspects of everything from airplane safety to air quality to drug approval. Instead of attempting to pass legislation with specific guidelines in these areas, Congress often creates specialized agencies, such as the Federal Aviation Administration (FAA), the Environmental Protection Agency (EPA), or the Food and Drug Administration (FDA), to address these issues. Technically, these agencies are part of the executive branch and are designed to implement laws already passed by Congress, but Congress often gives the bureaucracies a great deal of latitude. In sum, Congress delegates rulemaking power to agencies.

Delegation is tricky because the first section of the first article of the Constitution states that "all legislative powers" belong to Congress. The line between congressional legislating and bureaucratic rulemaking can be quite fine, but the Supreme Court has upheld delegation as long as Congress provides an "intelligible principle" in its enabling legislation. That is, the agency must be given some reasonable guidance. Furthermore, the bureaucratic rulemaking must be viewed as discretion in the implementation of legislation rather than the overt creation of new, independent law.[3] Congress may, for instance, pass clean air legislation, but it seldom stipulates how many parts per million of ozone, carbon monoxide, or various kinds of particulate matter are allowed. Those decisions are left to the EPA when it implements the clean air legislation. The EPA is not passing legislation, but in the process of implementing clean air legislation the EPA will inevitably make specific rules and guidelines about allowable levels of various pollutants. These rules will have the force of law, and they can have a profound effect on businesses and other interested parties.

Critics argue that this distinction between legislating and rulemaking is a sleight of hand, and they worry that Congress sacrifices accountability by giving bureaucrats too much power. The fear that bureaucracies make arbitrary rules without regard to their impact on people is commonplace. In short, some individuals fear that because bureaucrats are not elected by the people, bureaucracies are not accountable to the people. Participation of outside interests in bureaucratic rulemaking has been used as a means to monitor bureaucracies' activities and maintain accountability.

How do people, groups, or organizations participate in bureaucracies? Agencies establish working groups, advisory boards, and hold numerous quasi-legislative proceedings where these details, commonly called rules, are worked out. At this stage of the rulemaking process, agency officials often consult with affected groups to gain their expertise and gauge their reaction to proposals. In an excellent book on rulemaking, Cornelius Kerwin stated that "rulemaking is, in one sense, a process for changing information into law."[4] Where do bureaucrats secure information? Supreme Court Justice Stephen Breyer, who has written on this subject, says that there are four crucial sources for information.[5] (1) The regulated industries themselves have the best technical information about products and processes. (2) Bureaucratic agencies have considerable in-house expertise. (3) Outside experts from government, academia, or industry might be called upon for advice. (4) Public interest groups provide useful information about reactions to rules and procedures.

Kerwin documented instances of public participation in bureaucratic rulemaking dating back to 1902 when the Secretary of Agriculture was asked by Congress to consult with the Association of Official Agricultural Chemists to establish food purity guidelines.[6] The outside interest in that case lent expertise and enhanced the sense of the legitimacy of Department of Agriculture rulemaking. Public participation in agency rulemaking simply involves lobbying bureaucrats. This sort of participation in agency affairs was quite common though entirely informal until the 1946 Administrative Procedure Act (APA). Among other things, the APA mandated that agencies make an effort to inform the public of the nature and timing of their rulemaking. More specifically, agencies must post announcements of impending proceedings in the Federal Register. The APA formalized the procedures by which outside interests could offer information and communicate concerns, thereby opening up the bureaucratic decision-making apparatuses. The Negotiated Rulemaking Act of 1990 further institutionalized the process by which outside interests could participate in the rulemaking process. Those people advocating public participation adopted a prescriptive view of pluralism. Greater involvement from more interests was always preferred to fewer interests and less involvement.

During the 1960s and 1970s, Congress expanded the local-level opportunities to affect bureaucratic rulemaking and rule implementation to an unprecedented extent. Hundreds of programs required some type of public participation, and often the legislative guidelines asked for "maximum feasible participation." The thinking was fairly straightforward. Participation could enhance all aspects of a program. It would be better formulated because of the expertise of individuals and groups who entered into the rulemaking process. Legitimacy would be enhanced. Finally, the program would be better implemented, because the local individuals and groups could act as go-betweens, allowing federal agencies to find and serve their clientele more readily. In the third chapter, I referred to the summer jobs programs for at-risk teenagers. How does a federal bureaucrat find at-risk teenagers who might be helped by federal programs? Why not seek input from local groups and organizations that already work with at-risk teenagers?

Even with greater and greater access to bureaucratic rulemaking, some organized interests may still not have the means or expertise to participate in rulemaking processes. Biases may persist. Public interest groups face an ongoing collective-action problem. Even if they do overcome the collective-action problem, they often must subsist on a shoestring budget. Of course, technical and legal information do not come cheap, so some interests' abilities to participate in rulemaking are severely constrained by the collective-action problem. John de Figueiredo and Emerson Tiller argued that business interests also face a collective-action problem, but corporate interests are communicated regardless of whether the collective-action problem is solved.[7] Business firms must decide whether to work with trade associations or to use their own in-house lobbying personnel. Using in-house personnel is costly because the entire lobbying effort must be shouldered, but it ensures maximum control of the lobbying effort. Working with the trade association often reduces costs, but it also has drawbacks. First, firms lose control of the overall lobbying effort when they delegate responsibility to a trade association. Second, the strength of the trade association's lobbying campaign is affected by the collective-action problem. What de Figueiredo and Tiller found in their study of the Federal Communications Commission is that large businesses with proprietary information often used their own in-house lobbyists and that smaller firms often relied on trade associations. Note, however, that the strategic choice for the business firm is very different than the strategic choice for a public interest group. For the business interest, the choice is in-house or collective action through a trade association. For the public interest group the choice is collective action or bust. Even after opening up agencies and mandating participation from outside interests, biases may still persist because of the collective-action problem.

Partly because of these sorts of biases in participation, in 1974, the Federal Trade Commission began to provide intervenor financing to groups and individuals who were not, for whatever reason, able to provide for their own legal counsel. Groups receiving intervenor financing were typically broad-based citizens' groups—the same sorts of groups that are most likely to suffer from collective-action problems. During Jimmy Carter's presidency, all federal agencies were asked to simplify their procedures and language to facilitate greater participation from the traditionally underrepresented groups. In addition, intervenor financing was expanded across numerous agencies. Intervenor financing continued until 1981, when a federal court ruled that such procedures required specific and explicit support from Congress.[8] Up until that time, decisions about intervenor financing had been made predominantly at the agency level, with Congress playing no more than a limited role.[9] Though funding groups to engage in political advocacy through intervenor financing was always contentious, prior to 1981 no one had seriously challenged the practice.[10]

The groups that were mobilized to affect bureaucratic decision making during the Carter presidency were generally supportive of "big" government. President Ronald Reagan and officials in his administration looked askance at such groups and the governmental funding and promotion of their activities. The Carter administration had mobilized groups that were generally supportive of Democratic Party policies, and the new Republican administration sought to demobilize those groups that more often than not opposed the more conservative Reagan policies. The Reagan administration sought and found ways to limit intervenor financing and the ability of interest groups to affect agency rulemaking. In addition to simply asking agencies to end the practice, the Reagan administration reduced the funding for the Legal Services Corporation, which often supported public interest group activities. In addition, the Reagan administration mandated that all agency rulemaking be reviewed by the White House Office of Management and Budget (OMB). That is, even if a group had secured favorable results during the rulemaking process at the agency level, the OMB could reverse those decisions. A new important venue was established. Of course, groups could lobby the OMB, but the Reagan administration kept fairly tight reins on the OMB. Reagan detractors argued that the OMB allowed for backdoor influence of those people wanting to undermine stricter regulatory controls. Numerous scholars argued that intervenor financing rested on questionable constitutional grounds, but another lesson is told by the Carter and Reagan administrations. Elected officials often seek to mobilize their supporters and demobilize their detractors.[11]

After a rule has been established, organized interests may once again lobby federal agencies. For instance, if a group feels that a regulation has been violated, they may bring a claim before the relevant federal agency. The claim may be dismissed or heard by an administrative judge in the agency. These quasi-judicial proceedings provide one more opportunity for organized interests to affect policy at the agency level. Organized interests seeking access to an agency's quasi-judicial proceedings face many of the same difficulties as when they try to affect the rulemaking process. Expertise does not come cheap, so groups have sometimes used intervenor financing at this stage as well. If the administrative judges' rulings are unfavorable, there are often internal appeals that can be made. Once the appeals within the agency are exhausted, additional appeals are handled by the federal courts.

Some legislation has encouraged this sort of legal activity to encourage more effective monitoring of policies. For instance, the Clean Water Act of 1972 allowed for citizen suits, permitting private individuals or organized interests to sue water polluters. Monetary awards from successful claims would go to the U.S. Treasury rather than the individual or group, so the incentives to sue would not be strictly monetary. The reasonableness of these citizen suits was one of the issues at the heart of the *Friends of the Earth v. Laidlaw Environmental Services* case recently decided by the Supreme Court.[12] The Friends of the Earth lawsuit was initially permissible because of the way in which the Clean Water Act was written. However, Laidlaw contended that the legal action by Friends of the Earth was rendered moot, or no longer relevant, because new pollution devices were installed at the company to ensure compliance with the clean water legislation. Friends of the Earth argued that their actions were the catalyst that led to compliance and that current compliance did not limit legal redress.

Citizen suits affect both the regulators and the regulatees, though the first effect receives the most attention. Citizen suits open an additional avenue for influencing agencies and courts. Such suits shift some of the enforcement costs from the government agency to the individual or group bringing the citizen suit. Although monitoring costs for the executive branch agency may decline, citizen suits also shift power and responsibility from the executive branch to the courts, causing some people to question their constitutionality. In oral arguments for *Friends of the Earth v. Laidlaw*, Supreme Court Justice Scalia argued that citizen suits "usurped the ordinary function of the executive branch and brought about 'a major alteration of power between the various branches of government.'"[13] The effect on the regulatee is equally important. For the business or firm being regulated by the Clean Water Act, citizen suits increase the probability of being monitored. If clean water guidelines are not being followed, the increased probability of being monitored must also increase the chances of being caught. In sum, individuals and groups act as watchdogs, observing both potential polluters and federal enforcement of pollution regulations.[14] Citizen suits simply encourage the practice and require the federal courts to adjudicate. Ultimately, Scalia's arguments against citizen suits failed to sway a majority on the court. In its seven to two decision, the Supreme Court allowed citizen suits to remain in effect.

The Laidlaw case was complicated, but part of the case revolved around the issue of standing. Standing is simply the legal term for distinguishing those individuals who have an inherent interest in a case from those who do not. If one can show harm or imminent harm, then he or she can generally secure standing. The laws affecting standing are complex and always changing, because even simple terms such as *direct harm* are open to varying interpretations. Need the harm be physical or financial? Could it be psychic harm? Could it be aesthetic harm? How immediate need the harm be? Is the slow but steady development of harm sufficient?[15] If, for whatever reason, an agency refuses to allow the participation of some groups, those groups can sue in federal court. Once in federal court, every aspect of the agency's decision making is open to judicial review. Not only can the court assess whether the agency followed proper rulemaking procedures, the court can question the judgment of agency officials. Kerwin nicely summarized this as the "judicialization" of bureaucratic rulemaking.[16] "The scope of judicial oversight is broad. It encompasses every significant aspect of rulemaking. Courts are free to determine whether an agency has the authority to write a rule . . . whether it has observed proper procedure when doing so, and if the result is sound law and [sound] public policy."[17] In 1946, the APA began to open up the rulemaking processes in federal bureaucracies and provided for legal remedy if individuals or groups were prevented from stating their cases before the agency. Such procedures for judicial review were initiated to provide an important check on the powers of bureaucracies, but they have also created another opportunity for organized interests to affect public policy and they have increased the influence of the federal courts themselves.

Private interests and public policies: Dissenting views

Kerwin writes that "the legitimacy of the rulemaking process is clearly linked to public participation."[18] In a classic book on the organization of the federal government, Harold Seidman observed that long before laws formerly opened the executive branch to direct participation of organized interests, "President Truman thought it entirely proper that the Department of Commerce should be 'a channel to the White House for business and industry'" interests.[19] Federal agencies secure important information from such channels to organized interests. The participation of organized interests often enhances the legitimacy of the rulemaking process, and Congress is wont to reduce funding for those agencies with an expansive and active set of advocates in the interest group community. Organized interests are in a good position to lobby key congressional committees in lieu of the legal limitations on congressional lobbying by federal bureaucrats. The simple fact is that support from organized interests makes the interactions with Congress much easier for the bureaucracy.

There are, however, potential downsides. Regularized interactions between agencies, congressional committees, and organized interests may lead to agency capture or iron triangles. These terms have been used to describe situations when a relatively small set of individuals have dominated the decision making in a policy area. Members of Congress themselves often approve of the tight relations between agencies and organized interests.[20] Such tight relations may ease information-gathering problems, improve the chances that bureaucratic solutions remain workable, increase legitimacy, and decrease monitoring costs, but hazards certainly exist when such tight relations become too insular. Three problems are most commonly cited. First, public policy may become hopelessly fragmented as each minor agency supports its own clientele interests. Broader concerns about overarching policy goals become lost. Policy fragmentation further tightens these group-agency relations, leading to even more fragmentation. Writing about the Department of Agriculture during the early 1900s, Earl Latham noted that various interest groups competed for resources and attention within the same agency. Different bureaus within the Department of Agriculture highlighted different problems and advocated for different sets of interests. For instance, the Farm Security and Farm Credit Administrations did not always see eye to eye on agriculture issues. The Farm Security Administration sought ways to ease lending policies to small farmers, whereas the Farm Credit Administration sought to maintain fiscal responsibility first and foremost.[21]

A second point of concern revolves around congressional control. Does Congress maintain control of the bureaucracies? One might argue that Congress must lose some control over bureaucracies because it delegates authority to them. In theory, this delegation of authority is limited. Congress establishes some clear guidelines and then allows the bureaucracy discretion in its means of implementation.[22] Many scholars have argued that Congress has increasingly chosen to delegate to agencies because public policy issues are increasingly technical and complex.[23] Congressional authority can suffer because Congress does not have the expertise to monitor the increasingly technical affairs of the bureaucracies. By delegating authority, Congress simply trades expertise for control.[24] Accepting that Congress does forsake some control for expertise simply suggests that the pertinent question is whether Congress could regain control of the bureaucracy or redirect an agency's behavior. Delegation does not mean that Congress never revisits an issue. If legislators get the impression from individuals or organized interests that an agency is not implementing statutes in a reasonable fashion, Congress can respond in various ways. First, the House or Senate may use a legislative veto. That is, they may, by simple majority vote, direct the agency to change its policies.[25] Second, the chambers may pass new statutes to fine tune the original legislation. Third, Congress controls the purse strings, and no agency wants to risk reduced budgets year after year. Finally, Congress maintains numerous offices and agencies, such as the General Accounting Office, the Congressional Research Service, and the Congressional Budget Office, that can be used for information gathering. The point is that Congress has the means to revisit an issue that was delegated to a bureaucracy. The real question is whether they have the incentives to revisit the issue. For understanding these incentives, two points are most relevant. First, scholars have used signaling games similar to the one developed in the previous chapter to show that, as long as occasional auditing or verification is possible, a situation in which legislators rely on others for crucial information is often superior to a situation in which legislators can only rely on their own direct investigation of issues.[26] Second, organized interests are often well suited for affecting the incentives of legislators to regain control of bureaucracies.[27]

The third concern most frequently cited relates to the promotion of interests by government officials. Certainly, government agencies need to communicate with organized interests, but some organized interests have unique opportunities to communicate with policy makers. By providing channels for the easy communication of some interests, the overall balance of interests may be unfairly tipped in one direction or another. In addition to the larger, better known Washington bureaucracies, there are dozens of commissions, advisory boards, and special task forces. One such board illustrates how government bodies can channel the communication of private interests in public venues. In 1985, Congress established the National Pork Board to promote pork sales. The board coordinated advertising campaigns, funded research related to pork consumption, and distributed educational materials. Once established, Congress mandated that the board be supported by the farmers themselves. To avoid the pitfalls of the collective-action problem, a mandatory checkoff was used. Those farmers raising hogs had to contribute if they wanted to remain eligible for any sort of federal benefits. The National Pork Board was a fairly small operation, but it was not without friends in Washington. It shared offices and staff with the National Pork Producers Council, a private lobbying group. Critics contend that such arrangements amount to government-funded trade associations. There are at least half a dozen other boards established by Congress to promote other agriculture commodities. Nonagricultural products have also received the same royal treatment. Tight relations between organized interests and federal bureaucracies can create relations that are simply too cozy and too insular.

"Involvement of the public in rulemaking may be the most complex and important form of political action in the contemporary American political system," so it is not surprising to find some differences of opinion about the worthiness and impact of participation by organized interests.[28] There are numerous advantages to allowing, indeed encouraging, organized interests to participate in agency decision making, but it should not be surprising that private interests communicated in public venues can also lead to various problems.

The White House

The White House lobbies Congress for the same reasons that other organizations lobby: it needs congressional support to achieve its goals. The White House needs to lobby senators to ensure confirmation of justices and high-ranking executive branch nominees. The White House needs both branches to support its policy agenda. A president's success is often measured by his ability to move policy proposals through Congress. The chief congressional lobbyist for the White House heads the Office of Legislative Affairs, which has been a formal office in the White House since the Eisenhower administration.[29] Ironically, Eisenhower had little interest in interacting with members or senators and he used the office to insulate himself from congressional affairs.[30] More recently, the Office of Legislative Affairs is used to establish a two-way communication that involves listening as much as lobbying. Unless the president's party enjoys a large, unified majority in Congress, the White House needs to know the feelings of both supporters and detractors on the Hill; congressional liaison needs to hear from everyone.[31] White House lobbyists who show little regard for Congress, the concerns of the minority party, or the views of party mavericks are generally not well received. During eras of divided party control of the executive and legislative branches and narrow congressional majorities, lobbyists need to be willing to work with a broad range of legislators. In short, White House lobbyists need to know and respect the personal and institutional contexts in Congress. Perhaps the most important aspect of a legislator's institutional context is his or her next election. If the White House lobbyists ignore the electoral situations faced by legislators, trouble usually ensues. "We're giving him an earful of what we're hearing from our constituents; they want more spending cuts" said Representative David Mann (D-Ohio) in the spring of 1993.[32] House Democrats traveling in their districts sensed problems, problems that they feared the chief White House lobbyist was ignoring and failing to communicate back to the president. In the next election in the fall of 1994, the Republicans gained a majority in the House for the first time in decades.

Success on Capitol Hill sometimes requires success with the constituents. Presidential popularity is a great asset when bargaining with hesitant legislators. Of course, maintaining or increasing one's popularity is often times a tricky endeavor. The point to keep in mind is that a president's public popularity can either enhance or diminish his popularity in Congress. A popular president always has a stronger bargaining position than an unpopular president. To maintain his popularity and strengthen his bargaining position in Congress, a president must regularly reach out to the public. As Samuel Kernell has written, the president must "go public."[33] Going public simply involves taking a presidential message directly to the public. Writing about fifty years ago, David B. Truman stated that "the most notable change in the power of the president since the beginning of the twentieth century has been the enhancement of his ability to command a large public for his actions and utterances."[34] What Kernell notes is that presidents are increasingly going public.

Many of the twentieth century presidents required White House personnel to maintain informal liaisons with organized interests. Franklin Roosevelt is often considered the first president who had explicitly assigned liaison duties to White House staff.[35] Traditionally, the composition of a president's cabinet was devised to facilitate outreach.[36] Some cabinet nominees are informally vetted with particularly important organized interests. For instance, both Democratic and Republican presidents want their Labor Secretary to be able to communicate effectively with labor groups.[37] President Lyndon B. Johnson extended this outreach practice by developing a "'resident' concept whereby each White House assistant, in addition to his major responsibilities, served as liaison with some outside group."[38] Presidents Nixon and Carter extended the practice. Indeed, groups came to expect a certain amount of representation in the White House. Groups streamed to the small town of Plains, Georgia, to meet with President-elect Jimmy Carter, each demanding appointees somewhere in the new administration.[39] In addition to the cabinet positions, these groups were eyeing federal judgeships and the (literally) thousands of positions on executive department advisory commissions. When the outreach fails, for whatever reason, groups often make their dissatisfaction widely known. Veterans groups were skeptical of the elder President

Bush's Veterans Affairs Secretary. The Veterans for Foreign Wars (VFW) asked for a new secretary after the sitting secretary proved to be less than 110 percent supportive of VFW goals. Bush had received the VFW endorsement in his successful 1988 presidential bid, but a repeat endorsement in 1992 was not assured—especially because the group was not pleased with the sitting Veterans Affairs Secretary.[40]

Even informal ties between the White House and groups can be very effective if they can coordinate their efforts to convince Congress to pass particular legislation. President Johnson credited such coordinated efforts in the passage of landmark civil rights legislation. Johnson named appropriate lobbying targets in the Senate for civil rights groups to various civil rights leaders. Without such a coordinated effort, Johnson suggested that the 1964 Civil Rights Act would probably not have passed.[41] Such informal ties became increasingly institutionalized under Nixon, and in 1974 President Gerald Ford established the Office of Public Liaison (OPL) to formalize the outreach programs and cultivate group support. President Jimmy Carter initially sought to dismantle the office. Speaking before a group of Hispanic press reporters, Carter said,

> I don't intend to set up an administrative office in the White House for any particular group. . . . I wouldn't bring anyone on board to take care of a particular constituency group. . . . I don't like to segment my staff to be responsible for old people or farmers or labor or business or women or blacks or Spanish-speaking people.[42]

Carter recognized that group liaisons sometimes encouraged narrow assessments of broad policy goals, but before his term was over, Carter reversed himself and appointed numerous liaison personnel to maintain outreach to business groups; women's groups; and black, Hispanic, and white ethnic groups. Liaison was necessary for securing group support of presidential goals. Liaison personnel regularly mailed thousands of newsletters to important constituents and group leaders to help advertise the White House positions on issues.[43] Anne Wexler, Carter's director of OPL, described her job as "lobby[ing] the lobbyists."[44] Wexler reportedly was able to get hundreds of group and community leaders to lobby on behalf of Carter's energy proposals in Congress. Elizabeth Dole served in Ronald Reagan's White House in the same OPL position as Wexler. Dole managed to convince hundreds of groups, associations, and businesses to lobby in Congress on Reagan's behalf.[45] Carter's change of heart on the Office of Public Liaison was a nod to the changing nature of Washington politics. To be effective in Congress, the White House needs broad-based popularity and group support.

In addition to maintaining group liaisons, presidents now carefully cultivate their media image. FDR's fireside chats appear positively quaint in comparison to the apparatuses that presidents have established to communicate their message to the public. The Nixon White House fine-tuned relations with radio and TV outlets. The White House Office of Communications was established by Nixon, who long regarded the regular Washington press corps with disdain. The goal of the new office was to bypass the cynical, wizened Washington press corps and reach out to the more open, vibrant, and perhaps more manipulable, local press outlets. For radio outreach, Nixon's director of communications insisted on Spotmasters for several departments. These Spotmasters allowed radio stations to call the White House to secure excerpts from speeches made by high-ranking officials. In this way, radio stations could readily secure breaking news directly from the White House.[46] Of course, this news was completely controlled by the White House, insuring that it had just the right spin. The Department of Agriculture had established similar technical services in the 1950s to help to disseminate information.[47] The Nixon White House sought to extend and manage the practice to put the president in the most favorable light. Special briefings for local press, including radio, print, and TV, have been regular features of presidents' outreach efforts since the Nixon administration. By the Reagan presidency, Office of Communications directors were also contacting the big three news networks, seeking favorable coverage and opportunities to rebut unfavorable coverage.[48]

For the modern executive, there are various institutionalized offices to facilitate going public and controlling the public image of the president. Presidents are political beasts, so it is natural for them to communicate with and seek support from organized interests. Such regularized and ongoing outreach efforts insure that the White House will continue to interact with leaders of groups and organized interests. Groups are clearly important, but at the White House level the interactions are more one way. Messages more often go out than come in. No interest group is granted access unless it fits into a president's larger public appeals campaign. Even if they are not directly campaigning for votes, modern presidents' ongoing outreach efforts surely blur the distinctions between campaigning and governing.

Organized Interests and the Courts

A traditional view of the courts and the law holds that the legal process is unaffected by the hurly-burly of politics. The courts, some argue, are above politics. Is it reasonable to imagine court proceedings to be unaffected by politics? Lifetime appointments for judges and limits on the openness of court proceedings were meant to insulate the judicial branch from the hurly-burly of politics. However, many social scientists now realize that the courts and the legal process are indeed part of the political process. Indeed, the previous sections detailed how the federal courts are able to affect bureaucratic politics. Special interests may not lobby the courts in the same fashion that they lobby the other branches of government, but they do not ignore the courts in their efforts to influence policy.

Litigants

Groups can act as named litigants seeking redress of grievances before courts. For many years, scholars argued that groups that were locked out of the other branches were forced to use the courts as a strategy of last resort. Court scholars who promoted what became known as the political disadvantage theory most often referred to the experiences of the NAACP, a group that for much of the 1900s was locked out of the legislative and executive branches of government. A brief history of civil rights issues for black Americans can highlight key issues related to groups' interactions with the courts and the disadvantage theory. Legally speaking, the Fourteenth Amendment to the U.S. Constitution, adopted in 1868, protected black Americans from blatantly discriminatory black codes that were common in many southern states. The Fourteenth Amendment extended equal protection under the laws and due process to all U.S. citizens. Black codes were designed to limit the freedoms of black citizens, so they were clearly in violation of the equal protection language of the Fourteenth Amendment. However, immediately following the Civil War, blacks' civil rights were most directly protected by Reconstruction-era policies enforced by federal troops remaining in the southern states. Reconstruction, however, faded away after the election of Rutherford B. Hayes in 1876.[49] Indeed, some scholars contend that Hayes secured the presidency only after promising to end Reconstruction. Hayes had lost the popular vote to the Democratic Party nominee Samuel J. Tilden, but in the end Hayes secured a majority of electoral college votes. Before securing the electoral college majority, Hayes had to await the decision of a bipartisan commission evaluating questionable election returns in Florida, Louisiana, and South Carolina. Those states still had militarily reinforced Republican-backed Reconstruction governments. Not surprisingly, their reports favored the election of Hayes. However, the commission's report was still being held up by southern Democrats filibustering in the House. The private negotiations that ended the filibuster and allowed for the electoral vote to proceed may very well have included discussions of Reconstruction. With the end of Reconstruction and the removal of federal troops during the Hayes administration, Jim Crow laws were instituted in many southern regions to limit blacks' access to the polls and to segregate them from white society.[50] Jim Crow laws had a dramatic effect on black voters, reducing their numbers in southern states by the thousands and tens of thousands. Jim Crow laws were as discriminatory and as unconstitutional as the black codes that preceded them.

The Supreme Court did not redress the blatantly unconstitutional actions of southern states. Indeed, the Supreme Court supported Jim Crow. In its 1896 *Plessy v. Ferguson* decision, the Supreme Court instituted its separate but equal doctrine, paving the way for increased discrimination against blacks. Certainly, blacks were disadvantaged in that they were virtually locked out of the legislative and executive branches, but the courts offered little reason to be hopeful. In the late 1800s and early 1900s, most of the cases related to Fourteenth Amendment issues were decided in such a fashion as to provide "only a weak safeguard against discrimination."[51] Indeed, those cases directly addressing black civil rights issues were most often decided in favor of limitations on civil rights and civil rights protections.[52] The disadvantage theory offers the courts as a source for salvation, the branch of government that wisely disentangles issues that confound other political actors. Such a view of courts is simply not warranted. Judges reflect the mores of their day and are no wiser in their judgments than other political actors. Indeed, it is increasingly argued that judges pursue policy goals in much the same fashion as other political actors.[53] The point to keep in mind is that the courts may be no more receptive to the claims of organized interests than any other branch of government.

What aspect of the NAACP's history does provide support for disadvantage theory? In the early to mid-1900s, there was a string of court decisions more supportive of the group's goals. The NAACP closely followed *Guinn v. United States,* 238 U.S. 347 (1915), which ruled against the use of grandfather clauses to determine voting rights.[54] Grandfather clauses effectively limited the franchise to those citizens whose grandfathers had voted. Given the time period, such laws limited black voters much more than white voters. The NAACP successfully challenged city-sponsored segregation ordinances in *Buchanan v. Warley,* 245 U.S. 60 (1917). Discriminatory housing policy was again addressed in *Shelley v. Kraemer,* 324 U.S. 1 (1948), which limited state courts' abilities to enforce restrictive covenants. It too was brought by the NAACP. In 1923, the NAACP sponsored *Moore v. Dempsey,* 261 U.S. 86, which held that federal courts could scrutinize state court criminal proceedings to promote fairness in trails. The event leading to the trial was a 1919 riot in Phillips County, Arkansas, that had left around two hundred blacks and five whites dead. The state-court trials for six blacks accused of murder were frequently described as mob-dominated. The NAACP successfully argued that the federal courts had a role in monitoring state courts and in correcting gross deficiencies in state courts. Typically, the lawyers for the NAACP volunteered their services to the group, but in 1934 the NAACP hired its first full-time lawyer and in 1939 established its Legal Defense Fund (LDF).[55] The LDF gave the NAACP a greater ability to develop a long-range legal strategy to challenge discriminatory practices. In 1944, after earlier setbacks, all-white primaries were declared unconstitutional in a case sponsored by the NAACP.[56] As important as these decisions were, the landmark case that solidified the NAACP's legal reputation was the 1954 *Brown v. Board of Education* decision overturning *Plessy v. Ferguson.* With that decision, the NAACP's LDF secured its most important victory.[57]

Aside from the NAACP, how do other groups fare in the courts? As hallowed as the NAACP history is, it is not the norm. Susan Olson found that there was limited support for the disadvantage theory at the federal district court level.[58] Writing in the middle of the conservative Reagan era, Lee Epstein argued that "advantaged" groups were increasingly using the courts.[59] Even though they had strong ties to the legislative and executive branches, conservative groups were hardly averse to using the courts. Courts simply offer an additional venue for influence. The attractiveness of the courts as a venue for groups depends, at least to some extent, on the character and substance of the law. That is, as the law in an area changes, the sorts of organized interests that are actively pursuing cases in that area also changes.[60] The courts do not, however, appear to be dominated by a single type of group, advantaged or disadvantaged.

By some measures, the organized interests using the courts most frequently are institutions and unions and corporations, not citizen-based groups.[61] Generally speaking, the most successful litigants are the repeat players, whether they be groups or corporations. More experience with the courts leads to an even greater tendency to return to the courts. Finally, one might think that interest groups would pick and choose their cases so carefully that they could establish a strong win-loss record. However, Lee Epstein and C. K. Rowland find that groups are no more successful in federal district courts than other litigants.[62]

Friends of litigants

Groups need not be named litigants to affect a court case. Nonlitigants may attempt to influence the proceedings of a court with an amicus curiae. Amicus curiae are "friend of the court" briefs, offering advice and counsel to the jurists. Friend-of-the-court briefs often provide background information on the context of the case, including its legal, political, social, and economic implications. It has been long recognized that, even as friends of the court, they are advocating for one side in the case or another.[63] In the federal court system, amicus curiae are used almost exclusively at the Supreme Court level. Though less expensive than litigation, amicus curiae can still cost several thousand dollars. Amicus curiae briefs may affect the Supreme Court in at least two ways. First, the briefs are a signal of the salience of the issues at stake. Even the simple volume of briefs may provide an indication of the contentiousness of the issues related to the case. The Court seldom seeks to redress issues of little consequence for people, so the briefs can help bring attention to certain issues or cases. Greg Caldeira and John Wright found that the volume of amicus briefs affects the cases that the Court agrees to hear in full. Because the Court refuses to hear the vast majority of cases offered, amicus briefs maintain a demonstrable effect on the structuring of the Court's agenda.[64] Caldeira and Wright have also found that the Court is open to amicus briefs from a wide array of interests, including relatively penurious citizen-based groups.[65]

Groups are clearly becoming more savvy in their use of friend-of-the-court briefs. Both sides of the abortion debate file briefs whenever the federal courts hear an abortion case. For each side, the efforts behind these briefs are increasingly coordinated to create a coherent body of evidence rather than a set of redundant arguments. Friend-of-the-court briefs do not simply implore the Court to decide an issue in one way or another, they present legal, social, and scientific arguments to support their claims. Such friend-of-the-court briefs can affect the Court's interpretation of key legal or substantive issues. For instance, in the Supreme Court's 1961 *Mapp v. Ohio* case (367 U.S. 643), the counsel for Mapp argued that the mere possession of pornographic material was not in itself a crime. In a friend-of-the-court brief, the ACLU (the American Civil Liberties Union) argued in favor of Mapp on entirely different grounds. The ACLU argued that Mapp's pornographic material had been discovered illegally because the police had no warrant or cause to search the Mapp residence. In *Mapp v. Ohio*, the Court decided that illegally seized evidence was not admissible in a court of law. Of course, the exclusionary rule limits a federal courtroom's use of illegally obtained evidence, but the Mapp decision extended the rule to cover state laws. Interestingly, the Court never addressed the "mere-possession" issue raised by the Mapp counsel.[66] Although it has been weakened by subsequent cases, the Mapp decision remains a hallmark search and seizure case.

Confirming judges

Groups are no different than other political actors when it comes to following the nomination and confirmation process for the Supreme Court. Such close scrutiny of the confirmation process has made some Senate confirmation battles particularly tumultuous. Of all presidential nominees requiring Senate approval, Supreme Court nominees face the toughest confirmation battles, approaching a twenty-five percent failure rate during the last twenty-five years.[67] Groups may follow the confirmation process by simply taking a stand on the nominee or they may engage in costly advertising and lobbying campaigns.[68] The confirmation battles for Robert Bork, who was rejected in 1987, and Clarence Thomas, who was confirmed in 1991, were particularly grueling, and they still affect many people's view of the confirmation process. However, politics and interest groups have long been part of the confirmation process. Given that the courts themselves are increasingly viewed as political bodies, it should not be surprising that the confirmation process itself is an inherently political process.

The contentious, political slant of the Supreme Court confirmation process has always existed, but it often remained a bit more out of sight. Sometimes the Senate confirmation followed the presidential nomination so quickly that there was little time to organize any sort of lobbying campaign for or against the nominee. In 1881, the National Grange had a rather unique opportunity to lobby against the confirmation of Stanley Matthews twice. Both Presidents Hayes and Garfield nominated Matthews to the

Court. The first nomination by Hayes never made it out of the Senate Judiciary Committee, where it died. The concerns of the Grange, voiced in numerous Grange newspapers published throughout the country, appeared triumphant. The second nomination was more viable, in particular because of the change in the Senate. During the Hayes administration, Democrats controlled the Senate, whereas under Garfield the Democrats and Republicans controlled an equal number of seats. The relatively longer period of time between the initial mention of his name by President Hayes and his second nomination by President Garfield allowed the Grange enough time to mobilize an even larger scale lobbying campaign in opposition of Matthews.[69] Matthews' confirmation vote was ultimately successful, though only by a single vote.

In general, groups have less opportunity to lobby when the Senate process moves quickly or remains out of public view. In 1916, the Senate opened up its proceedings during the confirmation battle over Louis Brandeis. The Brandeis nomination came at an awkward time for some senators. The Seventeenth Amendment mandating the popular election of senators had been adopted just three years earlier. Senators were not used to popular elections and they were unsure of the electoral ramifications of a Brandeis vote. Brandeis was the first Jewish Supreme Court nominee. He was also ardently pro-labor and very suspicious of large corporations. For some senators, opening the proceedings to the public was simply a defensive move that allowed them to assess public opinion more accurately. The openness of the Brandeis proceedings was an anomaly, designed to protect senators. The Senate rule change mandating open proceedings was not adopted until 1929. In 1930, the nomination of John J. Parker was the first to proceed under the new rules. Even with the open hearings, groups were not regular players in the confirmation process until the late 1960s. Since that time, the confirmation process has become increasingly drawn out. As the elapsed time between the President's nomination and final Senate action has lengthened, the number of groups and individuals addressing the Judiciary Committee has increased and the amount of media attention has increased. Public opinion and group lobbying is now very much part of the process.[70] There is now solid evidence to suggest that, before voting, senators assess the ideological distance between the nominee and home state constituents, the qualifications of the nominee, the popularity of the president, and interest group activity, especially in opposition to the nominee.[71]

Conclusion

Congressional lobbying has received considerable media attention over the last several years, but we do not always hear very much about executive branch lobbying or group involvement in the courts. However, the federal structure of the U.S. government offers numerous lobbying venues for organized interests, and increasingly, organized interests are taking advantage of them all. Lobbyists and organized interests recognize that Congress, bureaucratic agencies, and the courts all have a role in the policy process. The intricate relations between the branches practically ensure that a group's hard-won legislative successes in Congress remain vulnerable. Legislative successes may be either supported or undermined by agency rulemaking and court actions.

As noted in the preceding chapter, lobbyists are an integral part of the congressional process. Lobbyists often follow-up legislative lobbying with agency lobbying to affect the rulemaking procedure. Indeed, organized interests have also become an integral part of the implementation process. Comment periods, advisory panels, and open hearings all encourage group involvement in the rulemaking process. Congress sought greater public involvement in rulemaking to promote bureaucratic accountability, to improve agency information, and to enhance the monitoring of agency behavior. In short, Congress sought broader involvement to gain expertise and to encourage watchdog activity. Just as Congress has sometimes promoted group access to bureaucratic agencies, it has also enhanced group access to the courts. Since 1946, federal agency decisions have been vulnerable to legal challenges. Increasingly, legislation allows for additional court challenges, say, by citizen suits. Of course, the design of this sort of judicial review is determined by Congress—the same Congress that is prone to group lobbying pressure.[72] Therefore, to understand Washington lobbying by organized interests, one must be sensitive to the complex relations between Congress, agencies, and the courts. After all, Congress has brought the bureaucratic agencies and the federal courts into the policy process and encouraged organized interests to operate in those same policy venues.

NOTES

1. Douglas Adams, *The Hitchhiker's Guide to the Galaxy* (New York: Harmony Books, 1979), 9–10.
2. Adams (1979), 35–36.
3. *J.W. Hampton Jr. & Co. v. United States*, 276 U.S. 394 (1928).
4. Cornelius M. Kerwin, *Rulemaking* (Washington, D.C.: Congressional Quarterly, 1994), 101.
5. This discussion relies on Kerwin (1994), 102.
6. Kerwin (1994), 164.
7. John M. de Figueiredo and Emerson H. Tiller, "The Structure and Conduct of Corporate Lobbying: How Firms Lobby the Federal Communications Commission," *Journal of Economics and Management Strategy* 10 (2001): 91–123.
8. *Pacific Legal Foundation v. Jere Goyan*, 664 F.2d 1221 (4th Cir. 1981).
9. See Joan B. Aron's "Citizen Participation at Government Expense," *Public Administration Review* (Sept/Oct 1979): 477–85, for a discussion of congressional statutes that addressed intervenor financing for particular agencies.
10. Aron (1979), 478–79.

11. See Mark A. Peterson's "Interest Mobilization and the Presidency," in *The Politics of Interests*, ed. Mark P. Petracca (Boulder: Westview, 1992).
12. *Friends of the Earth v. Laidlaw Environmental Services*, 528 U.S. 167 (2000).
13. Linda Greenhouse, "High Court Is Urged to Uphold 'Citizen Suit' to Curb Pollution" (*New York Times*, October 13, 1999), A-18.
14. David Epstein and Sharyn O'Halloran adopt the fire alarm analogy. Interest groups bear monitoring costs for other political actors and pull fire alarms to alert others to problems. See their "Theory of Strategic Oversight," *Journal of Law, Economics, & Organization* (1995) 11: 227–55.
15. Lief Carter and Christine Harrington's *Administrative Law and Politics* (New York: Longman, 2000) is one of the better resources for information on administrative law procedure.
16. Kerwin (1994), 56.
17. Kerwin (1994), 259. A common standard is "arbitrary and capricious," but the interpretation of the standard remains fairly open. Also see *Chevron U.S.A. v. Natural Resources Defense Council*, 467 U.S. 837 (1984). Of course, agencies may balk at court rulings, refusing to treat any judgment as a test case and not changing the fundamental manner in which it operates. Such agency reaction to court rulings is called nonacquiescence, which really means that the agency fulfills the court's mandate in the most narrow way possible. See Susan Haire and Stefanie Lindquist, "Social Security Disability Cases in the U.S. Court of Appeals," *Judicature* 80 (1997): 230–36.
18. Kerwin (1994), 161.
19. Harold Seidman, *Politics, Position, and Power: The Dynamics of Federal Organization* (New York: Oxford University Press, 1970), 126.
20. Joel D. Aberbach and Bert A. Rockman, "Bureaucrats and Clientele Groups: A View from Capitol Hill," *American Journal of Political Science* 22 (1978): 818–32.
21. Latham (1965), 48.
22. The most relevant court case related to congressional delegation and bureaucratic discretion is *J.W. Hampton Jr. & Co. v. United States*, 276 U.S. 394 (1928).
23. See, for example, Truman (1971), 396.
24. See David Epstein and Sharyn O'Halloran's *Delegating Powers* (New York: Cambridge University Press, 1999) for an excellent discussion of these issues.
25. To be certain, the Supreme Court rejected the legislative veto in 1983 in *INS v. Chadha*, 462 U.S. 919 (1983). The Court majority argued that directives to agencies must follow regular legislative procedures, thereby requiring approval by both chambers and presentation to the president. The Court, however, has no enforcement mechanism and Congress still uses the veto on a regular basis. See Louis Fisher's "The Legislative Veto—Invalidated, It Survives," *Law and Contemporary Problems* 56 (1993): 273–92.
26. The number of possible citations here is almost endless, but the interested reader can begin with Ainsworth (1993), Austen-Smith and Wright (1992), and Rasmusen (1993).
27. The list of relevant articles here is quite long, but it would certainly include Epstein and O'Halloran (1995); Randall L. Calvert, Mathew D. McCubbins, and Barry R. Weingast, "A Theory of Political Control and Agency Discretion," *American Journal of Political Science* (1989) 33: 588–611; and Mathew D. McCubbins and Thomas Schwartz, "Congressional Oversight Overlooked," *American Journal of Political Science* (1984) 28: 165–79.
28. Kerwin (1994), 116.

29. The office has had various names over the years, including the Congressional Liaison Office and the Office of Congressional Relations.

30. Nigel Bowles, *The White House and Capitol Hill* (Oxford: Oxford University Press, 1987), 16.

31. Clifford Krauss, "Clinton's Woes on Capitol Hill Spur Sharp Criticism of His Top Lobbyist" (*New York Times,* May 25, 1993a), A-7.

32. Clifford Krauss, "House Democrats Rush to Extinguish Rebellion" (*New York Times,* May 19, 1993b), A-8.

33. See Samuel Kernell's "The Presidency and the People: The Modern Paradox," in *The Presidency and the Political System,* ed. Michael Nelson (Washington, D.C.: CQ Press, 1984), and *Going Public: New Strategies of Presidential Leadership* (Washington, D.C.: CQ Press, 1986).

34. Truman (1971), 422.

35. See Joseph A. Pika, "Interest Groups and the Executive," in *Interest Group Politics,* eds. Allan J. Cigler and Burdett A. Loomis (Washington, D.C.: CQ Press, 1983), and "Opening Doors for Kindred Souls: The White House Office of Public Liaison," in *Interest Group Politics,* 3rd ed., eds. Allan J. Cigler and Burdett A. Loomis (Washington, D.C.: CQ Press, 1991).

36. Richard F. Fenno Jr., *The President's Cabinet* (Cambridge: Harvard University Press, 1959). However, Martha Joynt Kumar and Michael Baruch Grossman argue that cabinet positions do not facilitate outreach because of the presence of so many competing interests within the same agencies. See Kumar and Grossman's "The Presidency and Interest Groups," in *The Presidency and the Political System,* ed. Michael Nelson (Washington, D.C.: CQ Press, 1984), 285.

37. Presidents have also feared that their appointees would become little more than mouthpieces for outside interests. See, for example, Stephen Hess, *Organizing the Presidency* (Washington, D.C.: Brookings Institution, 1976), 128.

38. Hess (1976), 127–28, emphasis added.

39. Kumar and Grossman (1984), 291–92.

40. Bill McAllister, "Lobbied Out of a Cabinet Post" (*The Washington Post Weekly Edition,* October 5–11, 1992), 14. During President Richard Nixon's first term, the AMA was able to have a nominee to the HEW agency withdrawn. See Benjamin I. Page and Mark P. Petracca's *The American Presidency* (New York: McGraw-Hill, 1983), 150.

41. See, for instance, George C. Edwards, III's *Presidential Influence in Congress* (San Francisco: W. H. Freeman, 1980), 171, or Page and Petracca (1983), 159.

42. Quoted from Pika (1983), 317.

43. Kumar and Grossman (1984), 298.

44. Kumar and Grossman (1984), 302.

45. Page and Petracca (1983), 158–59.

46. The best source for information on the White House Office of Communications is John A. Maltese's *Spin Control: The White House Office of Communications and the Management of Presidential News* (Chapel Hill: University of North Carolina Press, 1992).

47. Maltese (1992), 155.

48. Maltese (1992), 194.

49. For more information on these issues and this fascinating time period, see Paul Leland Haworth, *The Hayes-Tilden Election* (Indianapolis: Bobbs-Merrill, 1906); Ari Hoogenboom, *The Presidency of Rutherford B. Hayes* (Lawrence: University of Kansas Press, 1988); and C. Vann Woodward, *Reunion and Reaction: The Compromise of 1877 and the End of Reconstruction* (Boston: Little, Brown, 1951).

50. For more information on Jim Crow laws, see C. Vann Woodward, *The Strange Career of Jim Crow* (London: Oxford University Press, 1966).
51. McAdam (1982), 71.
52. McAdam (1982), 71, 85.
53. See Richard A. Posner's "What Do Judges and Justices Maximize? (The Same Thing Everybody Else Does)," *Supreme Court Economic Review* 3 (1993): 1–41. Lee Epstein and Jack Knight address this same issue in *The Choices Justices Make* (Washington, D.C.: CQ Press, 1998).
54. The NAACP filed an amicus brief in the case. It was not a named litigant.
55. As noted in Chapter 2, patrons are important for groups working to overcome their collective-action problem. The NAACP received financial support to pursue its legal strategies from a liberal foundation. See Kermit Hall's *Oxford Companion to the Supreme Court of the United States* (New York: Oxford University Press, 1992), 497.
56. *Smith v. Allwright*, 321 U.S. 649 (1944). In earlier decisions, the Supreme Court had ruled that political parties could limit access to their own primaries. See *Grovey v. Townsend*, 295 U.S. 45 (1935).
57. In the mid-1950s, the NAACP and the LDF became increasingly distinct organizations. Ironically, the groups split along North/South lines, with the LDF concentrating on desegregation efforts in the South and the NAACP concentrating on desegregation efforts in the North. The splintering of the two groups provides another example of the unraveling concept discussed in Chapter 4.
58. Susan M. Olson, "Interest Group Litigation in Federal District Court," *Journal of Politics* 52 (1990): 854–82.
59. Lee Epstein, *Conservatives in Court* (Knoxville: University of Tennessee Press, 1985).
60. See, for instance, how groups affected by obscenity rulings changed their litigation strategies after *Miller v. California*, 413 U.S. 15 (1973). Joseph F. Kobylka, "A Court Related Context for Group Litigation: Libertarian Groups and Obscenity," *Journal of Politics* 49 (1987): 1061–78.
61. On the dominance of unions, see Kim Lane Scheppele and Jack L. Walker Jr., "The Litigation Strategies of Interest Groups," in *Mobilizing Interest Groups in America*, ed. Jack L. Walker Jr. (Ann Arbor: University of Michigan Press, 1991). Scheppele and Walker also provide a sound critique of the disadvantage theory.
62. Lee Epstein and C. K. Rowland, "Debunking the Myth of Interest Group Invincibility in the Courts," *American Political Science Review* 85 (1991): 205–17. If groups seek media attention from court cases, wins and losses inside the courtroom may be a secondary concern.
63. Samuel Krislov made this argument in "The Amicus Curiae Brief: From Friendship to Advocacy," *Yale Law Journal* 72 (1963): 694–721.
64. The Court typically hears around one hundred cases chosen from among a few thousand. Gregory A. Caldeira and John R. Wright, "Organized Interests and Agenda Setting in the U.S. Supreme Court," *American Political Science Review* 82 (1988): 1109–28.
65. Gregory A. Caldeira and John R. Wright, "Amici Curiae before the Supreme Court: Who Participates, When, and How Much?" *Journal of Politics* 52 (1990): 782–806.
66. See Shlozman and Tierney (1986), 370–71.
67. Maltese (1998), 2.
68. Gregory Caldeira, Marie Hojnacki, and John R. Wright, "The Lobbying Activities of Organized Interests in Federal Judicial Nominations," *Journal of Politics* 62 (2000): 51–69.

69. For more information on the Matthews confirmation battle, see Scott H. Ainsworth and John Anthony Maltese's "National Grange Influence on the Supreme Court Confirmation of Stanley Matthews," *Social Science History* 20 (1996): 41–62.

70. For histories of the role of groups in the confirmation process, see Maltese (1998) and Gregory A. Caldeira and John R. Wright's "Lobbying for Justice," in *Contemplating Courts,* ed. Lee Epstein (Washington, D.C.: Congressional Quarterly Press, 1995), 44–71.

71. Jeffrey A. Segal, Charles M. Cameron, and Albert D. Cover, "A Spatial Model of Roll Call Voting: Senators, Constituents, Presidents and Interest Groups in Supreme Court Confirmations," *American Journal of Political Science* 36 (1992): 96–121. Also see David Austen-Smith and John Wright, "Counteractive Lobbying," *American Journal of Political Science* 38 (1994): 25–44.

72. See, for example, Charles R. Shipan, *Designing Judicial Review: Interest Groups, Congress, and Communications Policy* (Ann Arbor: University of Michigan Press, 1997).

~8~

Organized Interests in the Electorate: Grassroots Politics

Introduction

The two preceding chapters focused on direct Washington lobbying. Washington lobbyists recognize that they must provide legislators with the local angle on an issue, because Washington lobbying has less impact when there are no clear connections between the lobbyist's client and the home state or district voting population. Sometimes organized interests work to reinforce that local angle through grassroots lobbying. Any sort of lobbying occurring beyond the Washington, D.C., beltway is typically called *grassroots*. Sometimes grassroots campaigns are virtually spontaneous, with numerous citizens responding to the same issue or problem even though there is little or no coordination of their activities. Increasingly, however, grassroots efforts are coordinated and organized by professional organizers or group entrepreneurs. By some accounts, "the golden age of grass roots has arrived," and just as there are more and more specialized lobbying firms, there are more and more professional contacting firms that specialize in little more than very sophisticated political contacting for organizing grassroots campaigns.[1] For instance, the Clinton Group (unrelated to the former president) maintains vast data banks to help identify people with specific reading and spending habits and particular political leanings. To this data, it may add aggregate-level data on the education and income profiles for different areas of the country.[2] Although one's actual vote remains secret, some states make records of voter turnout and party affiliations generally available. Aggregate voting records at the county or district level are even more readily available. By using aggregate-level data as well as data on the party identification and voting frequency of individuals, it is increasingly easy to target people with particular partisan leanings and group affiliations who happen to live in particular congressional districts. With automated phoning, thousands of just the right people can be contacted in a very short period of time. Once contacted, these people may be asked to contact elected officials about any number of issues. The most sophisticated operations can automatically transfer a caller to the appropriate Washington office.

This chapter addresses several issues. How have new technologies affected grassroots campaigns? Do grassroots techniques now dominate other lobbying tactics? Who uses grassroots campaigns, why, and when? Finally, this chapter will address whether grassroots efforts can avoid the pitfalls of traditional interest group politics. Can some form of direct democracy do any better?

Early Examples of Grassroots Campaigns

Writing in the 1950s, David B. Truman opined that "groups . . . make limited use of letters, telegrams, and petitions." Truman contended that "personal contacts" were "of far greater value than a hundred letters or telegrams from persons unknown to the legislator."[3] Direct lobbying was no doubt more commonplace in the 1950s than grassroots efforts, but some very important movements in the United States, affecting everything from alcohol to veterans, had strong grassroots components. Abolitionists seeking to end the practice of slavery inundated the Capitol with petitions. During the early 1800s, the rules of the U.S. House required that all petitions had to be read aloud to the chamber. Large numbers of petitions could literally stall the work of the entire House for days and weeks. The onslaught of abolitionists' petitions made it impossible to ignore the slavery issue. Slowly, the House changed its rules to limit the amount of time and energy it devoted to petitions, but the slavery issue and disagreements about how best to respond to abolitionists continued to charge many House debates.

After the Civil War, the G.A.R. was for several years the largest and most powerful interest group in the United States.[4] Comprising Union veterans, the G.A.R. was originally a philanthropic group, highlighting camaraderie through social gatherings. For several years, its only foray into politics was to ask for a Memorial Day to honor those Union soldiers who had died in the conflict. The G.A.R. became politically charged when it decided to push for more generous pensions for former Union soldiers. Grassroots activities always played a key role in the life of the G.A.R. The *National Tribune*, published by the G.A.R., always listed those representatives and senators who were friends of the soldiers. Virtually every edition of the weekly paper informed the reader of Washington events and suggested appropriate courses of action. In short, the *National Tribune* facilitated the coordination of the grassroots efforts. G.A.R. officials recognized that the soldiers' vote was crucial to the success of their direct lobbying in Washington. For a time, the *National Tribune* was the most widely circulated weekly in the United States, so it is not surprising that representatives and senators were sensitive to how they were portrayed in the paper.[5]

A grassroots campaign was also integral to the success of the prohibitionists' cause in the early 1900s. The Anti-Saloon League was one of the most prominent prohibitionist groups and it remained actively engaged in both direct congressional lobbying and grassroots lobbying.[6] Records of the League's activities suggest that their grassroots campaign was in many regards quintessential. First, the League worked through existing organizations to minimize collective-action problems. Few collective efforts start from scratch, and the League's was no different. The League recognized that its natural clientele resided in Protestant church members. With churches as their partners, the League organized huge rallies.[7] At the League's insistence, when the collection plate was passed, the contributions were for the League, not the church. To be certain, some churches winced at the idea of raising money for secular affairs, but whichever church hosted the League was guaranteed the largest Sunday turnout. After all, the League *hired* very popular figures to speak on its behalf. The two most successful speakers were Richmond P. Hobson, a Spanish War hero and a member of Congress, and William Jennings Bryan, a lawyer in the Scopes Monkey Trial and a four-time presidential candidate. The League rallies were big-time affairs that raised both money and media attention, coupling preaching and politics.

Registration drives were key elements of Anti-Saloon League rallies. As people were registered to vote, they were also asked to fight the evils of alcohol by pledging to vote dry. As it registered people to vote, the League developed a very detailed house list, similar to the house lists discussed in Chapter 4, with party identification, address, church affiliation, and telephone numbers in those rare instances in which the individual actually owned a phone.[8] For its time, the League's house list was very impressive, especially since all records had to be maintained by hand. With an effective connection to voters, the League could employ its Select/Elect/Defeat strategy. The League decided which candidates to select for election or defeat by their willingness to pledge support for the dry cause. The League's actively maintained house list and the popularity of its rallies made the electoral consequences clear to the candidates without threats and bribes. The League realized that if they could select and elect the proper candidates, then direct lobbying would be less necessary and when necessary more effective. In 1920, Prohibition was enacted, lasting for thirteen years.

Grassroots Today

Given the nature of these earlier grassroots campaigns, why do some people think today is the golden age of grassroots politics? What makes grassroots lobbying campaigns so different today? Grassroots politics has become easier and comparatively less expensive, largely due to technological advances. Huge house lists can be maintained on simple desktop computers with tailor-designed software. Point-and-click technologies have affected countless aspects of our interest group society, not the least grassroots campaigns. The tactics are the same, but their relative costs and ease are changed.

The brief overviews of earlier grassroots campaigns highlight certain commonalities that continue today. Grassroots lobbying is almost always used in conjunction with direct lobbying.[9] The reverse, however, is not true. Most direct lobbying is unconnected to grassroots campaigns. One of the all-time great lobbyists, Thomas H. Boggs Jr., noted that most direct lobbying addresses small, technical details, albeit details with considerable impact for certain people. People involved in direct lobbying often prefer working beyond public view. Too much attention may lead opposition forces to mobilize. Whenever choosing the blend of direct and grassroots lobbying to employ, organized interests are very sensitive to the scope of the debate. Grassroots campaigns tend to expand rather than limit the scope of conflict.[10] "Where . . . grass-roots campaigns have been used a lot are the big public policy debates."[11] Other issues are better suited to smaller, more intimate venues. If a lobbyist is seeking a minor change in a rather arcane piece of legislation, a full grassroots campaign will do no good.

Many groups and organized interests prefer to work behind the scenes where there is less public exposure. Simply put, the publicity and media attention that come with grassroots campaigns fit some groups better than others. Using Jack Walker's data referred to in the second chapter, Thomas Gais and the late Jack Walker found that centralized groups tend to prefer more direct insider strategies, while more decentralized groups tend to favor outsider, grassroots strategies.[12] Overall, citizen-based groups prefer outsider strategies more than profit sector groups do. However, when a group has the support of a patron, both insider and outsider strategies are adopted. The patron's backing makes the strategic balancing of direct and grassroots efforts less problematic because there are fewer financial constraints. With sufficient backing, groups use all available lobbying strategies.

Effects on the issue agenda

Grassroots campaigns and the media attention they garner affect what social scientists often call the *issue agenda,* which is simply the set of issues that people are thinking about. Not all issues are prominent at all times in people's minds. Disturbances affect our view of the interest group society. We may think of farm policies more during a drought, or environmental groups more after an oil spill. Grassroots events are designed to produce the same effect. Grassroots organizers try to affect the issue agenda to make their issues more salient or prominent in citizens' minds. In that regard, grassroots campaigns typically focus more on mobilizing latent supporters than on converting opponents. One need not always change people's views on an issue; often one must simply convince people that an action must be taken. For instance, during its heyday in the 1980s, few weeks went by without a major news story about MADD or the dangers of drunk driving. MADD's grassroots campaign had no obvious opponents—there were, after all, no *proponents* of drunk driving. MADD's grassroots efforts focused on its latent supporters, opponents to drunk driving who seldom thought about drunk driving and who were therefore largely inactive on the issue. Only when supporters are thinking about the right issue will they consider acting on the issue.

Affecting the issue agenda or the salience of an issue in people's minds is a relatively short-term goal. However, some grassroots efforts focus on the long-term goal of educating people. Of course, the distinctions between long-term education goals and shorter-term issue agenda goals are sometimes blurry. For instance, MADD's education efforts about alcohol-related driving fatalities and the impairment of driving linked to even moderate levels of alcohol in the blood served dual purposes. Yes, people were educated, but the education increased their awareness of the problem and affected the issue agenda. Other educationally oriented grassroots efforts take a longer-term approach. Teachers' unions and oil industry corporations have long used advertisements in prominent news magazines and newspapers to present their interpretation of policy debates. Often these advertorials appear much like regular articles or editorials. In addition to the print media, groups such as the NRA also use television infomercials in some markets to communicate their message. Support for research centers and think tanks perhaps best exemplifies the long-term approach to affecting a policy debate. Jeffrey Berry describes traditional think tanks as research "universities without students."[13] Recently, however, think tanks and research centers have become increasingly partisan, often taking clear stands on policy debates.[14] When their policy stands are clear, corporate support for their research efforts is more forthcoming. Corporations affect the issue agenda by funding research that is linked to partisan-oriented research centers and think tanks. Most recently, "several big weapons builders have financed research centers to shape the debate" over the missile-defense system.[15] Though it is a long-term approach to affecting the issue agenda, funding research centers and think tanks has a distinct advantage over other grassroots strategies. Unlike other grassroots tactics, funding research allows corporations to stay out of the limelight.

Effects on individuals

Many interest group scholars address the issue agenda in broad terms without ever addressing the affects of grassroots lobbying on individuals. In a broad sense, one can talk about the issue agenda being changed, but affecting the issue agenda is worthwhile only because of the impact on individuals.[16] Throughout this book, the analysis has been primarily at the individual level, not the group level. How are goal-oriented individuals affected by groups and grassroots campaigns? Political psychologists often note that individuals are sensitive to the presentation or framing of issues. Facts in and of themselves are devoid of meaning; it is the presentation of the facts that affects our interpretation of them. Consider views on alcohol and alcohol consumption. Alcohol consumption was long considered a rite of passage for young adults and a key ingredient for the successful business lunch. MADD wanted to change those views. It presented facts about alcohol and drunk-driving fatalities so that alcohol consumption would be linked first and foremost to tragedy. MADD successfully reframed the issue from one of personal freedom or thrill seeking to one of tragedy.

Political psychologists Thomas Nelson and Donald Kinder have shown that if issues are framed in an us-and-them fashion, people are more apt to adopt a group-oriented view of society.[17] Depending on how one frames an issue, people are more or less beholden to a group centric view of their world. A group-oriented view of society can be very helpful to people who have limited or incomplete information about many political issues and events. Indeed, a long-standing lament among the civic minded is that American voters are amazingly ignorant of politics. Such concerns are largely misplaced. Individuals themselves have only limited information about politics because they choose to remain "rationally ignorant."[18] No one can gather information about everything. At various times, we delegate responsibilities to others or glean information from second- or third-hand sources. Being less informed on some issues is not a problem if one can rely on others to provide reasonably accurate information. When choosing to remain rationally ignorant, one balances the costs of becoming personally informed with the costs associated with perhaps being misled by others. Groups can inform rationally ignorant people as long as the people themselves know something about the groups. As it happens, political scientists Henry Brady and Paul Sniderman found that individuals do know where major groups stand on various issues. That is, the groups' stands are known by individuals even if the individuals themselves know little about the issues. Indeed, in this regard individuals are "remarkably accurate."[19] Individuals can develop an "accurate map of politics, of who wants what politically, of who takes the same side as whom and of who lines up on the opposing side of key issues."[20] Such an accurate map allows one to act in a reasonable, rational fashion. For instance, Arthur Lupia has found that when California voters could identify the sponsors of ballot initiatives, they could vote in their own self-interest.[21] In-depth knowledge of the initiative itself was not necessary for one to make an appropriate vote choice. Elisabeth Gerber and Lupia further showed how competing messages from conflicting groups help voters gain an increasingly accurate view of their political circumstances.[22] The gist of these results is that groups help citizens navigate their political worlds so that they may take appropriate actions.

Effects on legislators

As noted earlier, most organized interests that engage in outside grassroots lobbying also engage in direct lobbying. How does grassroots lobbying affect legislators? In the two preceding chapters, the informational impact of direct lobbying was stressed. University of Michigan political scientist Ken Kollman built on some of the models of insider lobbying discussed in Chapter 6 to explain how outside grassroots lobbying can also play an informational role. Outside grassroots lobbying is a costly signal to decision makers that reinforces insider lobbying. Grassroots lobbying can inform legislators about the popular support for issues. Legislators can glean electoral information from grassroots activity whenever there is a direct correspondence between grassroots activity and grassroots support. Organizing any grassroots activity is expensive, but it is reasonable to suppose that grassroots efforts are particularly expensive for unpopular causes and relatively less expensive for popular ones. If the supposition does indeed hold, then organized interests with little popular support may find grassroots efforts prohibitively expensive. Depending on the *relative* costs of grassroots lobbying for popular and unpopular issues, legislators may be able to gauge citizen support for issues accurately by evaluating grassroots efforts.

To be certain, grassroots lobbying does sometimes occur with rather unpopular, narrow issues. Kollman argues that grassroots efforts may be designed to increase the saliency of an issue among supporters. In some ways, popularity is a crude measure, only roughly indicating support for an issue. Support for an issue may be widespread but not very deep. A standard example often used here is the gun-control issue. For many years public opinion has supported stricter gun-control regulations. Opponents of gun control are, quite simply, outnumbered. The salience of the gun-control issue is, however, very different for these two groups. The salience of the gun-control issue for those opposing restrictions is considerably greater than the salience of the issue for those supporting stricter regulations. In an interest group society, preferences alone—for or against—do not provide the same sort of information as the strength of those preferences. Legislators can also learn about issue salience from grassroots campaigns.

Grassroots efforts provide information to legislators that is not readily available from other sources. To some extent, popular support for issues could be ascertained from public opinion polls, but not all issues receive regular attention from pollsters. In addition, polls seldom provide information about salience. That is, how much does an issue stand out from other issues? How important is the issue relative to others? Simply stating an opinion on an issue is very different than acting on an issue. Participants in grassroots campaigns indicate a willingness to act on their preferences. John Wright refers to "grassroots lobbying campaigns . . . as miniexperiments in political mobilization, reveal[ing] important information to legislators about how constituents might react . . . on Election Day."[23]

Groups and the Media

Grassroots lobbying campaigns are most successful when the media gives them special attention. In his work on political protests, Michael Lipsky noted that protest organizers focused much of their efforts on securing favorable media coverage.[24] It is virtually impossible to affect the issue agenda or expand the scope of conflict without extensive media coverage. The media will define the issues at stake and the terms of the policy debates. The media will label individuals as participants in grassroots campaigns or as political protesters. Are protesters breaking the law or bravely standing on principles? The media may suggest that efforts are either noble or silly and futile. The media will report whether the Million Man March has one million marchers or only twenty-five thousand. If the media attention is favorable, then grassroots participants may feel greater solidary, expressive, and purposive benefits. With favorable media coverage, organizers may attract larger and larger numbers of participants.

Clearly, the media plays a central role in the functioning of an interest group society. Media outlets are not, however, neutral players in the interest group environment. Some issues and some organized interests receive more coverage than others.[25] In a series of working papers, James Snider and Benjamin Page illustrate why the media's lobbying campaigns can be particularly troublesome.[26] Elected officials and the media have an unbalanced relationship. Certainly, those people working in the media appreciate lively news events, but news comes from many sources, both political and nonpolitical. News outlets do not need to cover every political event. In contrast, elected officials need media outlets to get their message out. By some counts, House members appear about twice a month on local television stations, and members and senators generally view such opportunities as far more important to their careers than similar opportunities on the national outlets.[27] Partly for these reasons, the head of the National Association of Broadcasters (NAB), "a Southern gentleman not given to braggadocio," can credibly state that "'no one has more sway with members of Congress than the local broadcaster.'"[28] The NAB keeps its members apprised of Washington affairs. It distributes weekly, monthly, and twice-yearly reports on legislative issues to its members. The NAB develops legislative liaison committees for each of the fifty states. Every year the liaison committee members travel to Washington to visit every member of Congress.[29] The NAB and its members are, in short, politically savvy.

What issues do media outlets themselves choose to lobby on? How do they report on those issues that they themselves are also lobbying on? Many news outlets establish what is sometimes called a wall of separation between a media outlet's business decisions and financial affairs and its editorial and reporting policies. To help to maintain the wall, different staffs are used to run the financial affairs and to structure the reporting policies. Such a wall might allow owners of television stations or newspapers to lobby on issues that their own reporters deem unworthy. Financial stakes would not cloud reporters' coverage. Without a wall, the reporting on the lobbying issues might be skewed or one-sided. Of course, there is a widely held feeling that journalists should endeavor to present the news fairly, which is to say most folks would support a wall-of-separation policy.

Consider, however, the Telecommunications Act of 1996. This act gave established broadcasters free access to new air space (or spectrums) on publicly regulated airways. The value of the spectrum was judged to be somewhere between $10 billion and $70 billion. In the past, such items had been auctioned off rather than given away. The print media repeatedly reported on the "spectrum give-away" or the "super highway robbery."[30] The print media was overwhelmingly opposed to the act as unnecessary corporate welfare. Indeed, Snider and Page found that the only newspapers supporting the act were owned by companies that also secured considerable revenue from their ownership of local television stations.[31] How did the television media report on the issue? They didn't at all. In the words of Snider and Page, there was bias by omission.

Former Senator Robert Dole (R-Kans.) complained about this blackout—this bias by omission. Though the House had passed the measure, Dole blocked the measure from consideration in the Senate. Dole was also running in the Republican presidential primaries. Of course, one of the most important resources in the presidential primaries is media attention. Media attention is crucial for solidifying a candidate's momentum and gathering greater support. Just prior to the Iowa caucuses, Dole received a hand-delivered letter from Nick Evans, the president of a firm owning eleven local stations in the Midwest and South. Evans was also on the NAB TV Board. In the letter, Evans states that no threats are implied, but he also states that

> this is where the hard part comes into play. If over the next few days your position on spectrum has not changed and been made public, you will have lost my support. I will be forced to use our resources to tell the viewers in all of our markets of your plan to destroy free over-the-air television. . . . My plan is to start our campaign against spectrum auctions and its supporters in the next ten days.[32]

Consider the pressure on Dole. He needed media coverage. Dole remained quiet about the issue until his nomination was fairly sewn up. In April of 1996, Dole attacked the NAB and the media blackout of the issue on the floor of the U.S. Senate. Dole titled his speech the Broadcast Blackout.

Of course, Dole and the print media may have been wrong. The NAB position may have been the proper one. However, the more important lesson is that the media, like the government, is not always a neutral player in the interest group environment. The wall of separation that some journalists speak so nobly of is sometimes dramatically breached.

Ballot Initiatives and Referenda

Many states allow their citizens to initiate public policy proposals through the use of ballot initiatives or allow citizens to decide the fate of legislative proposals through referenda.[33] Though their uses vary considerably from state to state, initiatives and referenda allow citizens to vote on basic policy proposals without interference or involvement of state legislatures. Initiatives and referenda were especially popular among progressive reformers in the early 1900s. If corrupt politicians dominated state legislatures, then one means of either bypassing or countering state legislators was to promote the wider use of initiatives and referenda. The simple presence of ballot initiative opportunities can affect legislators' behaviors. For instance, legislators might alter legislative proposals so that citizens would be less apt to attempt ballot initiatives to undo legislative outcomes.[34] These progressive reforms remain very popular in some states, such as California, and most states permit either one or the other procedure.[35]

Ballot initiatives may bypass legislatures, but they do not evade group influence. Anyone can start an initiative campaign—individuals, citizen-based interest groups, corporations, trade associations. The process is the same for any initiator. Before an initiative is placed on the ballot for voter approval, a set number of signatures from registered voters must be collected. Signature requirements vary by state, but in 1996 they varied from over 10,000 to almost 700,000.[36] Thousands of signatures do not appear out of thin air, so not surprisingly, there are firms that initiative organizers can hire to help collect signatures. The rate is around seventy cents per signature.[37] Anyone can start an initiative campaign, but the signature requirements do make ballot measures expensive to organize. Attempts to limit the role for professional organizers run into questions of constitutionality, and for the most part the Supreme Court has ruled against such limitations.[38]

Three issues are addressed in the remainder of this section. First, is there equal access to the ballot initiative process? Just as some organized interests might find legislative lobbying difficult, some interests might find the initiative process too expensive or cumbersome. Second, are the results coherent and meaningful? That is, after all the votes on ballot initiatives are counted, can one make sense of the whole collection of adopted policies? Would voters approve of the collection of successful initiatives in a simple up or down vote? Finally, is there any evidence of a tyranny of the majority surfacing in ballot-initiative campaigns?

Access to state ballot initiatives

Given the expenses associated with signature requirements, one might reasonably wonder whether economic interests have an easier time affecting the policy process through initiatives than do citizen groups. In essence, Gerber raised the same sort of questions that critics of pluralism raised in the 1960s. Is the group environment inclusive of most interests or dominated by only a few? To answer this and other questions, Gerber collected data on 168 ballot-initiative campaigns from eight states. Gerber found that citizen-based groups and economic interests used very different strategies. Not surprisingly, economic interests prefer to use strategies that are resource rich. They rely on money. Citizen groups prefer strategies that rely on personnel resources. They rely on people. Powerful economic interests certainly use the initiative process, but citizen-based groups are actually more successful than economic interests in securing voter approval of initiatives. Although economic interests appear to have distinct advantages when it comes to blocking ballot initiatives, Gerber suggested that overall the playing field is fairly level.

The paradox of multiple elections[39]

Does fairly equal access to the methods of direct democracy lead to fairly reasonable results? There is no way to provide a universal answer, but this section does illustrate some of the possibilities for anomalous results. For present purposes, suppose there are three propositions on the ballot. Voters must vote yes or no on each of the three proposals. A completed ballot, therefore, has one of eight possible combinations of yeas and nays. Only those propositions with majority approval will become law. Although propositions are voted on singly, the body of laws under which one lives is the combination of winning propositions. Of course, no single proposition can win unless it receives majority support, but what about the entire set of winning propositions? How many voters must necessarily approve of the body of laws or the set of winning propositions?

For simplicity, suppose there are just thirteen voters. One voter filled her ballot YYY, voting yes on all three propositions. The other ballots were filled as follows, YYN (1), YNY (1), NYY (1), YNN (3), NYN (3), NNY (3), where the number in parentheses indicates the number of ballots so marked. No voter opposed each of the three ballot initiatives, so there were no ballots marked NNN. Table 8.1 provides the tallies.

Each of the three propositions fails by a six to seven tally, forcing our imaginary society to live under the laws mandated by this combination of no votes. It is indeed paradoxical that *no one* marked a ballot NNN. Whether one is bothered by this paradox may largely depend on whether the propositions should be taken as a whole or considered separately.[40] Propositions are, however, often related to one another. General levies for school districts, funds for targeted education programs, and support for other social or

TABLE 8.1
An Illustration of the
Paradox of Multiple Elections

Number of Voters	Voters' Ballots
1	Y Y Y
1	Y Y N
1	Y N Y
1	N Y Y
3	Y N N
3	N Y N
3	N N Y
0	N N N
Number of N votes by proposition	7, 7, 7
Number of Y votes by proposition	6, 6, 6
Winning "slate" of propositions	N N N
Number of ballots marked N N N	0

educational affairs, such as library and museum funding, often appear on the same ballot.

The anomalies in Table 8.1 are stark, but even more stark examples are readily available. For the next example, imagine a setting with four ballot proposals and thirty-one voters. The ballots are displayed in Table 8.2. In this situation, each proposition wins even though the YYYY slate received no votes and the NNNN slate received more votes than any other slate. That is, the plurality winner is the exact opposite of the propositions approved.[41]

Are there real-life examples of the paradox? Although they are difficult to document, one example involves voting on propositions in California.[42] In the November elections of 1990, California voters faced a series of twenty-eight statewide propositions, affecting everything from health care to law enforcement. In their analysis of the votes just in Los Angeles County, three formal theorists, Steven Brams, Marc Kilgour, and William Zwicker, found that the winning combination or slate of the twenty-eight propositions (NNNYNNYNYNNNNNNYNYYYNYYNNYNY) received absolutely no votes.[43]

TABLE 8.2
Another Illustration of the Paradox of Multiple Elections

Number of Voters	Voters' Ballots
0	Y Y Y Y
4	Y Y Y N
4	Y Y N Y
4	Y N Y Y
4	N Y Y Y
1	Y Y N N
1	Y N Y N
1	Y N N Y
1	N Y Y N
1	N Y N Y
1	N N Y Y
1	Y N N N
1	N Y N N
1	N N Y N
1	N N N Y
5	N N N N

Number of Y votes by proposition	16, 16, 16, 16
Number of N votes by proposition	15, 15, 15, 15
Winning "slate" of propositions	Y Y Y Y
Number of ballots marked Y Y Y Y	0
Number of ballots marked N N N N	5

Tyranny of the majority

Direct democracy has not always worked out well for political minorities. Being on the losing side politically need not be the end of the world, but attempts to infringe on constitutional rights through the initiative process are unsettling. In some of the starkest instances, courts have voided the results of initiatives on constitutional grounds. In 1964, California voters approved a ballot initiative that allowed for "'private' discrimination in the housing market."[44] Supporters of the initiative sought to undo California's fair-housing laws. In California, ballot initiatives can overturn legislative proposals, but no legislative action can undo popularly approved ballot initiatives. The courts were the only recourse. After hearing the case, the Supreme Court ruled that constitutional rights could not be subject to popular approval.[45] When are voters most apt to restrict the rights of political minorities? Two prominent scholars of the initiative and referenda processes note that larger, more heterogeneous communities are less likely to limit the rights of minorities and more likely to extend rights to minorities.[46]

The Representation Problem Revisited: Organizing Others' Grassroots

A recurring lesson from this book is that no group emerges out of thin air. The collective-action problem is simply too onerous. Of course, the collective-action problem does not curtail the presence of groups, but as Jack Walker's work reminds us, groups need sponsors.[47] Sometimes one group's sponsor is itself another group. It is quite natural for organized interests to work with one another. When, however, is the support for other groups legitimate and when are groups simply creating fronts, or the appearance of legitimacy? The people who can most afford grassroots campaigns may or may not have genuine grassroots support. Is grassroots lobbying free from the representation problem first discussed in Chapter 6? Can one necessarily know who is behind a grassroots lobbying campaign?

Consider the following background. The NRA and police groups have often been on opposite sides of gun-control issues. Police groups felt increasingly wary of the NRA as it moved away from its sportsmen and law and order traditions, but the NRA's stand on "cop-killer" Teflon bullets finalized the split in 1982. Teflon-coated bullets have armor-piercing capabilities, making bullet-proof vests useless. After 1982, police unions became more active in politics, often providing cover to legislators voting for limits or outright bans on various types of guns or ammunition. In 1982, one union official stated that the "NRA is no longer a friend of law enforcement."[48] Of course, it does not help the NRA to be perceived as an enemy of the police. In 1991 the Law Enforcement Alliance of America (LEAA) was formed with $100,000 of start-up money from the NRA. A year later, the NRA closed its own internal law-enforcement liaison division. The first executive director of the LEAA came directly from the NRA's closed division. The LEAA has in turn been linked to the Southern States Police Benevolent Association, which has also been very supportive of NRA positions. Most readers of this book will not be NRA members, so it might seem that the NRA is creating fronts for their own interests. Perhaps the NRA created fake allies or perhaps it is providing a voice for those police who do not feel that limits on the second amendment yield any safeguards for law enforcement officials. The array of interest group voices is complex and often overlapping. Interpreting these voices is difficult at best. The representation problem that affects direct lobbying also affects grassroots lobbying campaigns.

Conclusion

Lobbyists for organized interests have three general means of affecting policy: they can elect the right people so no lobbying is ever necessary, they can lobby elected officials directly, or they can organize grassroots efforts, hoping that the grassroots activists will in turn pressure their elected officials. Grassroots strategies may appear to be indirect and poorly focused, but grassroots efforts bolster the impact of other lobbying strategies. Electing the right people requires a successful voter mobilization drive. Grassroots lobbying campaigns are dry runs for vote drives. Direct lobbying is enhanced by grassroots efforts when those efforts illustrate the likely electoral ramifications of legislators' decisions.

Grassroots lobbying campaigns remain expensive, but technological advances have considerably reduced their costs. In addition, more and more firms specialize in grassroots-related services. Virtually every issue of *Campaigns and Elections* contains articles designed to help the grassroots novice. Each issue contains advertisements for political consultants, political public relations firms, and specialized software. Not surprisingly, more and more organized interests are adopting grassroots strategies. Readers of the *New York Times* are used to seeing advertisements from oil corporations on the editorial page, but corporations are increasingly becoming players in every aspect of the grassroots environment. William Browne uses the term *all-directional advocacy* to describe the tendency of organized interests to adopt a full array of both insider and outsider lobbying strategies.[49] One cannot understand American politics today without understanding the struggle to affect both constituents in the electorate and elected officials.

NOTES

1. Jack Bonner, head of Bonner Associates, quoted by Stephen Engelberg, in "A New Breed of Hired Hands Cultivates Grass-Roots Anger" (*New York Times,* March 17, 1993), A-1, A-11. Also see Kenneth M. Goldstein's *Interest Groups, Lobbying, and Participation in America* (New York: Cambridge University Press, 1999).
2. Individual-level data is data that can be linked to a particular person. Aggregate-level data is data that can only be linked to a large group of people, say those living in a particular congressional district. For instance, the average income per family for the congressional district may be helpful aggregate-level information, but it is important to remember that it will fit some individual citizens of that district better than others.

3. Truman (1971), 391.
4. There are numerous works addressing the political activity of the G.A.R. Two articles by Ainsworth (1995a and 1995b) provide a good starting place.
5. Today, *Modern Maturity*, the magazine produced by the AARP, is one of the most widely distributed magazines in the United States.
6. The best works on the Anti-Saloon League are Peter C. Odegard's *Pressure Politics: The Story of the Anti-Saloon League* (New York: Columbia University Press, 1928), and K. Austin Kerr's *Organized for Prohibition: A New History of the Anti-Saloon League* (New Haven: Yale University Press, 1985).
7. See, for instance, Kerr (1985), 81.
8. Recall from Chapter 4 that house lists are lists of the most active and generous supporters of a group or cause.
9. See Marie Hojnacki and David C. Kimball's "The Who and How of Organizations' Lobbying Strategies in Committee," *Journal of Politics* 61 (1999): 999–1024, for a recent look at this issue.
10. Many of these issues are addressed more extensively in Kollman (1998).
11. Thomas H. Boggs Jr. quoted in Joel Brinkley, "Cultivating the Grass Roots to Reap Legislative Benefits" (*New York Times,* November 1, 1993), A-14.
12. Thomas L. Gais and Jack Walker, "Pathways to Influence in American Politics," in *Mobilizing Interest Groups in America,* ed. Jack L. Walker (Ann Arbor: University of Michigan Press, 1991), 112–13.
13. Berry (1997), 126.
14. Andrew Rich and R. Kent Weaver, "Advocates and Analysts: Think Tanks and the Politicization of Expertise," in *Interest Group Politics,* eds. Allan J. Cigler and Burdett A. Loomis (Washington, D.C.: CQ Press, 1998).
15. Leslie Payne, "After High Pressure Years, Contractors Tone Down Missile Defense Lobbying" (*New York Times,* June 13, 2000), A-6.
16. For a lobbyist's view of this process, see Susan Herbst's *Reading Public Opinion: How Political Actors View the Democratic Process* (Chicago: University of Chicago Press, 1998).
17. Thomas E. Nelson and Donald R. Kinder, "Issue Frames and Group-Centrism in American Public Opinion," *Journal of Politics* 58 (1996): 1055–78.
18. This term was coined by Anthony Downs in his classic *An Economic View of Democracy* (New York: Harper & Row, 1957).
19. Henry E. Brady and Paul M. Sniderman, "Attitude Attribution: A Group Basis for Political Reasoning," *American Political Science Review* 79 (1985): 1061.
20. Brady and Sniderman (1985), 1061.
21. Arthur Lupia, "Shortcuts versus Encyclopedias: Information and Voting Behavior in California Insurance Reform Elections," *American Political Science Review* 88 (1994): 63–76. Also see work by Susan A. Banducci, "Searching for Ideological Consistency in Direct Legislation Voting," in *Citizens as Legislators,* eds. Shaun Bowler, Todd Donovan, and Caroline J. Tolbert (Columbus: Ohio State University Press, 1998).
22. Elisabeth R. Gerber and Arthur Lupia, "Campaign Competition and Policy Responsiveness in Direct Legislation Elections," *Political Behavior* 17 (1995): 639–56.
23. Wright (1996), 71.
24. Michael Lipsky, "Protest as a Political Resource," *American Political Science Review* 62 (1968): 1144–58.
25. Lucig H. Danielian and Benjamin I. Page, "The Heavenly Chorus: Interest Group Voices on TV News," *American Journal of Political Science* 38 (1994): 1056–78.
26. James H. Snider and Benjamin I Page, "Does Media Ownership Affect Media Standards?" paper presented at the Annual Meeting of the Midwest Political Sci-

ence Association, Chicago, April 10–12, 1997a; "The Political Power of TV Broadcasters," (Evanston: Working Papers, Institute for Policy Research, 1997b); "Measuring Information and Money as Interest Group Resources," paper presented at the Annual Meeting of the Midwest Political Science Association, Chicago, April 15–17, 1999.

27. Snider and Page (1997b), 18.
28. Edward O. Fritts quoted in Paul Taylor's "Superhighway Robbery" (*New Republic Magazine,* May 5, 1997), 20.
29. Snider and Page (1997a), 4.
30. See, for instance, Leslie Wayne's "Broadcast Lobby's Formula: Airtime + Money = Influence" (*New York Times,* May 5, 1997), C-1.
31. Snider and Page (1997a), 10–11.
32. Snider and Page (1997b), 25–26. Snider received a copy of the Evans letter after the 1996 general election
33. See Shaun Bowler, Todd Donovan, and Caroline J. Tolbert, eds., *Citizens as Legislators* (Columbus: Ohio State University Press, 1998); John Haskell, *Direct Democracy or Representative Government?* (Boulder: Westview, 2001); or David D. Schmidt, *Citizen Lawmakers: The Ballot Initiative Revolution* (Philadelphia: Temple University Press, 1989), for good overviews of various states' experiences with initiatives.
34. The second chapter in Elisabeth R. Gerber's *The Populist Paradox* (Princeton, NJ: Princeton University Press, 1999) nicely details these issues.
35. On the continuing popularity of ballot initiatives, see Todd S. Purdum, "Ballot Initiatives Flourishing as Way to Bypass Politicians" (*New York Times,* March 31, 1998), A-1.
36. Gerber (1999), 40.
37. Gerber (1999), 40.
38. *Meyer v. Grant,* 486 U.S. 414 (1988).
39. This section and its examples are based largely on work by Steven J. Brams, D. Marc Kilgour, and William S. Zwicker. See their work entitled "The Paradox of Multiple Elections," *Social Choice and Welfare* 15 (1998): 211–36.
40. This issue is addressed by Dean Lacy and Emerson Niou in "A Problem with Referendums," *Journal of Theoretical Politics* 12 (2000): 5–31. If preferences are nonseparable, then one's evaluations of one initiative is affected by which other initiatives win. That is, it may be difficult for individuals to consider the initiatives separately. If preferences are nonseparable, ballot procedures may lead to pareto inferior outcomes. That is, *everyone* would be made better off and no one worse off by adopting some other combination of initiatives.
41. These voting procedures might even reject combinations of winning proposals that could defeat all other combinations in simple pairwise voting. For more details, see Lacy and Niou (2000).
42. See Lacy and Niou (2000) for an example from voting on the Internet.
43. Some would argue that this is not a surprising result since $2^{28} = 268.4$ million. Therefore, most combinations would receive no votes. This is all true, but it does not affect the paradox. Deciding on propositions singly may or may not yield a combination of propositions that are favorable to a majority of people. Marco Scarsini shows that even the slates similar to the winning slate may receive no votes. See "A Strong Paradox of Multiple Elections," *Social Choice and Welfare* 15 (1998): 237–38.
44. Lucius J. Barker and Twiley W. Barker Jr., *Civil Liberties and the Constitution: Cases and Commentaries,* 2nd ed. (Englewood Cliffs, NJ: Prentice Hall, 1975), 369.
45. *Reitman v. Mulkey,* 387 U.S. 369 (1967).

46. Shaun Bowler and Todd Donovan, "Direct Democracy and Minority Rights," *American Journal of Political Science* 42 (1998): 1020–24.
47. Walker (1983).
48. Osha Gray Davidson, "Guns and Poses" (*The New Republic*, October 11, 1993), 12. Also see Davidson's *Under Fire: The NRA and the Battle for Gun Control* (1993).
49. William P. Browne, "Lobbying the Public: All-Directional Advocacy," in *Interest Group Politics*, eds. Allan J. Cigler and Burdett A. Loomis (Washington, D.C.: CQ Press, 1998).

~9~

Elections, Groups, and Money

Introduction

The last three chapters analyzed both direct and grassroots lobbying. Elected officials are the ultimate targets of any direct or indirect lobbying effort. A lobbyist might try to change a legislator's mind to secure new-found support, or a lobbyist might try to encourage a legislator to stay the course and refuse to yield to pressure from the opposition. Sometimes lobbyists simply try to turn erstwhile supporters into more active supporters.[1] In any event, such lobbying efforts are costly. Suppose, however, groups could simply ensure that the right legislators were elected in the first place. If the right legislators were elected, then lobbying efforts might not be necessary; or if they were still necessary, they might be much less costly. Groups' roles in elections create another avenue for influence, supplementing and extending lobbying influence.

Often interest group influence is viewed with suspicion, but disgust over campaign money linked to organized interests is perhaps most common. Disgust over campaign-finance methods led a ninety-year-old great grandmother to raise awareness of the issue by trekking across the entire United States. Mrs. Haddock refers to herself as Granny D—the D represents democracy. After fourteen months and 3,200 miles of walking, Granny D arrived in Washington, D.C. For Mrs. Haddock, large unregulated donations, known generally as soft money, are ruining American democracy. In her view big money dwarfs little money, thereby limiting the impact of one person one vote, and only by "reforming" campaign finance can one preserve that central tenet of democracy. Upon arriving in Washington, in the spring of 2000, Granny D spoke as a true populist. "If I have offended you . . . that is as it should be. You have offended America . . . You have somewhere on your desks, under the love letters from your greedy friends and co-conspirators against representative democracy, a modest bill against soft money. Pass it."[2]

On March 27, 2002, Granny D's pleas were answered by President Bush's signing of the McCain-Feingold legislation, banning soft-money contributions to political parties.

Why are we so sensitive to campaign contributions and less sensitive to other forms of political activity? Overall, the campaign finance system is highly regulated, and much more regulated than any other form of political activism. As one scholar stated, "it is curious [that] . . . strong legal restrictions are imposed on the sources and levels of support for electioneering but not on those for [court] litigation, legislative lobbying, administrative lobbying, public education, or any other political activity."[3] Why the discrepancy? First, U.S. citizens are taught to admire and even revere their electoral system. Other aspects of government may be suspect, but elections are not. Second, most people do not like the idea of money corrupting any sort of competition or contest—political or not. This chapter highlights the role of money in elections. Who can and who cannot give? How is campaign money regulated? Why is it sometimes left unregulated? What are the distinctions between regulated and unregulated money? What are the effects of the campaign contributions and campaign finance regulations? Does the cliche about a level playing field fit or does big money indeed dominant?

A Brief History of Money and Elections

Elections have never been free of money. Campaigning costs money. The questions are who should provide the money, and is the recipient of the money beholden to the contributor of the money? The federal government has regulated money in elections for almost one hundred years. Although it is difficult to declare definitively, concern about money and elections was probably first linked to the growth of large trusts and corporations after the Civil War. Thomas Nast, the nineteenth-century political cartoonist, often caricatured the power and influence of large corporate donors to legislators' coffers. The drive to restrict corporate influence began in the late 1800s, but it was not until 1907 that the Tillman Act forbade all corporate contributions to federal campaigns. The Tillman Act, however, had no effect on state elections, and the federal–state distinction was important because U.S. senators were still elected by their state's assemblies. Indeed, the corrupting influence of money in state legislatures led many people to prefer the direct election of U.S. senators. In 1910, 1911, and 1925 federal legislation limiting spending on elections and requiring the disclosure of large contributors was passed. However, these acts, including the 1925 Corrupt Practices Act, had little impact on either contributors or candidates. Though Congress passed the acts, it did not pass legislation to establish any sort of enforcement agency to implement the laws. The end result was that these acts had no real effect.[4]

There were, however, important congressional actions limiting the ability to raise money from government workers and limiting the role of unions in elections. The Hatch Acts of 1939 and 1940 limited political party fundraising among government employees and forbade individual contributions of more than $5,000 to any sort of national campaign committee or federal candidate. These acts were considered important tools for limiting the possibility of returning to corrupt patronage systems. World War II–era legislation also affected numerous aspects of unions' activities. The Smith-Connally Act of 1943 prohibited strikes and restricted union campaign money.[5] The Taft-Hartley Act of 1947 made the wartime provisions of Smith-Connally permanent. Neither unions nor corporations were to contribute money to federal campaigns. John Lewis, the head of the CIO (the Congress of Industrial Organizations), had shown a steady interest in campaign politics throughout his career.[6] In his view, labor struggles were ultimately electoral struggles.[7] The same year that the Smith-Connally Act became law, the CIO created what it called the CIO-PAC. PAC is an acronym for political action committee. Technically, PACs are neither interest groups nor corporations. PACs are organizations that are established to work in and influence electoral politics. Interest groups and corporations engage in numerous activities that have nothing to do with electoral politics. In contrast, PACs only engage in electoral politics. Though affiliated with the CIO, the CIO-PAC was separate and segregated from the union itself so that it was not in violation of the Smith-Connally Act.

There were, to say the least, very fuzzy legal lines surrounding campaign fundraising in the early and mid-1900s. Union and corporate contributions continued, however furtively. Unions skirted the laws by arguing that the CIO-PAC and later the AFL-CIO's Committee on Political Education (COPE) raised funds that were entirely separate and segregated from general union coffers. Union dues went into one account and COPE contributions went into a separate account. Not all union members necessarily contributed to COPE and not all COPE contributors were necessarily union members. A corporation could remain electorally active by coordinating the efforts and contributions of corporate officials. Indeed, corporate officials honed the strategy of bundling individuals' contributions. Rather than receiving a check from the corporate accounts, a candidate might receive a bundle of contributions from a large number of officers from the same corporation. Technically, the contributions were from individuals, but clearly corporate officials coordinated the contribution effort. Indeed, corporate structures facilitate this sort of fund-raising. If the chief officer at a meeting pulls out her checkbook and declares that she is supporting a particular candidate, the hint to others attending the meeting is obvious. Alexander Heard, a longtime scholar of money in elections, repeatedly noted the ease with which some interests could raise money.[8] Indeed, from time to time letters from corporate heads detailing such efforts have been leaked to the public. The message from bundling is clear: whoever bundled the checks was driving the money-raising efforts.

Usually when one reads or writes about PACs, the focus is on the period from the 1970s to the present.[9] The early union PACs are overlooked, not because they were unimportant, but because records on early PAC activity are not readily available. The wealth of publicly available data on PAC contributions is linked directly to the 1971 and 1974 Federal Election Campaign Acts (FECA). The 1971 act established individual contribution limits and explicitly allowed for the establishment of separate and segregated funds—or PACs.[10] Individuals could contribute $1,000 per candidate per election and $5,000 per PAC, the PACs themselves could contribute $5,000 per candidate per election, and the language "separate and segregated" had the imprimatur of law. Two points deserve attention: (1) primaries, general elections, and run-offs are all treated as separate elections, and (2) the term PAC is informal and does not have the imprimatur of law. Campaign finance laws use the term SSF, separate segregated fund, not PAC. The 1971 legislation did not, however, restrict the establishment of separate and segregated funds (SSFs) to unions, and corporations slowly began to take advantage of their new political opportunities. The slow growth in corporate PACs (or SSFs) was a direct consequence of the continuing restrictions on campaign activity for any corporation with federal government contracts. That limitation, similar in spirit to the Hatch Act, limited corporate activity considerably. The government has hundreds of contracts with private corporations. The explosion in the number of corporate PACs began after the 1974 FECA legislation, which lifted the ban on government contractors. The 1974 act also created the the Federal Election Commission (FEC), to implement and oversee these new electoral laws. As described in Chapter 7, bureaucratic agencies promulgate various rulings as they implement congressional mandates, and so the FEC itself has greatly affected campaign finance in the United States. For instance, when the Sun Oil Company sought a clarification from the FEC on various matters related to the 1974 legislation, the FEC made one of its most important rulings ever. In 1975 the FEC ruled that administrative and fund-raising costs for a PAC could be covered by the parent organization. This ruling opened the proverbial floodgates, and corporate PACs exploded in number. Corporations could use their own funds and resources to raise money for their PACs. PACs affiliated with a union or a corporation were technically separate and segregated, but in reality they were intimately connected. Corporate and union PACs had little to worry about—all expenses could be covered by the parent organization.

Who Forms PACs?

Pluralists and group scholars have long asked who gets represented. That question was asked in one form or another in almost every one of the preceding chapters. Who forms PACs and who is represented by these PACs? Is the PAC environment representative of many interests or is it biased toward a few interests? The most important distinction for PACs is whether they are connected or nonconnected.

Connected versus nonconnected PACs

The FEC's Sun Oil ruling amplified a distinction that was already in existence, namely, the distinction between nonconnected and connected PACs. Nonconnected PACs have no parent organization to look to for support. Nonconnected PACs must start from scratch, often employing the lengthy and costly direct mail tactics explained in Chapter 3. Nonconnected PACs have to resolve a collective-action problem. Connected PACs have a much easier life. Their parent organization can cover *all* overhead costs of the PAC. Salaries and accounting and legal fees are covered by the parent institution. Even the fund-raising itself is easier for a connected PAC. A union or corporate PAC already has an established house list: their members, employees, and stockholders. Unions and corporations can also use a check-off system by which means a regular contribution is drawn directly from a paycheck. Securing check-off approval for automatic withdrawal is generally easier than securing separate contributions each month. With automatic withdrawals, the PAC is less vulnerable to members' forgetfulness. In addition, the check-off system is deemed relatively painless by contributors. In sum, solving a collective-action problem is easier when a parent organization covers virtually all of the costs and maintains a pre-established house list.

In the world of connected PACs, there are PACs affiliated with interest groups, unions, and corporations, but the corporate PACs dominate. There are various ways to illustrate this. First, only six to seven percent of citizen-based PACs are connected, whereas over ninety percent of the corporate and union PACs are connected. Second, as seen in Table 9.1, among all PACs, connected and nonconnected, the connected PACs dominate.

Still, not all corporations form PACs. Firms that are most able to work by themselves in a particular market niche are more apt to form a PAC. Firms in this situation do not face a collective-action or freerider problem. Strong trade associations may not be established. Firms in industries that are heavily regulated and firms that rely on government contracts are also more apt to form PACs.[11]

Disadvantages for citizen-based PACs

Thomas Gais analyzed the PAC environment in a very clever way.[12] Gais compared the PAC environment with the environment of organized interests first discussed in Chapter 2. The membership associations discussed in Chapter 2 were grouped into two broad categories: those that were occupationally

TABLE 9.1
Percentage of PACs Registered by Legal Affiliation, 1978–1992

| | | | | *Election Year* | | | | |
Legal Affiliation	1978	1980	1982	1984	1986	1988	1990	1992
All Connected	87	83	75	74	72	72	72	71
Corporate	42	45	42	42	42	42	42	41
Trade	28	23	18	17	17	18	17	18
Labor	14	12	11	10	9	8	8	8
Other	2	3	4	4	4	5	4	4
All Nonconnected	13	17	25	26	28	28	28	29
Total Number	1,949	2,785	3,722	4,347	4,596	4,832	4,677	4,729

Note: Adding all connected to all nonconnected yields the total number. The connected are broken down further into corporate, trade, labor, and other categories.

Source: Reproduced from Gais (1996), Table 3.1, p. 49.

based and those that were nonoccupational, citizen-based groups. The occupationally based groups were further broken down according to the economic sector of the members. That is, were the members working in the profit-oriented, nonprofit-oriented, or mixed sectors? Gais then asked, "Given what we know about the environment of associations and groups, how does the PAC environment compare?" One of the things that we know about the interest group environment is that the collective-action problem is easier for some groups to overcome than it is for others. Though empirically minded, Gais did more than just survey the PAC community. He took the collective-action problem seriously. Gais asked whether the small numbers of citizen-based PACs can be linked to the collective-action problem.

The general rationale behind all campaign finance regulations has been the need, real or perceived, to give the little guy a chance. In the PAC community, the little guy is the citizen-based PAC forced to confront the collective-action problem. Not surprisingly, connected PACs have an easier time overcoming the collective-action problem. That alone might create some bias in the PAC community. However, nonconnected PACs face additional hurdles because the common solutions to the collective-action problem are not available to them. Recall from Chapter 2 the importance of patrons for interest group formation. Connected PACs have patrons by definition, and ninety percent of the time these patrons are either corporations or unions. Nonconnected PACs are prohibited from developing patron support. Individuals' contributions are capped at $5,000. Would patron support make any difference? Are not all the big contributions linked to corporations? The short answer to the second question is that citizen-based PACs rely more heavily on big contributors than any other type of PAC. From Table 9.2, one can see that citizen-based PACs received over a third of their funds from large contributions (defined as $500 or more). In contrast, connected PACs linked to the profit sector received only about sixteen percent of their revenue from large donations. Citizen-based PACs rely on big contributions to minimize their shortfalls.

TABLE 9.2
PAC Reliance on Large Contributions

Institutional Base	Percentage of PACs that are Separate Segregated Funds (Connected)	Mean Percentage of Contributions in Amounts Greater Than $500.00	Number of Cases
Profit Sector	94.3	16.2	1,565
Mixed Sector	93.8	1.6	16
Nonprofit Sector	81.3	.6	32
Labor	99.2	.5	244
Citizen	6.9	35	333
All PACs	81.4	17	2,190

Source: Reproduced from Gais (1996), Table 3.9, p. 71.

Interest groups might be natural patrons for some nonconnected PACs, but groups and organizations with tax-deductible status (501(c)(3)) may not use any of their resources to establish SSFs. Many research institutes, schools, charities, and interest groups enjoy the benefits of 501(c)(3) tax status, but that status means that they must forgo electoral activities. Indeed, a 501(c)(3) organization cannot even use funds to engage in any sort of partisan communications with its own members. Of course, 501(c)(4) organizations can engage in lobbying because they have no tax-deductible status. These 501(c)(4) organizations could then form SSFs. However, even the 501(c)(4) groups face unusual hurdles. By law, the 501(c)(4) groups may not encourage contributions or thank contributors with any form of selective incentive.[13] In sum, the only way for 501(c)(3) organizations to play a role in electoral politics is to establish a 501(c)(4) organization, which then creates an SSF. However, the 501(c)(4) organization may not use any selective incentives as inducements for contributing to the PAC.

Given such hurdles for citizen-based PACs, it is not too surprising that they are very weak by some measures. Three measures help one to assess a

PAC's strength or weakness: debt, longevity, and total receipts. Citizen-based PACs are weak on all counts. They are more likely to be debt ridden, they are less likely to survive from one campaign cycle to the next, and they are least likely to have receipts in excess of $10,000. Nonconnected PACs do, however, show certain strengths. Although about two-thirds of all PACs are linked to the profit sector, PACs from the profit sector generally raise less than half of the PAC receipts. However, rough equality in contributions need not lead to equality of interest representation if expenditures are unequal, and Gais made this point repeatedly. Just because two PACs receive the same amount of funds does not mean they disburse the same amount. Although they raise less than half the total PAC receipts, profit sector PACs account for over half of all PAC expenditures. Because their costs are entirely absorbed by their parent organization, profit sector PACs can distribute more of what they raise. Nonconnected PACs are much less efficient at distributing their resources to candidates than connected ones because nonconnected PACs have to cover their own operating expenses.[14]

Ostensibly, the 1971 and 1974 FEC legislation was meant to allow the little guy a voice. However, by ignoring the collective-action problem for nonconnected PACs, legislative proposals have created a campaign-finance system with little autonomy. There is little autonomy because "PACs do not create wholly new collections of individuals . . . as much as they build on" and amplify existing organized interests.[15] Those interests that are amplified the greatest are tied to institutions or organizations that manage the collective-action problems associated with PACs.

Unions and corporations benefit the most, whereas citizen-based groups suffer the most. Though campaign finance is highly regulated, there is still considerable dissatisfaction with the results. What are the most basic reasons for the dissatisfaction? First, FEC legislation was oriented around organized interests, so it was nonmajoritarian from the start. Nonmajoritarian influences are not generically bad or good. We promote nonmajoritarian influence in various aspects of U.S. politics. By the same token, however, many people are unsettled by any nonmajoritarian electoral structure. Second, campaign-finance laws amplify the biases that already exist in the group environment. Organized interests are unlikely to forgo the pursuit of their self-interests in electoral politics. The question is whether one can structure rules affecting the organized interests' activities in electoral politics in a simple straightforward way.

Cash Flow: Who Gets PAC Money?

Who is represented by the PAC environment is, of course, only one part of the concern about PAC influence. There is a second element central to the issue of money and electoral politics. Who gets the money? In a classic text from the 1930s, Harold Lasswell argued that politics could be understood by assessing who gets what, when, and how.[16] Although Lasswell wrote long before PAC influence raised so many concerns, his simple aphorism seems particularly appropriate for this section. After all, the concerns about interest group influence are marked by who gets contributions, when, and how.

What sort of candidate gets PAC money? PAC money is most important to House candidates, accounting for approximately one-third of all House candidates' campaign receipts. PAC contributions account for about one-fifth of all senate candidates' funds. The balance of funds is generally raised from individuals—including contributions from the candidates themselves. At the presidential level, public funding through matching grants is crucial for most candidates, readily overwhelming the importance of direct PAC contributions. However, organized interests, as distinguished from PACs, do not simply sit out the presidential elections.[17] For instance, the two contenders for the White House in 2000 each raised over half a million dollars during 1999 from individual lobbyists. However, of the total amount raised by Vice President Gore ($27 million), only two percent could be linked to registered lobbyists. Of Governor Bush's $67 million raised, only 0.8 percent was linked to registered lobbyists.[18] PACs' most important and influential roles at the presidential level develop indirectly. Since 1979, limits on contributions to political parties for get-out-the-vote drives, voter education, and general party-building efforts were lifted. During presidential election years, the fates of a party and its presidential candidate are closely tied, so the major parties and their candidates work hard to build their party's coffers. Prior to the recent adoption of McCain-Feingold, these soft-money party contributions were unlimited, and millions of dollars were raised. Although the contributions were made to a party, the parties structured their voter education and mobilization drives to highlight the strengths of their own candidates and the weaknesses of the other party's candidates. Given the coordinated efforts between a party and its major candidates, many people—including Granny D—viewed unlimited soft-money contributions as nothing more than a gaping loophole in campaign finance law.

Increasingly, PACs and interest groups spend their money independently, avoiding direct contributions to candidates. That is, a group may engage in an independent issue advocacy campaign, promoting one policy stand over another, while never contributing to or communicating with a candidate directly. Once again, voter education is the stated goal, but it is often difficult to distinguish voter education from voter mobilization efforts—especially when the policy stand advocated by the group is also advocated by one of the candidates. Issue advocacy advertisements raise the most suspicion when they are overly negative in tone, attacking a particular candidate.[19] It is difficult to judge the impact of issue advocacy campaigns, but the candidates themselves view them as effective, either providing great help or creating a great hindrance.[20] One of the most recent empirical analyses of an independent issue advocacy campaign focused on the AFL-CIO's voter-education drive in the 1996 U.S. House elections. The results from that study suggested that the AFL-CIO voter-education drives were effective against freshman House Republicans, but not more senior Republicans.[21] Of course, in the end, Republicans retained the House despite the efforts of the AFL-CIO.

Direct PAC contributions play the greatest role in U.S. House elections, which provide the primary focus of the next two sections.

Cash and the congressional context

The institutional context that is so important for direct lobbying, as discussed in Chapter 6, is also important for electoral contributions. Many contributors focus as much on a member's institutional positions as they do on a member's ideology or voting record. Chairmanships of key committees or subcommittees and leadership positions can be very valuable characteristics for fund-raising purposes. Money generally follows influence, and in the U.S. Congress leaders and committee chairs have more influence than other members.[22] Indeed, as members' committee assignments change, so too do contribution patterns.[23] Particular examples are easy to find. Former Senator Alfonse D'Amato (R-N.Y.) was never a slacker when it came to raising campaign funds, but his ascendance to the chairmanship of the Senate Banking Committee led to even greater contributions, making his "previous fundraising seem almost pedestrian."[24] At times, his reelection coffers were the largest in the Senate. Chairing the Banking Committee gave him an enviable position and allowed him to make small amendments to banking legislation that could have a huge impact on financial institutions. From the time of his ascendance, the MBNA Corporation, a leader in the credit card industry, channeled over $500,000 to campaign committees headed by D'Amato.[25]

The greatest PAC windfall is bestowed on majority party leaders. The majority party dominates the chamber and each committee and subcommittee. It controls all the most important leadership positions. If money follows influence, then the majority party members should do quite well. As it turns out, majority party status is worth about $36,000 in PAC contributions for House members, even after controlling for voting records.[26] For a new Speaker of the House, the windfall can be much larger. Dennis Hastert (R-Ill.) was not especially well known prior to his sudden ascendance to Speaker in 1999. In all of 1998, Hastert raised about $85,000, but after becoming Speaker he was able to raise $200,000 in just one week.[27]

It would be unfair and inaccurate to say that all PACs pursue influential members and ignore basic ideological issues such as a member's party affiliation or voting records. Nonconnected PACs tend to be more ideologically oriented and more willing to focus on policy positions.[28] However, as noted earlier, the PAC environment is dominated by connected PACs, so the behaviors of nonconnected PACs do not set the tone for the overall fundraising environment.

Cash and the electoral context

The most important congressional context that affects the flow of PAC money has not yet been introduced. Although it is obvious, it is important to remember that not all candidates have positions in the U.S. House of Representatives. Challengers do not have the luxuries of wide name recognition or House committee positions, causing their fund-raising to suffer considerably. Indeed, one of the greatest fears related to PACs stems from the strongest trend in PAC giving: PAC contributions flow predominantly to incumbents. The disparities between PAC contributions to incumbents and challengers is so large that many fear that the PAC system simply reinforces the incumbency advantages already in place. Since World War II, long before the rise of the present PAC system, House incumbents who chose to run for reelection were successful more than ninety percent of the time. When aggregate PAC contributions to incumbents dwarf contributions to challengers, that incumbency advantage increases. Why is there an incumbency advantage in PAC contributions? Four different angles are developed to highlight the varied strategic concerns related to PAC contributions.[29] Although these approaches are not mutually exclusive, their theoretical foundations are sufficiently distinct to merit separate attention.

Nolan McCarty and Lawrence Rothenberg's analysis begins with the assumption that contributions are used to secure either favorable election outcomes or access to the winning candidate's offices.[30] That is, PACs' strategic concerns are simple. They can contribute to gain access to the winner's office after the election, or they can contribute to secure the election of the right candidate so that access is no longer an issue. For clarity of argument, McCarty and Rothenberg suggest that there are two different goods that PACs may attempt to purchase. The first good, access, is a private good. As noted in the second chapter, private goods are excludable and they have rivalrous consumption. That is, if a PAC can buy access, then it is buying a private good over which it has complete control. The idea is that no one secures access to an elected official because of someone *else's* contribution. The second good a PAC may buy, electoral success, is a public good because it is characterized by nonexcludability and nonrival consumption. The benefit that one person receives from a candidate's election does not affect any other person's benefits, and no person can be excluded from the benefits. Public goods are, however, vulnerable to freeriding. Any PAC's effort to elect the right candidate allows others to freeride on those efforts. McCarty and Rothenberg argue that the purchase of electoral outcomes is an unlikely goal for PACs, not because it is amoral, but because it is a public good. If PACs are as devious and conniving as newspaper accounts might lead one to believe, then they would certainly avoid attempts to buy public goods and would prefer investing in private goods whenever possible. If access is indeed the overarching goal, then the actual occupant is less important than your own access to that occupant. If one simply desires access, then betting on and contributing to an incumbent, rather than a challenger, is the best strategy.

John Wright evaluates the access versus electoral success issue somewhat differently than did McCarty and Rothenberg. Wright notes that the costs of campaigning have dramatically increased, but that these costs have not affected challengers and incumbents in the same way. The candidates who are in greatest need of expensive television and radio time are the challengers, not the incumbents who already have name recognition. The challengers need the money, but the incumbents get it. One might argue that donors are sensitive to the marginal impact of their contribution on a candidate's ability to be successful. It is well established that incumbents can attract more voters with small expenditures than challengers can. Wright, however, makes a different claim. He argues that the cost of access has increased more slowly than the cost of electoral success for a challenger. Therefore, the cost of access is cheaper and cheaper relative to the costs associated with campaigning, and the contributions simply flow where their marginal impact is greatest.[31] Once again, if access is the goal, then one must bet on and contribute to incumbents.

James Snyder takes a very different approach to PAC contributions.[32] Snyder argues that different types of PACs are motivated by different goals. Ideologically oriented, citizen-based PACs should operate differently than corporate or labor PACs. Snyder, therefore, distinguishes "ideological" PACs from "investor" PACs. Citizen-based ideological PACs are less concerned about access and are more concerned about having the right issues receive their due attention. Ideological PACs are beholden to ideas, not access to incumbents. Investor PACs provide a different story. Investor PACs seek regular channels of access and are willing to make long-term investments to solidify their access. Incumbents secure the bulk of PAC contributions because investor PACs dominate the PAC environment, as Gais has illustrated, and investor PACs seek long-term access that incumbents can best provide.

Frank J. Sorauf simply contends that incumbents became more aggressive in their pursuit of PAC money.[33] At some point, "buddy can you spare a dime" changed to "show me the money." Indeed, many scholars are now suggesting that legislators are as much responsible as PACs for the current state of campaign finance.[34] Consider, for instance, that legislators write the campaign-finance laws and control the access to their own offices. Access cannot be bought by PACs unless legislators are selling it. Basically, some scholars accuse legislators of shaking down PACs for money. How does such pressure for contributions really work? Legislators cannot simply demand money from PACs, but PAC employees do often suggest that campaign staffs have fund-raising "'down to a science.'"[35]

Incumbents' fund-raising benefits from two conditions not explicitly detailed by Sorauf. First, if groups and PACs develop long-term relationships with legislators, then the PACs are vulnerable to what economists affectionately call a *hold-up potential.*[36] The generic hold-up occurs as follows: Suppose someone makes a long-term investment in a very nice car, a computer designed for a specialized operating system, or a specialized manufacturing device. After the initial investment is made, one still has to purchase operating supplies and perform some simple maintenance or repairs. To retool the manufacturing equipment, learn a new operating system, or buy a new car takes time and money. Of course, the suppliers for operating and maintenance equipment and repair parts know this, so they are in a position to charge a little more for their unique goods and services. Depending on the transaction costs associated with making a change, the hold-up potential can be considerable. The higher the transaction costs, the higher the hold-up potential. How does such a hold-up occur with PACs? Incumbency advantage and the control of access to the policy process put legislators in an enviable position. To work long and hard to unseat incumbents is very expensive, as Wright noted, and risky. To maintain access is a less expensive, defensive strategy.[37] Legislators can be more aggressive in their fund-raising because the high costs associated with electing challengers creates a hold-up potential for incumbents.

In addition to the hold-up potential, incumbents may benefit from another condition: access is not a pure private good because there is the possibility of a crowding effect. That is, a legislator has only twenty-four hours in a day, so not all contributors can secure access at any given time. There is a crowding effect if a contributor is lost in the shuffle due to the large number of other contributors. Anecdotal evidence suggests that contributors seek to match the contributions of their potential rivals for access. Candidates typically use very simple actions to signal information to their contributors so that everyone gets to know what everyone else has contributed. The seating assignments at gala campaign events are hardly random. The more one contributes, the closer that individual is seated to the person of the moment. Even at informal affairs, such information is sometimes signaled. The reelection committee for former Representative Dan Rostenkowski (D-Ill.) provided different colored "Rosty" pins at a mix and mingle. The pins' colors—white, red, or blue—signified the level of contribution made by the pin's wearer.[38]

One way for a contributor to stand apart from the crowd is to give more. Most PAC contributions fall well below the $5,000 limit per election, so it is not clear that the crowding effect has yet affected many contributors. If an incumbent legislator was already overbooked, PACs used to be able to make soft-money contributions to a party to show their interest. Prior to the passage of the McCain-Feingold legislation, there were those who contended that soft-money contributions to parties were less and less voluntary. An interest group called the Committee for Economic Development, comprising officers from standard corporations such as Merck and General Motors, had been publicizing the issue, using both insider and outsider tactics. In a *New*

York Times op-ed piece, Edward A. Kangas, chairman of Deloitte Touche Tohmatsu and a member of the committee, made the following points:

> (1) It is hard to say no to a request for a contribution because the financial success of one's company may be linked to governmental action or inaction. (2) Fund-raisers "make sure you know that your competitors have contributed, implying that you should pay a toll in Washington to stay competitive." (3) Corporate donations are not made as "gestures of good will or for ideological reasons. Corporations are thinking of the bottom line. Will the contribution help or hurt the company?"[39]

Senator McConnell (R-Ky.) wrote to ten members of the Committee for Economic Development, urging the business executives to resign from the group. McConnell suggested that it would be impossible for the Republican Party to hold forth against antibusiness proposals without soft-money contributions to its own coffers.[40] Given that soft-money contributions have now been eliminated, McConnell's contention can be tested.

Effects of Group Money on Elections

Increasingly, campaigns are viewed as being composed of two crucial elements: attracting contributions and attracting votes. From a purely strategic standpoint, candidates may shift their platforms to secure contributions if those contributions can then be used to attract votes. Big contributors secure the platform shifts, and candidates secure the contributions that can then be used to advertise to the more traditional voters.[41] Elections are costly, so candidates may have a difficult time ignoring the big contributors. How might a focus on big contributors affect the representation of interests? John Wright investigated one means by which PAC money in congressional elections might distort the representation of interests.[42] Wright's analysis began with the simple observation that PACs and groups represent functional interests—teachers, farmers, environmentalists, and so forth—but members and senators represent geographic areas that encompass diverse interests. PACs are essentially asking the recipients of their contributions to consider functional representation rather than geographic representation. Do PAC contributions reinforce functional representation and distort or undermine geographical representation? Wright found that PACs focused their efforts on members who came from districts wherein the group had a strong organizational presence. That is, the geographic and functional interests largely coincided.

PAC money does affect the ability of candidates to appear competitive. It is difficult to run any sort of race for elective office without spending money on campaign materials and advertisements. Contributors, whether they are PACs or individuals or parties, pay some attention to a candidate's actual prospects for winning, and the ability to raise PAC money early in a campaign is considered one indicator of a candidate's viability. There is some evidence that successful fund-raising early on makes fund-raising later easier. Emily's List is a nonconnected PAC that developed its name from the dynamics of campaign finance. Emily is an acronym for Early Money Is Like Yeast (it makes the dough rise).

Can campaign money really buy citizens' support in the voting booth? Although the debates about the links between campaign expenditures and electoral fates are rich and detailed, the main thing to focus on is that contributions lead to visibility and visibility leads to votes.[43] More money and more advertisements yield more votes. Early money for little-known challengers is especially important.[44] However, indirect effects also exist. Large campaign chests can scare off potential challengers, leaving incumbents the good fortune of having relatively weak or inexperienced challengers.[45] Many candidates establish war chests, large amounts of campaign money that they do not actually spend. Such war chests provide legislators considerable discretion in their Washington activities. For instance, if large war chests scare off strong challengers, then legislators have more leeway to vote as they see fit, regardless of the current cycle of campaign contributions. Legislators with large campaign chests can also curry favor within the chamber by redistributing funds to other less fortunate party members. As a final note, PACs do seem to know who needs the money the most. Those U.S. Senate candidates who do receive PAC money are apt to use it rather than save it to develop some sort of campaign war chest. PACs prefer contributing to those legislators who need the money. Legislators who do not have the cushion of a war chest are desperate for cash, and they also, presumably, have less discretion in their Washington activities.[46]

Vote Buying in the House

Efforts to find empirical evidence of the influence of money on legislators' votes have yielded mixed results. Though some influence is found on some issues,[47] just as often scholars find that money has limited direct influence on legislators' votes,[48] or they argue that contributions are most useful as predictors of access rather than votes.[49] In one of the few analyses of the effects of lobbying contacts and contributions, successful lobbying efforts were found to follow contributions. This analysis found that the number of lobbying contacts made with a legislator was more important than contributions to a legislator.[50] Lobbying patterns of groups seem to mimic the contribution patterns of groups, but the lobbying appears to be most influential.[51] Recent work has also shown that PAC access to legislators does not curtail constituents' access.[52] Indeed, the constituency link remains particularly helpful when trying to gain access to a legislator's office. One can only conclude that money may not be the most effective currency when seeking access or lobby-ing for legislators' votes.

Why is it so difficult to find evidence of vote buying? David Austen-Smith (1993) developed a formal model of the legislator–lobbyist interaction that suggests that lobbyists are often better off attempting to alter a congressional agenda rather than buy a legislator's vote.[53] That is, we may have looked for influence in the wrong areas of congressional activity. Empirical work by Richard Hall and Frank Wayman appears to lend some support to Austen-Smith's main conclusions.[54] Hall and Wayman found that monetary contri-butions were most closely related to legislators' efforts or "legislators' in-volvement" rather than their votes. PAC contributions appear to affect legislators' efforts, inspiring advocacy for an issue rather than simple acquies-cence. Money does not seem to change minds, but it may change a legisla-tor's level of effort.[55]

William Mitchell and Michael Munger provide a nice synthesis of some of the issues discussed so far.[56] Mitchell and Munger make three observations. First, they argue that untoward interest group activity is less likely when con-stituents are well informed. Second, they note that congressional scholars generally agree that members of the U.S. House seek particular committee assignments, at least in part, to serve their constituents' interests. Finally, they discuss a point raised here earlier: committee memberships affect how and where legislators raise campaign funds. The last observation allows legis-lators to raise campaign funds from PACs, but the first two observations work together to limit the likelihood of undue influence or vote buying.

Conclusion

The area of campaign finance is ever changing. New legislation, FEC rulings, and Court decisions affect campaign finance on a yearly or even monthly ba-sis, ensuring that campaign-finance strategies are ever changing as candidates and PACs seek new ways to raise funds. Campaign finance is also an area where virtually everyone is a reformer, because few people are perfectly satis-fied with the present campaign-finance system.

The first real attempt to limit contributions occurred in the 1970s. Re-formers of that era wanted to ensure that small contributions would not be crowded out by large contributions. Originally, the FECA statutes limited contributions from groups, parties, and individuals and expenditures by can-didates; but in 1976 in *Buckley v. Valeo,* the Supreme Court ruled that limita-tions on expenditures violated first amendment rights.[57] To mandate any sort of financial constraints on expenditures related to electoral challenges jeop-ardized free speech in electoral politics. The Court, however, upheld limita-tions on contributions, arguing in part that a lack of any limit on contribu-tions would infringe on the first amendment rights of small contributors. Big money would drown out small money. Furthermore, the Court reasoned, the $1,000 limit on contributions did not render the political activity of big-time contributors meaningless. In consideration of contributions, the Court sought to balance the first amendment rights of small and large contributors.

At various times, the federal courts have ruled on issues related to the FECA statutes or the *Buckley v. Valeo* decision. In 1998, the United States Court of Appeals for the Eighth Circuit struck down the $300 limits in Arkansas' statewide races. In 1996, Arkansas voters had approved a referendum to limit individual contributions to $300 for most statewide races and $100 for judicial contests. The Eighth Circuit argued that such limits were "'too low to allow meaningful participation.'"[58] Small contributors might not have been affected, but large contributors were, and the balance between large and small contributors was deemed inappropriate. The Supreme Court was asked to revisit the issue, but it declined to hear the appeal. The federal courts have consistently accepted the $1,000 limits, but not necessarily lower limits, even for state rather than federal races. The Supreme Court has, however, ruled that the $1,000 limits established in the 1970s remain a reasonable upper limit, even though their current inflation-adjusted value is about $400.[59] The federal courts also appear willing to let candidate expenditures remain unlimited.[60] In 1998, the Supreme Court declined to reassess circuit court rulings that rejected attempts to limit a candidate's expenditures.[61]

Given most people's visceral reactions to PACs, it is worth repeating a few general points from the chapter because the myths and the realities surrounding PACs are distinctly different.[62] For instance, it is especially easy to lose sight of the simple fact that the sums of individuals' contributions typically exceed PAC contributions.[63] Simply put, most campaign money comes from small, individual contributions. In addition, electoral contributions are not at the forefront of political activity for groups or corporations. Groups and corporations generally spend more money on lobbying than on electoral activity. For instance, there has long been a sense that corporations prefer less visible strategies to more visible strategies, but now the evidence is particularly strong. Corporate spending on lobbying is higher than corporate spending on PAC giving, which in turn is higher than corporate spending on charities and nonprofits.[64] This pattern of spending is true for established Washington players and for newcomers. New, burgeoning industries fighting to catch up with Washington politics also favor lobbying over electioneering. By most standards the high-tech companies are behind in the Washington influence game, and at present they are beefing up their lobbying much more quickly and substantially than their campaign contributions.[65] Campaign contributions are just one way to affect public policies, and, as one scholar forcefully stated, "it is ridiculous to identify PACs as the center of 'special interest' spending."[66]

Even after separating the myths from the realities, many people remain reform minded when it comes to campaign finance. Many novel proposals have been made, but few, if any, implemented. Some reform proposals focus on the high costs of televison advertising and recommend regulating air time for the candidates to ensure greater access.[67] Other reforms explore the possible use of campaign vouchers to ensure that every eligible voter has the same amount of voucher money to distribute among the various candidates for office.[68] Finally, one's reform efforts need not be merely academic proposals. Given the heated arguments related to campaign finance, one might wonder how best to affect FECA statutes and FEC rulings. One could pursue policy change through the FEC, Congress, or the courts. In the preceding chapter, the issue of standing was addressed. Could an ordinary citizen secure legal standing simply because of incredible disgruntlement with campaign finance? Taxpayer lawsuits are seldom recognized when individuals have general grievances, rather than proof of direct harm. However, in *FEC v. Akins*, 524 U.S. 11 (1998), the Supreme Court ruled that voters have an inherent interest in the operation of the Federal Election Commission. Voting is the bare bone standard for standing when it comes to campaign finance.

NOTES

1. See, for instance, Hall and Wayman (1990).
2. "Backers Hope Presidential Race Confers Front-Burner Status on Campaign Finance Overhaul" (*CQ Weekly*, March 4, 2000), 464.
3. Thomas Gais, *Improper Influence: Campaign Finance Law, Political Interest Groups, and the Problem of Equality* (Ann Arbor: University of Michigan Press, 1996), 40.
4. Karen Foerstel and Peter Wallsten, with Derek Willis, "Campaign Overhaul Mired in Money and Loopholes" (*CQ Weekly*, May 13, 2000), 1084–93, briefly detail the events surrounding these earliest pieces of legislation.
5. John R. Wright (1996), 116–19, provides more details on regulations on unions. Also see Robert K. Goidel, Donald A. Gross, and Todd G. Shields, *Money Matters: Consequences of Campaign Finance Reform in the U.S. House Elections* (Lanham, MD: Rowman and Littlefield, 1999).
6. At this time, the AFL (the American Federation of Labor) and the CIO had not yet merged.
7. In 1936, Lewis gave over $1 million to support the election of FDR and a Democratic Congress. See Wright (1996), 117.
8. Alexander Heard, *The Costs of Democracy* (Garden City, NY: Doubleday, 1962).
9. Frank J. Sorauf's *What Price PACs?* (New York: Twentieth Century Fund, 1984) provides good background information on the history and development of PACs.
10. Two important Supreme Court rulings affected campaign finance law during this period. In 1972, the Supreme Court ruled that unions could solicit voluntary contributions to their segregated funds (*Pipefitters Local Union No. 526 of St. Louis v. United States*, 407 U.S. 385, 1972). However, legislative attempts to limit candidate expenditures were ruled unconstitutional (*Buckley v. Valeo*, 424 U.S. 1, 1976).
11. See Kevin B. Grier, Michael C. Munger, and Brian E. Roberts, "Industrial Organization of Corporate Political Participation," *Southern Economic Journal* 57 (1991): 727–38, and Craig Humphries, "Corporations, PACs, and the Strategic

Link between Contributions and Lobbying Activities," *Western Political Quarterly* 44 (1991): 353–72.

12. Gais (1996).

13. See Chapter 5 of Gais (1996).

14. Several scholars have noted this receipt/expenditure discrepancy. See Gais (1996), 59.

15. Gais (1996), 61.

16. Lasswell (1958).

17. For more information on presidential fund-raising, see Anthony Corrado's *Creative Campaigning: PACs and the Presidential Selection Process* (Boulder: Westview, 1992), and Clifford W. Brown Jr., Lynda W. Powell, and Clyde Wilcox, *Serious Money: Fundraising and Contributing in Presidential Nominating Campaigns* (New York: Cambridge University Press, 1995).

18. Don Van Natta Jr. and Douglas Frantz, "Lobbyists are Friends and Foes to McCain" (*New York Times,* February 10, 2000), A-23.

19. For information on issue advocacy during the recent presidential primaries, see David Magleby, ed., *Getting Inside the Outside Campaign* (Brigham Young University: Center for the Study of Elections and Democracy, 2000).

20. Richard L. Berke, "Sierra Club Ads in Political Races Offer a Case Study in Issue Advocacy" (*New York Times,* October 24, 1998), A-12.

21. Gary C. Jacobson, "The Effect of the AFL-CIO's 'Voter Education' Campaigns on the 1996 House Elections," *Journal of Politics* 61 (1999): 185–94.

22. Janet Box-Steffensmeier and Tobin Grant argue that most PAC money goes to the most effective House members, but of course most influential people tend to be very effective as well. Janet M. Box-Steffensmeier and J. Tobin Grant, "All in a Day's Work: The Financial Rewards of Legislative Effectiveness," *Legislative Studies Quarterly* 24 (1999): 511–24.

23. Thomas Romer and James M. Snyder Jr., "An Empirical Investigation of the Dynamics of PAC Contributions," *American Journal of Political Science* 38 (1994): 745–69.

24. Clifford J. Levy, "D'Amato Campaign Awash in Donations by Hopeful Lobbies" (*New York Times,* June 2, 1998), A-1.

25. Levy (1998), A-1.

26. Gary W. Cox and Eric Magar, "How Much is Majority Status in the U.S. Congress Worth?" *American Political Science Review* 93 (1999): 299–310.

27. Juliet Eilperin, "Hastert Drawing Crowds—of Lobbyists, With Eager Audience, Speaker Builds a Fund-Raising Machine" (*Washington Post,* March 10, 1999), A-1.

28. James M. Snyder Jr., "Long-Term Investing in Politicians: Or, Give Early, Give Often," *Journal of Law and Economics* 35 (1992): 15–43, and "The Market for Campaign Contributions: Evidence for the U.S. Senate 1980–1986," *Economics and Politics* 5 (1993): 219–40.

29. The literature in this area is voluminous, to say the least. Rebecca Morton and Charles Cameron provide a solid review of the area. "Elections and the Theory of Campaign Contributions: A Survey and Critical Analysis," *Economics and Politics* 4 (1992): 80–107.

30. Nolan McCarty and Lawrence Rothenberg, "Contributions, Candidates, and the Nature of Electoral Support," Mimeo, Princeton University, n.d.

31. Wright (1996), 135.

32. Snyder (1992) and (1993).

33. Frank J. Sorauf, *Inside Campaign Finance: Myths and Realities* (New Haven: Yale University Press, 1992). In particular, see Chapter 3.

34. Fred S. McChesney, *Money for Nothing: Politicians, Rent Extraction, and Political Extortion* (Boston: Harvard University Press, 1997).

35. See Charles R. Babcock and Richard Morin, "Following the Path of Self-Interest" (*The Washington Post National Weekly Edition,* June 25–July 1, 1990), 14.

36. One of the best works on hold-up potential remains Benjamin Klein, Robert G. Crawford, and Armen A. Alchian, "Vertical Integration, Appropriable Rents, and the Competitive Contracting Process," *Journal of Law and Economics* 21 (1978): 297–326.

37. Janet M. Grenzke, "PACs and the Congressional Supermarket," *American Journal of Political Science* 33 (1989): 1–24.

38. See Larry J. Sabato's, *PAC Power: Inside the World of Political Action Committees* (New York: W. W. Norton, 1985) for more information on this specific instance and other instances.

39. Edward A. Kangas, "Soft Money and Hard Bargains" (*New York Times,* October 22, 1999), A-29.

40. "A Letter and Its Response" (*New York Times,* September 1, 1999), A-16.

41. See, for instance, David Austen-Smith's "Interest Groups, Campaign Contributions, and Probabilistic Voting," *Public Choice* 54 (1987): 123–39.

42. Wright (1989).

43. The list of relevant and important work is much too long to provide here, but the interested reader can get started with Donald Philip Green and Jonathon S. Krasno, "Salvation for the Spendthrift Incumbent," *American Journal of Political Science* 32 (1988): 884–907, and "Rebuttal to Jacobson's 'New Evidence for Old Arguments,'" *American Journal of Political Science* 34 (1990): 363–72; Gary C. Jacobson, "The Effects of Campaign Spending in House Elections: New Evidence for Old Arguments," *American Journal of Political Science* 34 (1990): 334–62, and *The Politics of Congressional Elections,* 3rd ed. (New York: HarperCollins, 1992); and Christopher Kenny and Michael McBurnett, "A Dynamic Mode of the Effect of Campaign Spending on Congressional Vote Choice," *American Journal of Political Science* 36 (1992): 923–37.

44. At least one study suggests that veteran incumbents can reap electoral rewards from PAC money. Robert K. Goidel and Donald A. Gross, "A Systems Approach to Campaign Finance in U.S. House Elections," *American Politics Quarterly* 22 (1994): 125–53.

45. These issues are developed more fully in Jan M. Box-Steffensmeier, "A Dynamic Analysis of the Role of War Chests in Campaign Strategy," *American Journal of Political Science* 40 (1996): 352–71, and Gary W. Cox and Jonathon N. Katz, "Why Did the Incumbency Advantage in U.S. House Elections Grow?" *American Journal of Political Science* 40 (1996): 478–97.

46. James L. Regens and Ronald Keith Gaddie, *The Economic Realities of Political Reform* (New York: Cambridge University Press, 1995).

47. John P. Frendreis and Richard W. Waterman, "PAC Contributions and Legislative Behavior," *Social Science Quarterly* 66 (1985): 401–12; Laura Langbein, "PACs, Lobbies, and Political Conflict: The Case of Gun Control," *Public Choice* 75 (1993): 254–71; Langbein and Mark A. Lotwis, "The Political Efficacy of Lobbying and Money," *Legislative Studies Quarterly* 15 (1990): 413–40; Lawrence S. Rothenberg, *Linking Citizens to Government* (New York: Cambridge University Press, 1992); Jean R. Schroedel, "Campaign Contributions and Legislative Outcomes," *Western Political Quarterly* 40 (1987): 371–89.

48. Grenzke (1989). John R. Wright, "PACs, Contributions, and Roll Calls," *American Political Science Review* 79 (1985): 400–414, and "Contributions, Lobbying, and Committee Voting in the U.S. House of Representatives," *American Political Science Review* 84 (1990): 417–38.

49. Grenzke (1989). James F. Herndon, "Access, Record and Competition as Influences on Interest Group Contributions to Congressional Campaigns," *Journal of Politics* 44 (1982): 996–1019. Laura Langbein, "Money and Access," *Journal of Politics* 48 (1986): 1052–62. Wright (1990).

50. Wright (1990).

51. Wright also suggests that lobbyists for groups or corporations with an associated PAC have better information about electoral issues than those lobbyists working without PACs. The mere presence of a PAC insures that group leaders and lobbyists are in constant touch with their members, thereby minimizing the representation problem spoken of in Chapter Six. See Wright (1996), 149.

52. Michelle L. Chin, Jon R. Bond, and Nehemia Geva, "A Foot in the Door: An Experimental Study of PAC and Constituency Effects on Access," *Journal of Politics* 62 (2000): 534–49.

53. Austen-Smith (1993).

54. Hall and Wayman (1990).

55. For a related argument, see Richard L. Hall's "Lobbying as an Informational Subsidy," paper presented at the Annual Meeting of the Midwestern Political Science Association, Chicago, 1998.

56. William C. Mitchell and Michael C. Munger, "Economic Models of Interest Groups," *American Journal of Political Science* 35 (1991): 512–46.

57. *Buckley v. Valeo*, 424 U.S. 1 (1976).

58. Linda Greenhouse, "Justices Reject Appeals in Two Cases Involving Limits on Political Money" (*New York Times*, November 17, 1998), A-18.

59. *Nixon v. Shrink Missouri Government PAC*, 528 U.S. 377 (2000).

60. Expenditure limits are more readily accepted when public financing is involved. A Federal District Court in Maine has upheld a Maine law that provides candidates with strong incentives to accept public financing and expenditure limits. See Carey Goldberg, "Court Upholds Maine Campaign Law" (*New York Times*, November 9, 1999), A-13.

61. Greenhouse (1998), A-18.

62. This phrasing—*myths and realities*—is drawn from Sorauf (1992).

63. Robert Biersack, John C. Green, Paul S. Herrnson, Lynda W. Powell, and Clyde Wilcox, "Individual Congressional Campaign Contributors: A Preliminary Report," paper presented at the Midwest Political Science Association Meeting, Chicago, April 15–17, 1999.

64. Wendy L. Hansen and Neil J. Mitchell, "Is Corporate Political Activity Cumulative?" paper presented at the Annual Meeting of the American Political Science Association, Atlanta, Georgia, September 2–5, 1999. Also see Hansen and Mitchell's "Disaggregating and Explaining Corporate Political Activity," *American Political Science Review* 94 (2000): 891–905, and Kevin B. Grier, Michael C. Munger, and Brian E. Roberts' "The Determinants of Industry Political Activity, 1978–1986," *American Political Science Review* 88 (1994): 911–26.

65. Jim VandeHei, "K Street Booms with Computer Cash: Technology Industry Emphasizing Lobbying over Campaign Giving," (*Roll Call Monthly*, rollcall.com/newscoops/leadscoop, April 6, 1999).

66. Gais (1996), 77.

67. See, for instance, Norman Ornstein's "Bad Contribution" (*The New Republic*, June 10, 1995), 14–16.

68. See, for instance, Richard L. Hasen, "'Clipping Coupons for Democracy'—An Egalitarian/Public Choice Defense of Campaign Finance Vouchers," *California Law Review*, January (1996): 1–59, and Edward B. Foley, "'Equal Dollars per Voter'—A Constitutional Principle of Campaign Finance Reform," *Columbia Law Review*, May (1994): 1204–57.

∼10∼

Conclusion

Introduction

To understand the many subtleties of our interest group environment, it is important to consider both groups and individuals. Groups' roles in our socialization, our day-to-day lives, and in our political lives are very important. Groups affect our social existence from birth to death. However important groups are, individuals provide the micro-foundations for all groups and all group activities. Therefore, when studying groups, one should not lose sight of individuals. The emphasis in this book on individuals' goal-oriented behavior provides a micro-foundation for group activities.[1] Unfortunately, for some group scholars a formal theoretic approach that highlights individuals' goal-oriented behavior is regarded as fundamentally incompatible with group studies. This reputed incompatibility between the study of goal-oriented individuals and the study of groups stems largely from overemphasizing their distinct traditions, rather than from insurmountable conflicts.

One's abilities to choose group affiliations varies. We are born into various social, geographic, ethnic, economic, gender, and religious groupings, and such early groupings are not a product of conscious choice. Even as young adults, we may become affiliated with a group or association with little recognition of our choice. For example, when choosing a university, students are also choosing an alumni association, which will keep graduates' addresses and phone numbers for many, many years to facilitate regular university fundraising calls. However the environment may constrain our choices, it does not preordain our desires to make certain choices. We do choose whether we want to identify with the geographic, ethnic, or religious groupings into which we are born. We choose to associate with various professional, social, and ideological groups. In addition, we choose a level of activism. We may choose to freeride, contribute a small amount of money, contribute only time, or contribute a large amount of time and provide large sums of cash to support a group effort. The composition of groups and the mobilization of group interests in a society are affected by individuals' choices. In sum, *organized* interests, a term adopted by many scholars of groups, require conscious choices on the part of individuals.[2]

The composition and mobilization of groups is deemed important because organized interests affect governmental policy. Indeed, groups influence every stage of the policy process. Groups affect grassroots mobilizations throughout the country. Many groups establish permanent homes in Washington, D.C., to be better positioned when they seek active roles in the legislative process. Groups are key players in the bureaucratic implementation of legislation. Even the courts provide a venue for group influence. Given that organized interests are a product of our own choices, why are we leery of group influence on the policy process? In this final chapter, various contradictions, problems, and possible solutions are examined in greater detail.

Governmental Responsiveness and Contradictory Demands

Democratic governance requires some level of governmental responsiveness to citizens' demands. Oddly enough, concerns about governmental responsiveness often creates contradictory demands. An unresponsive government is unsatisfactory, but so too is a government that is too responsive to demands. This is the overarching question: How broad-based should the interests be before a government takes action? When a government is responsive to an organized interest with considerable numerical strength, then few questions are raised. But must the organized interest constitute a majority before a government responds? Numerous policies are designed to help relatively few individuals. Consider disaster relief, school loan programs, measures to protect political minorities, or farm programs. The immediate beneficiaries hardly constitute a majority. Indeed, one might find governmental programs that are weakened by attempts to broaden the base of beneficiaries. Consider a proposed missile defense system. If the Department of Defense and the primary contractor secure subcontractors in a majority of the congressional districts, then the implementing legislation is more likely to pass. After all, a majority of districts will benefit. But how should one choose subcontractors? Are the subcontractors chosen for political exigencies or for their technical expertise? Would a small handful of subcontractors do a better job? Demanding that governments respond only to majority interests is most likely impossible and quite likely unwise.

The following four simple scenarios illustrate how difficult determining the appropriate level of governmental responsiveness to organized interests and unorganized interests can be.

Scenario 1: Majoritarian interests

Demanding that a government respond to majoritarian interests presumes that there is a single majority. Chapter 4 presented the possibility of a majority-rule voting cycle. If there is a majority-rule voting cycle, then every alternative can be defeated by majority rule by some other alternative. In other words, no matter what the outcome might be, a majority of people, and not just a small group of malcontents, is dissatisfied. In addition, the dissatisfied majority can point to an alternative on the table that they prefer. They are not dreaming of "pie-in-the-sky" alternatives. Majority rule does not always lead to majority-rule voting cycles. Sometimes there are clear-cut majority-rule winners; but when majority-rule cycles do exist, it is impossible to pinpoint *the* majoritarian interest. In addition, majority-rule cycles are almost certain to occur when there are many alternatives and many people involved. With its manifold interests and myriad participants, a pluralist society is well suited for majority-rule voting cycles.[3]

Scenario 2: Changing circumstances

Whether the government is too responsive or too resistant to change depends on how one interprets the groups and issues at hand. How does one distinguish between government fortitude against interest group meddling and government nonresponsiveness to legitimate interests? We tend to love groups when their activities suit our own interests. However, groups become the enemy when circumstances change and their goals come to oppose our own. Consider the recent history of two groups, U.S. Term Limits and Americans for Term Limits. Both of these groups were very active in supporting the Republican Party and were partly responsible for the improving fortunes of congressional Republicans in the early 1990s. The U.S. House of Representatives had been dominated by Democrats for most of the second half of the twentieth century. The term-limits proponents were particularly concerned about those members who had served for fifteen, twenty, thirty years, or more. Incumbents had developed clear electoral advantages over their challengers, allowing incumbents to retain their seats with greater and greater ease.[4] Since the 1950s, House incumbents who chose to run were reelected about ninety percent of the time. Of course, this incumbency advantage translated into an advantage for the Democrats because they controlled the House for most of the last half of the twentieth century. Not surprisingly, for many years Republicans allied themselves with term-limits proponents. Republicans promised better responsiveness to the interests of term-limits proponents. In the record-breaking 1994 elections, Republicans took over both chambers of Congress, unseating many prominent Democrats, including the Democratic Speaker of the House. Now, several election cycles later, the Republicans who these groups helped in the early part of the 1990s are the incumbents who, according to U.S. Term Limits and Americans for Term Limits, should not stay too long. Indeed, numerous Republican incumbents face the prospect of negative advertising campaigns funded and organized by their old friends the term-limits proponents. The Republicans were erstwhile advocates of term limits when the Democrats controlled the Congress, but they are now less impressed with the idea. In some states, leaders of conservative groups that benefited from coalitions with term-limits proponents in the early 1990s are now saying, "You don't bench champions," or, "In six years you barely get your feet wet," or simply, "Let the people . . . decide." [5]

Scenario 3: What about the little guy? Formal procedures versus informal bargaining

Theodore Lowi's *The End of Liberalism* remains one of the sharpest critiques of interest group influence in American politics.[6] Among other things, Lowi fears that due process and formal procedures are irrevocably undermined by petty group bargaining. Rules and procedures lose their meaning because everything is negotiable in an interest group environment. It would be hard to overstate the importance of due process for governments and citizens. However, the structure and nature of due process is defined by political winners, not political losers. One should not be surprised to learn that political winners sometimes alter rules and procedures to preserve their own stakes. Sometimes formal procedures undermine the political viability of the proverbial little guy, and in the United States many voters and politicians root for the little guy.

As noted in Chapter 5, colleges and universities are increasingly active players in Washington politics. Colleges and universities are affected by federal policies addressing equal-opportunity and equal-access issues, tuition-assistance programs, and funding for research and development (R&D). Numerous federal agencies, such as the National Science Foundation (NSF) and the National Institute of Health (NIH), distribute research funds to colleges and universities through a peer-review process. That is, every request for money is reviewed by one's own peers in the scientific community. Peer review is the established, formalized process. For some colleges and universities fighting to gain broader acceptance, peer review can be a problem. Consider the pecking order among colleges and universities. If Harvard looks askance at Princeton and Yale, what chance does Boston University have? What if peers consider themselves superior? Not surprisingly, some schools seek to bypass toe-to-toe peer review.[7] Schools such as Boston University can secure federal money for research effort if their lobbyists are adept and know the legislative process. Schools may be able to secure earmarked funds. *Earmarking* is the term used to describe how legislators attach money for special projects to any sort of spending legislation. Earmarked money for university research bypasses the review process of the NSF or NIH. Perhaps one dislikes the upstarts for circumventing the peer-review process or dislikes the dominance of older, stodgy universities. However, one should not be surprised that some universities favor peer review more than others or that universities use various tactics to support their research endeavors. In sum, institutionalized rules and procedures are important, but they can also have a restricting and calcifying effect limiting some political actors more than others.

Scenario 4: Widespread panic at my daughter's wedding! Political action in social and economic groups

Many local governments rely on social and economic groups to maintain and enhance a strong community. Social groups reinforce a sense of connectedness in the community, creating what scholars now like to call social capital.[8] Many critics of the political influence of groups somehow see social groups in an entirely different light. Churches, sports leagues, neighborhood watch groups, and other social groups are typically considered good for a community because their interests are not overtly political. Local governments also rely on economic groups and associations to promote the economic vitality of the community. However, as noted in Chapter 4, under certain circumstances nonpolitical social or economic groups become politically active. Hirschman's discussion of groups' shifting involvements and Truman's discussion of groups' gravitation toward government relate to this theme—social or economic groups sometimes become political groups. Sometimes the line between good social or economic groups and bad political groups becomes blurred.

Even the most unlikely events can become politically charged, leading groups to gravitate to governments to solve thorny problems. Consider the following series of events. A couple frets over their daughter's wedding for months, planning (almost) every detail. Many a parent frets over a child's wedding, but few parents need fear widespread panic at the event. However, for an Athens, Georgia, couple, that fear was real. Widespread Panic might have literally ruined their daughter's wedding, long scheduled at a downtown Athens church. As it happens, the church is only fifty to one hundred yards away from the 40 Watt Club, world-famous in the alternative music scene and a regular venue for a wide array of rock bands ranging from the B-52s to R.E.M. to the Violent Femmes to Widespread Panic. Ordinarily, the 40 Watt is very quiet during the day, but Widespread Panic, in conjunction with the 40 Watt Club and various business associations, planned a free, outdoor CD release party. A crowd of more than twenty thousand was expected, and many downtown streets were to be closed to regular traffic.[9] The concert would be a boon for downtown businesses, so the city obligingly approved the necessary permits. Everything appeared straightforward for both events—until the wedding group learned of the outdoor concert. No wedding could proceed within one hundred yards of a huge outdoor rock concert. What was at stake? One rock 'n' roll concert. Thousands of dollars in revenue for city merchants. The sanctity of one church wedding. The sanity of a wedding party. Thousands of dollars and hours of planning for two wedding families.

Undeniably, the concert was going to create what many scholars refer to as social costs or negative externalities—costs of production that are not borne by the producers themselves. What was to be produced? A rock 'n' roll concert. What costs associated with the concert would not be borne by the 40 Watt Club or Widespread Panic? The social costs or negative externalities from the Widespread Panic concert might include traffic jams, litter, and noise. Who should bear the costs of these negative externalities? Only those who have never planned a wedding would suggest that the wedding party move to another week. Such events are planned six months to a year in advance. Guests had already booked flights and hotel rooms. Moving the wedding would not be easy. The church and the wedding party were most concerned about noise, music fans overwhelming church grounds, and closed streets. Some of those negative externalities are readily accounted for in negotiations with the city. The city can mandate policies to ensure that the concert promoters pay most of the costs associated with traffic and crowd control and litter pick up. That is, the city can ensure that the concert promoters bear the bulk of the costs linked to some of the negative externalities. Noise, however, remained the fundamental impasse. An outdoor CD release party with a live band requires a certain level of noise.

There were no established procedures for bargaining over who should bear the social costs of the noise production. Recall the discussion of Ronald Coase's work in Chapter 2.[10] To use the terminology of the Nobel Prize–winning Coase, there were no established property rights over the air and bargaining costs were high. If property rights had been well established and negotiation costs relatively low, then the wedding group and the concert promoters would have been able to negotiate an agreement among themselves. Private negotiations were, however, fruitless, and for several weeks it looked as though the wedding group would directly bear the costs of the noise production. What happened to the purely social wedding group? It transformed for a short period of time into a politically active group, led by the mother of the bride. The mother of the bride used insider and outsider lobbying tactics. She contacted every local office directly or indirectly overseeing the outdoor concert. She contacted the local media. The wedding party did not want to cancel the concert, but by the same token they did not want to bear the social costs related to the concert.

How should a local government respond to such a problem? Initially, neither group was particularly demanding or politically oriented. They were both good groups—groups that might actually strengthen the community. For a time, they were also at loggerheads. The concert revelers were a larger group than the wedding party, but neither group constituted a majority of

Athens residents. Indeed, both groups were dominated by out-of-towners. Why did the wedding party become politicized? Neither group was politically oriented prior to their scheduling conflict, but gravitation to government was inevitable because of the poorly defined property rights and the high bargaining costs. How did the local government establish property rights over the air? Simple—the local Athens, Georgia, government forbade sound checks and warm-ups for a set period of time. The church and wedding party "owned" the air during that time. Wedding bells pealed. A clear concert starting time was established. From that time on Widespread Panic "owned" the air.[11] The solution might seem painfully obvious, but it was not secured by the two groups negotiating alone. Each party in the dispute became politically active and, in looking for a solution, gravitated toward government.

Groups and the Distribution of Social Costs

We often think of winners and losers in the policy process in group terms. Who gets what, when, and how is explained in group terms, not on an individual-by-individual basis. To the extent that groups affect the policy process, they often affect the distribution of social costs. Virtually every governmental policy and program creates a negative externality for some set of individuals. The costs associated with negative externalities are social costs, and the distribution of social costs is a key concern for groups. How do governments respond to social costs? To say that governments should reduce social costs or distribute social costs fairly simply evades the issue. Social costs do not disappear, and questions of fairness are open to considerable debate. Governments may be able to distribute social costs so widely among members of society that the impact of the costs is barely noticed, but such a distribution is not necessarily fair, and the reduction in the visibility of costs is not the same as a genuine reduction of the costs. The aggregate costs may still be considerable, even if the costs for any one individual are minimal.

One of the strongest attacks against an interest group society is posed by Mancur Olson in his book, *The Rise and Decline of Nations.*[12] Olson contended that concerns over distribution, rather than production, lead to greater and greater inefficiencies. Politically entrenched groups reduce the ability of a society to reallocate resources efficiently, and they slow the adoption of newer, more efficient technologies. The reallocation of resources or the adoption of new technologies may enhance efficiency, but they also create social costs. Olson contended that too much emphasis on the distribution of social costs ensures that the opportunities for gains from greater efficiency are lost. Productivity goes down as more and more groups focus narrowly on the distributional issues alone.

Consider, for instance, free trade legislation linked to the North American Free Trade Agreement (NAFTA) or the World Trade Organization (WTO).

Economists have long promoted free trade on efficiency grounds, but free trade will shift jobs and may undermine the effectiveness of environmental standards. Not surprisingly, labor and environmental groups are often the most vocal critics of relaxed tariffs. Consider, however, who bears the costs of the shift in jobs. The gains in productivity and efficiency linked to free trade mean that there are resources available to ease the burden of social costs. Suppose a retraining program was linked to the passage of free trade proposals. Such programs redistribute the social costs connected to job losses in certain sectors when trade is free and open. Throughout the 1990s, labor groups argued that they wanted free trade, but they were also worried about the distribution of the social costs associated with job losses. The redistribution of social costs is simply one aspect of the costs associated with political bargaining. At one level it is inefficient, but there are very few perfectly competitive settings in the world of politics or economics.[13] Second best may have to do.[14]

Problems Associated with an Interest Group Society and Their Possible Solutions

In an interest group society, virtually everyone is a reformer. Here the focus is on three standard complaints about an interest group society. Do the standard solutions promoted to address these complaints yield clearly better outcomes?

Narrow-minded groups versus broad-based organizations

In *The Rise and Decline of Nations,* Olson held out hope for group-oriented societies if the groups were large and more encompassing of broad interests. The larger, more all-encompassing groups are less detrimental to society because they internalize the externalities. Larger, more all-encompassing groups recognize that they will not be able to shield all their own members from social costs, so they are more restrained in their demands. Political parties exemplify these larger, more comprehensive organizations, and scholars, at least since the time of de Tocqueville, have considered parties as a natural balance to groups.[15]

Parties may internalize externalities, but they do not eliminate externalities. Parties may or may not reduce total social costs. It is premature to suggest that, by their very nature, parties somehow reduce externalities or deadweight losses. Indeed, there are reasons to believe that parties may increase social costs. Political parties recognize that they control access to the political marketplace. The fact that there are only two major parties and numerous groups seeking to interact with party officials ensures that parties have the upper hand in the relations between themselves and groups.[16] Partisan legislators devise the campaign laws and tax codes that affect the ability of organized interests to gain political leverage. Some scholars argue that the massive restructuring of the congressional committee system in the mid-1970s was driven by the desire for campaign dollars.[17] The revamped committee structures facilitated greater fund-raising from groups. Writing about the early 1900s, E. E. Schattschneider, a prominent political parties scholar of his day, argued that political parties are not "an association of men who have agreed on some principle . . . [instead] parties are held together by the 'cohesive power of public plunder.'"[18] Parties may or may not be the saving grace.

Shadow organizations versus membership lists

Some critics argue that many "groups" are not groups at all, and all groups exaggerate their claims. There are indeed groups and associations that are not membership based. Some groups embody little more than one person's drive for political glory.[19] In regards to the exaggeration of claims, groups are probably little different from any other political actor who claims to represent some sort of silent majority.[20] These very issues are aspects of the representation problem discussed in Chapter 6.

Securing membership lists is one way to uncover shadow-group operations and claims of massive memberships. Who should uncover shadow organizations? To what lengths should one go? These are not idle issues. Recall the discussion in Chapter 7 about the interactions between groups and courts. Judges assess standing. Before granting standing to an interest group, judges may consider whether the group members themselves are harmed.[21] If the members themselves could not secure standing, then it is unlikely the interest group will be granted standing. That is, there is a distinction between the group and the individuals comprising the group. Recall from Chapter 8 that new legislation requires IRS 527 organizations to reveal their contributors. Indeed, the lobbying regulations discussed in Chapter 6 are aimed at securing the same sort of openness.

But again, to what lengths should one go? Regulations do have costs. Many critics of present campaign-finance regulations acknowledge that 527 organizations most likely will find other avenues for influence that are not as closely monitored. The regulations may simply remove political activity even further from view. The release of membership lists can also have a chilling effect on one's freedoms of speech and association. In the 1950s, the state of Alabama sought the membership lists of the NAACP. Alabama sought to establish that the Alabama NAACP chapters were dominated by out-of-state money and influence. The state of Alabama argued that it did not want to limit Alabamians from joining, they simply wanted to uncover out-of-state meddling. Groups working to reopen Arkansas schools closed by Governor Orval Faubus during racial strife in the 1950s worked underground to avoid detection.[22] The state of Mississippi maintained a State Sovereignty Commission to monitor the activities of civil rights activists in the 1950s, 1960s, and

1970s. "Investigators made note of the skin color, associations, religious beliefs and sexual proclivities of the civil rights workers they tracked." "They
jotted down the license plate numbers of cars parked at civil rights meetings."[23] In each instance, the state argued that it had to protect itself from
improper group influence and shadow organizations, but the constitutional
right of free association means little if states are in a position to monitor that
association.

Growth in government versus contracting out

Various organized groups have demanded more and more from the government: more money for agriculture, defense, education, the environment, and
so forth. Governments have also become responsible for more and more
services that used to be privately provided. Some critics of group influence
argue that groups lead to wasteful government growth and undue expansion.
One way to limit the size of government is to contract out for goods and
services. That is, a government could hire a private firm or group to take over
certain tasks. As noted in Chapter 3, at the close of the twentieth century,
there was a drive afoot to increase the role of private charities in the provision
and distribution of goods and services. In 2000, presidential aspirants Al
Gore and George W. Bush both called for increased reliance on church organizations. Many prominent politicians continue to call for the privatization
of Social Security. Contracting out may reduce the size of government, but it
also changes our views of citizenship, and it legitimizes those organizations
that secured the government contracts.[24] Groups are already "of the same genus, although a different species, as the state."[25] Government contracts simply strengthen those groups that, literally, deliver the goods. Certainly, contracting out has merits, but it does affect the absolute and relative strengths
of groups. Some groups may push for bigger government, but governments
cannot contract out without strengthening some of those very same groups.

Are Groups Solely Responsible for the Problems within an Interest Group Society?

It is easy to link problems with interest group activity. The question raised
here is whether group culpability is unique to them or common to other political actors or perhaps inherent in the federal political structure of the
United States. Of course, there is simply no way to address all the problems
associated with groups, but some of the most common concerns are addressed here.

Vote buying

PACs are regularly accused of buying or attempting to buy legislators' votes
with campaign contributions. PACs' coffers, however, are seldom overflow-

ing, and PACs are not the only political actors engaged in the strategic distribution of money and resources. Legislators with little electoral competition but large campaign chests frequently contribute to other legislators' campaign efforts. Legislators with leadership positions have been especially generous in this regard. During the 1993 debates surrounding NAFTA, Vic Fazio's vocal support for the accord was especially effective with Democratic legislators because Fazio (D-Calif.) was on the very influential House Appropriations Committee and was the chairman of the Democratic Congressional Campaign Committee. Fazio was well positioned to control two sets of purse strings. During his last few years in the U.S. House, Newt Gingrich (R-Ga.) was a tireless fund-raiser for his party and Republican candidates. By voting against Gingrich's desires, a member risked losing his formidable fund-raising prowess. If the strategic distribution of money and resources to influence legislative activity is reprehensible, then does it matter whether the money or resources come from a group or another legislator?

Policy gridlock

Some interest group critics contend that the government is hamstrung by groups. Gridlock, in these critics' eyes, is a product of interest groups. This critique invites two responses. First, is all gridlock bad? Proponents of nationalized health insurance and health care often point to the power of interest groups when asked to comment on the shortcomings of the U.S. policies. Nationalized health insurance, they contend, is killed by powerful interest groups in the insurance and medical communities. Of course, for opponents of nationalized health insurance, group power is viewed somewhat differently. Gridlock is a good or bad thing, depending on one's view of the policies at stake, so by extension interest group pressure is a good or bad thing depending on the policies at stake. Second, is gridlock pervasive and long lasting or relatively temporary? Many scholars have argued that any sort of equilibrium in politics is uncommon.[26] New issues create new cleavages that can always undo the old equilibrium. As the number of issues and the number of individuals increases, the likelihood of disequilibrium is even greater. New majorities unseat old majorities. The mobilization of new groups unsettles established policies. Given the presence of collective-action problems, not all interests are organized, so the mobilization of new interests is always possible.[27] The presence of groups may create more disequilibrium rather than gridlock.

Once upon a time, there were iron triangles, or so the lesson goes[28]

The essence of an iron triangle is that the relations between organized interests, committees in Congress, and agencies work to lock out competing interests from the policy process. Concerns about access still pervade the interest group literature, and at times organized interests may still dominate points of access to legislators and bureaucrats. However, two points should be kept in mind. First, lobbyists cannot demand access to legislators. Legislators are the linchpin for access. Second, the empirical evidence for iron triangles has never appeared weaker. In *Cultivating Congress,* William Browne notes that the agriculture policy domain, a policy area well suited for the presence of iron triangles, is more open than it has perhaps ever been.[29] An ever-increasing number of participants has opened up the policymaking process. Browne and Won Paik refer to legislators as unconstrained entrepreneurs able to get information from a multitude of sources.[30] Groups no longer hold a lock on access to information or voters, and legislators are eager to establish their own set of wide-ranging contacts.

Parochial interests

Critics often contend that groups are so narrow and parochial in their focus that concern for the common good is lost. However, Andrew McFarland, a noted scholar of public interest groups, states pointedly that a common mistake of reformers is their naive "Belief in an Objective Public Interest."[31] Many terms are used synonymously for the public interest, including the common interest, the common good, the general will, or the public interest. Regardless of the term used, the common interest is hard to define. Former Speaker of the House Tip O'Neill often said that all politics is local. One might just as easily say that all interests are parochial. The question is whether group interests are any more parochial than other political actors.

Consider two recent legislative events. Former Senate Majority Leader Trent Lott (R-Miss.) displayed some parochial interests when he "tucked into the military authorization bill . . . $50 million to buy parts for a $1.5 billion helicopter carrier [that would be built in Mississippi and] that the Navy did not request."[32] One commentator said there was no lobbying, "this is all Lott."[33] The lobbyists never showed up, and parochialism survived just the same. Lott was parochial in his views, which is to say that he represented the interests of his state. Military authorizations are not unique in this regard. Recent medicare legislation allowed parochial interests to shine. Medicare reimbursement is linked to hospital costs, which vary considerably by region. Large city hospitals typically have higher costs than small city hospitals, so they receive larger reimbursements. What about those small cities close to large urban areas? They sometimes have high costs too. What about a small town in northwestern Vermont? To help it secure a higher rate for Medicare reimbursement, a hospital in a small town in northwestern Vermont was linked to the Boston metropolitan area—about 175 miles away. Who engineered that geographical feat? Speculation is that James Jeffords, then a Republican senator from Vermont, asked for the change. Was it undue group influence or was Jeffords simply representing the interests of Vermont? Is it reasonable policy? Maybe, maybe not. The bill made six such allowances, including a hospital one hundred miles west of Chicago—in Speaker Dennis Hastert's district (R-Ill.).[34] Whether groups or legislators or voters, political actors in the United States naturally display parochialism. Our federal system of government is well suited to ensure the representation of parochial interests.

The fragmentation and incoherence of policy

Theodore Lowi's critique of interest group influence is multifaceted. In addition to undermining due process, Lowi contends that group influence also creates jurisdictional disputes and fragmented policy. Inevitably, governments lose the ability to plan, and policy incoherence results. Consider the following series of events.[35] Over the last several years, schools, states, and the federal government have urged more students to go into the sciences, and, in particular, computer science. There is such a dearth of programmers that everyone is scrambling to keep up. Congress has considered ways to relax foreign immigration procedures to allow more programmers from abroad into the United States, and former President Clinton was "pouring millions of dollars into federal initiatives to train more" software developers.[36] Why, then did Congress pass a tax law that has forced the IRS to disallow individual programmers to incorporate themselves as independent businesses? Why encourage and discourage software developers at the same time? Clearly, there is policy incoherence.

Are groups solely to blame for such incoherence? IBM had its fingerprints on the tax code and Microsoft wanted to attract more programmers from abroad. However, the structure of the U.S. government is as much at fault as are corporate interests. Senator Daniel P. Moynihan (D-N.Y.) pushed for the changes in the tax code to offset revenue losses from a tax break that he wanted to secure for IBM, which is headquartered in New York. We have already seen that parochialism needs little prodding from lobbyists. Moynihan simply sought a quick fix for the revenue losses. As if to highlight Lowi's discussion of jurisdictional disputes, just as Congress was assessing immigration procedures, the Department of Justice pursued antitrust actions against the Microsoft Corporation. That is, Congress considered expanding the labor pool for Microsoft, while the Department of Justice claimed that Microsoft was too prone to developing and exploiting its monopoly power. Of course, to win in Congress is not the same as to win in the Department of Justice or in the federal courts. Some policy incoherence is inevitable in a large federal system, with a balance of powers between the legislative, executive, and judicial branches.

To guarantee policy coherence there must be one, and only one, individual making all decisions. If policy decisions are made in a serial fashion by many different individuals, some incoherence is almost inevitable. Political scientist J. Leiper Freeman used the term *creeping pluralism* to describe such disjointed policy processes in which different groups make different policy demands at different times and in different governmental venues.[37] However, does policy coherence naturally exist in other settings that allow for democratic governance? Consider the ballot initiatives in Chapter 8. Even direct democracy may lack coherence. The aggregation paradox in Chapter 8 and the voting cycle first presented in Chapter 4 are akin to the policy incoherence that Lowi and others have highlighted. Lowi is partially correct, but the only way to avoid any possibility of incoherence is to restrict individual input into the governing process. Lowi himself seemed to recognize this when he stated that the "more government operates by the spreading of access, the more public order seems to suffer."[38] Even if limiting access to a single individual is the only assured way to avoid policy incoherence, such a drastic step is hardly wise.

What Is to Be Done?

Given all that has been discussed, how should one make sense of groups and organized interests?

(1) Consider the good that group affiliations do provide to individuals. Group affiliations do connect us. "Amongst the laws which rule human societies there is one which seems to be more precise and clear than all others. If men are to remain civilized, or become so, the art of associating together must grow and improve."[39] Groups also provide a voice and allow their members "to combine their own advantage with that of their fellow citizens."[40]

(2) Do not forget the predominance of individuals in an interest group society. There is a natural limit on the influence of membership-based interest groups because of individuals' overlapping memberships. Few individuals consider themselves fully and wholly members of only one group. Individuals themselves provide an important check on group influence.

(3) Recognize that there are sham organizations and groups that make inflated claims. Having a state uncover group memberships to check inflated claims may not be wise, but individuals themselves can question group goals and claims.

(4) Interest group scholars have sought to highlight the role of groups in government and to detail the many diverse connections between individuals and groups in society. The state, however, cannot be entirely forgotten. The state is a player too. The state determines such basic rules of the game as the tax status of businesses, groups, and charities.[41] It affects the ability of unions to organize and corporations to form PACs. Therefore, it is wise to keep Earl Latham's descriptions of interest groups and the state in mind. As noted previously, interest groups and the state are of the same genus though

different species. To study only the state, as early institutionalists did, is a mistake. By the same token, to highlight groups, while ignoring the state, is also a mistake.

(5) The state, corporations, and large interest groups are established players in our interest group environment, but their powers and influence can be countered. Jeffrey Berry notes what a *Washington Post* writer referred to as the "dirty little secret about high-priced Washington lobbyists. . . . They lose a lot."[42] Therefore, be willing to consider ways to mobilize forces to counteract institutionalized influence. Consider varied direct and indirect strategies, and be willing to work in different venues within the federal political system. One may not need to counter another's institutionalized presence toe to toe in the same venue.

(6) Remember that your vote is a blunt instrument. Social commentator Andrei Codrescu suggested that we are "too complex" for one man–one vote.[43] Codrescu wonders why he cannot divide his vote, giving some support to more than one candidate. His allegiances to the candidates are ambiguous. He likes some candidates on certain issues and other candidates on other issues. Why not split the vote accordingly? In some ways, an interest group society tries to accomplish exactly what Codrescu suggests, tongue in cheek. Our votes remain blunt, but our contributions of time and money to groups can be more finely adjusted.

Conclusion

Although the terms we use to name and define them have changed over the years, organized interests have long captured the attention of both social science scholars and casual observers of politics. Both scholars and lay people are often apprehensive of interest group activity, but their critiques of interest groups are seldom well structured or carefully reasoned. Even among scholars, critiques are more often instinctively rather than intellectually oriented. As scandals develop, people tend to assess and judge group activity on a case-by-case basis. One could rely on any number of accounts for simple descriptions of one-time political events. An event-driven, case-by-case analysis leads to a slow accumulation of isolated facts and details, but it does not lend itself to an overall understanding of interest group politics or the effects of groups on American democracy. Unfortunately, the media does not always clarify such issues. The events that are of most interest to media outlets are usually atypical. As readers and viewers, we are often more struck by the atypical than the typical. The science of political science involves more than being reasonably objective when describing isolated political events. If explanation is the goal, then one must structure generalized models to yield more comprehensive results.

A formal theoretic approach to the study of pluralism and interest group activities is both objective and consistent. Consistency is derived from the fact that the core assumption of goal-oriented behavior is not altered. Ancillary assumptions may vary, but not the core assumption of rationally oriented behavior. Objectivity is maintained because all key players are presumed to be goal oriented and rational in their choices. Formal theory is particularly well suited to the study of interest groups because groups are unabashedly goal oriented and strategic. The core assumption underlying formal theory is wonderfully transparent, and partly for that reason, formal theoretic reasoning is increasingly popular. Little by little, terms from formal theory are used more widely in newspaper accounts of strategic world events. Legal scholars and judges increasingly write and speak of externalities and social costs. Even the president of the United States sometimes has to brush up on his understanding of game theory.[44]

At best, individuals are ambivalent toward groups, and at worst, they are steadfastly suspicious. In a wonderfully eloquent piece in the *American Political Science Review,* Nicholas R. Miller applies the following three qualities to characterize a pluralist or interest group society. First, there are numerous and varied preferences. Second, these manifold interests are genuinely meaningful because there is also dispersed power. If all power and influence were concentrated, then the presence of varied interests would be less important than the interests of the most powerful. Third, interest group activity defines the push and pull of politics. If there is an accepted policy, it is the balance of competing interests. Miller then asks what the results of pluralism are. Three results deserve particular attention. First, there is a moderation of attitudes and behaviors due to individuals' multiple memberships and the subsequent cross-cutting cleavages. Second, there is a heavy reliance on political stratagems. In the absence of clear majorities, temporary group coalitions are glued together with log-rolls, vote trades, agenda manipulation, and other stratagems. Third, the lack of clear majorities may actually promote stability because losers at one point in time recognize that they can be winners at the next turn. Perhaps we must satisfy ourselves with the simple fact that pluralism in an interest group society "distributes political satisfaction" by allowing ever-shifting interest group coalitions of winners and losers to secure small gains.[45]

NOTES

1. Frans van Winden, a European scholar of groups and formal theory, argues that formal theory would yield even greater advances if there were a greater recognition among formal theorists of groups and group influence. See his article, "On the Economic Theory of Interest Groups: Towards a Group Frame of Reference in Political Economics," *Public Choice* 100 (1999): 1–29.
2. In their book *Organized Interests and American Democracy* (1983), Kay Lehman Schlozman and John T. Tierney argued that the term *interest group* was too narrow for American politics. Their work did much to popularize the use of

organized interest. In addition to Mancur Olson, other prominent scholars writing about group politics noted the role for individuals in a group-oriented view
of society and politics. See, for instance, Earl Latham's "The Group Basis of
Politics: Notes for a Theory," *American Political Science Review* 46 (1952):
376–97, and Schattschneider (1960).

3. Miller's (1983) work provides an excellent analysis of these issues.
4. A full discussion of the incumbency advantage is beyond the scope of this work,
but the interested reader can find more information in Fiorina (1989) or Jacobson (1992).
5. Thomas B. Edsall, "Coming to Term Limits" (*Washington Post,* May 12, 1998),
A-4.
6. Theodore J. Lowi, *The End of Liberalism: Ideology, Policy, and the Crisis of Public
Authority* (New York: W. W. Norton, 1969).
7. Tim Weiner, "Lobbying for Research Money, Colleges Bypass Review Process"
(*New York Times,* August 24, 1999), A-1.
8. Robert Putnam reinvigorated popular and scholarly interest in groups' roles in
promoting social connectedness and social capital. For a nice overview of his
work in this area, see Putnam (1995a; 1995b; 2000).
9. The actual crowd was several times larger than the projected twenty thousand.
10. Coase (1960).
11. For more information on these events, one can refer to the March 1999 archives
of the *Athens Banner Herald.*
12. Mancur Olson, *The Rise and Decline of Nations* (New Haven: Yale University
Press, 1982).
13. There are now two books that directly address this issue: John E. Mueller, *Capitalism, Democracy, and Ralph's Pretty Good Grocery* (Princeton, NJ: Princeton
University Press, 1999), and Donald A. Wittman, *The Myth of Democratic Failure: Why Political Institutions Are Efficient* (Chicago: University of Chicago
Press, 1995).
14. There is a well-established theory of second best in economics. One general result is that an economy with $n - 1$ distortions or politically constrained transactions is not generically better than an economy with n distortions. See Chapter 7
in Jean-Jacques Laffont, *Fundamentals of Public Economics* (Cambridge: MIT
Press, 1990).
15. Tocqueville (1961). Also see Charles W. Wiggins, Keith E. Hamm, and Charles
G. Bell, "Interest Group Influence and Party Influence Agents in the Legislative
Process," *Journal of Politics* 54 (1992): 82–100 for a more recent analysis.
16. Viable third parties may provide relief, but for a number of reasons third parties
are seldom viable in the United States.
17. Wright (2000). Also see Ainsworth (1997).
18. Schattschneider (1942), 37.
19. See Salisbury (1984) for more on this topic.
20. Barry Goldwater's claims of support from a silent majority failed to prevent his
landslide defeat to Lyndon B. Johnson in the 1964 presidential election.
21. *Sierra Club v. Morton,* 405 U.S. 727 (1972).
22. Kevin Sack, "Mississippi Reveals Dark Secrets of a Racist Time" (*New York
Times,* March 18, 1998), A-1, A-15.
23. Sack (1998), A-15.
24. See, in particular, Smith and Lipsky (1993), 207.
25. Latham (1965), 12.
26. Work by Miller (1983), Riker (1982), and Schattschneider (1960) immediately
come to mind.

27. Partitioning games provide another means to analyze the opportunity for new group emergence. Individuals cannot always partition themselves into a set of groups such that no individual seeks to leave one group and join another. For recent work with numerous helpful references in this area, see Igal Milchtaich and Eyal Winter's "Stability and Segregation in Group Formation," *Games and Economic Behavior* 38 (2002): 318–46.

28. This subtitle is the first sentence of Browne and Paik (1993).

29. Browne (1995). Hugh Heclo's "Issue Networks and the Executive Establishment" in *The New American Political System,* ed. Anthony King (Washington, D.C.: American Enterprise Institute, 1978), is also helpful.

30. Browne and Paik (1993), 1057.

31. See McFarland (1984), 26–29.

32. Eric Schmitt, "Lott Pushes New Warship for Home State Contract" (*New York Times,* June 23, 1998), A-12.

33. Schmitt (1998), A-12.

34. See Robert Pear's "Health Industry Sees Wish List Made into Law" (*New York Times,* December 6, 1999), A-1, A-26, and Al Kamen's "Going the Distance for Medicare Money" (*The Washington Post,* December 6, 1999), A-25.

35. For more information on this situation, see David Cay Johnston's article, "How a Tax Law Helps Insure a Scarcity of Programmers" (*New York Times,* April 27, 1998), C-1, C-12.

36. Johnston (1998).

37. J. Leiper Freeman, *The Political Process: Executive Bureau—Legislative Committee Relations* (New York: Random House, 1965).

38. Lowi (1969), 292.

39. Tocqueville (1961), 133.

40. Tocqueville (1961), 145.

41. For more information on the impact that public policies have on charities' abilities to raise funds, see Charles T. Clotfelter's *Federal Tax Policy and Charitable Giving* (Chicago: University of Chicago Press, 1985).

42. Berry (1997), 115.

43. Andrei Codrescu, "1 Man–1 Vote," *All Things Considered,* March 2, 2000.

44. The Clinton White House often released the names of the books on former President Clinton's summer reading lists. Among the books on his 1999 list was one that covered various topics central to modern political analysis, including game theory. Katherine Q. Seelye "President Hits the Golf Course, and the Books" (*New York Times,* August 24, 1999), A-12.

45. Miller (1983), 736.

Glossary of Formal Terms

Arrow's Paradox: Kenneth Arrow, a Nobel Laureate in economics, is credited with formalizing the conditions that allow for the possibility of *voting cycles*. A paradox occurs when a group of individuals are unable to order a set of alternatives from best to worst. Though the individuals themselves have well-ordered preferences, the group's preferences may cycle, such that alternative A is preferred by the group to B, B to C, and C to A.

Black's Theorem: Duncan Black showed that if all members of a group in a one dimensional policy space have symmetric, *single-peaked preferences*, then the *median* voter's ideal point is the unique *equilibrium*.

By-product Theory: Mancur Olson argued that the demand for *public goods* cannot foster group formation because of the possibility of *freeriding*. Groups must offer selective incentives to attract members. The sale of *selective incentives* provides the group with resources to fund the public good, thereby making the group a by-product of the selective incentives.

Collective-Action Problem: This term is used to indicate the difficulties associated with collective efforts. Sometimes used synonymously with *freeriding*.

Coordination Problem: This term is used to indicate the difficulties associated with coordinating two or more individuals' actions. Whenever a *game* has more than one *equilibrium*, one is likely to face a coordination problem.

Crowding Effect: Whenever goods shift from being *nonrivalrous* to rivalrous, a crowding effect is occurring. Although pure *public goods* have *nonrivalrous consumption*, hybrid goods may exhibit rivalrous consumption as more and more people partake of the good. For instance, a public beach has nonrivalrous consumption if only a few individuals are present, but a crowding effect occurs as more and more people arrive. The value of a good is diminished by the crowding effect.

Equilibrium: An equilibrium is a steady state. Consider strategic interactions among people. An equilibrium occurs whenever no one wants to change his or her *strategy* given what everyone else is doing.

Excludable: See *nonexcludable*.

Freeriding: Some collective efforts are vulnerable to freeriding. That is, a freerider is able to benefit from the efforts of others while not fully contributing oneself.

Game: Games provide a means of formalizing the strategic interactions between people. The simplest games include players, *strategies*, and outcomes. A game may have any number of players who must make a single choice from a set of available strategies. Outcomes, per se, are not chosen. Outcomes are a product of every player's chosen strategy.

Ideal Point: Consider an individual's preferences over a set of alternatives. The most preferred alternative is his or her ideal point. One's utility is maximized at his or her ideal point.

Incomplete Information: In some *games*, a player may take on different attributes. That is, the same player may take on one of two or more different *types*. Different types of players have different characteristics, and they often have slightly different goals. In games with incomplete information, at least one player does not know what type some other player is. Consider a high-priced lobbyist representing a single client from a wide array of possible clients. One can think of the client as defining the lobbyist's type. If a legislator knows the lobbyist, but does not know the lobbyist's client (or type), then the legislator and lobbyist are in a game with incomplete information.

Majority: For a group with N individuals, $N/2 + 1$ or more is a majority.

Median: Array a group of individuals by their *ideal points*. The median individual in the group is the one whose ideal point is middle-most. If the group is odd in number, the median has an equal number of people on each side. For odd numbered groups of size N, the median is $(N+1)/2$. For even numbered groups, the two middle-most members are $N/2$ and $N/2 + 1$.

Mixed Strategy: See *Strategy*.

N-Person: Though two-person games are commonplace, there is no reason to limit oneself to games with only two players. Indeed, some strategic interactions are much more interesting when there are more than two individuals. *N-person* simply refers to an interaction with N players, where N is any whole number greater than or equal to 2.

Nonexcludable: Goods are nonexcludable if one cannot be prevented or excluded from benefiting from the good. Television programming is nonexcludable, whereas cable programming is excludable. Grades for group projects are often nonexcludable. Everyone in the group secures the same grade whether they contributed or not. Pure *public goods* are nonexcludable.

Nonrivalrous Consumption: A good has nonrivalrous consumption if there is no diminution in benefits as more and more people benefit from the good. Television broadcasts have nonrivalrous consumption. As more and more people watch a show, no one individual's reception becomes fuzzier. Pure *public goods* have nonrivalrous consumption. Pure private goods have rivalrous consumption.

Nonseparable: See *Separable*.

Pareto Inferior: This term is named for the Italian scholar Vilfredro Pareto (1848–1923). Consider a set of possible outcomes of interest to two or more people. An outcome is Pareto inferior if there is some other outcome that would make everyone better off and no one worse off.

Pooling Equilibrium: Pooling equilibria are those equilibria in games of *incomplete information* in which each *type* chooses the same *strategy*. Therefore, even if one is able to see another player's choice of strategy, one still cannot induce the *type* of that player.

Principal-Agent Theory: Principal-agent theory is a broad term now encompassing a wide array of relationships. Generally, one entity, the principal, hires another entity, the agent, to work on his or her behalf. The principal secures the expertise of the agent but is not always able to monitor the agent's work. Some principal-agent interactions can be formalized as a *game*, allowing one to analyze the strategic opportunities available to the principal and the agent.

Private Goods: Private goods have two features. They have *rivalrous consumption* and are *excludable*.

Property Rights: Property rights are those rights allowing for the use of goods and services or resources. Ownership has a clear connection to property rights, but ownership does not imply an absence of restrictions on use. For example, owning a lake does not allow someone to dump wastes into it. The ownership of the lake does not typically include a property right to "store" wastes at the lake's bottom. When property rights are not well defined, conflicts often ensue. For instance, does Smokestack, Inc., have property rights over its airspace? Does anyone else?

Public Goods: Public goods have two features. They have *nonrivalrous consumption* and are *nonexcludable*.

Pure Strategy: See *Strategy*.

Rivalrous Consumption: See *Nonrivalrous*.

Selective Incentives: Mancur Olson argued that groups must provide selective incentives to overcome *freeriding*. Selective incentives are available only to those people who join a group. They are *excludable*. The sale of selective incentives is central to Olson's *by-product theory*.

Separable Preferences: Preferences can be either separable or nonseparable. Consider two issue dimensions, X and Y. Preferences are separable if one's utility for X is unrelated to the level or amount of Y. Preferences are nonseparable if the utility of X is linked to the level or amount of Y. For instance, a voter's utility derived from new public school facilities may or may not be linked to the type of curriculum offered in the new schools. If the voter views the facilities and the curriculum independently, then the voter has separable preferences. If the utility of the new facilities is affected by the type of curriculum offered, then the voter has nonseparable preferences.

Separating Equilibria: Separating equilibria are those equilibria in games of *incomplete information* in which each *type* chooses a different *strategy*. Therefore, if one is able to see another player's choice of strategy, one can induce the *type* of that player.

Single-Peaked: Single-peaked preferences have a global maximum and no local maxima. Smooth bell-shaped utility functions are single peaked.

Signaling Game: Signaling games include any *game* in which one player tries to signal important information to another player. The signals may or may not be truthful, and they are seldom readily verifiable. That is, some sort of cost is typically borne if one wants to uncover the truthfulness of a signal.

Social Costs: Costs that are not borne by the private producer of a good yield a social cost. Social costs are often called externalities.

Step Good: Step goods are most easily understood in contrast to discrete or continuous goods. Discrete goods only yield a benefit if a given amount or level of the good is provided. A continuous good provides additional utility for even the smallest of increases in the level of the good. Step goods are intermediary, providing additional utility at given intervals.

Strategy: Every player in a *game* has a set of available strategies. Each player chooses one strategy from his or her set of available strategies. Technically, a strategy can be either pure or mixed. In a contribution game as described in the third chapter, an individual's set of available pure strategies might be fairly summarized as {Contribute, Don't Contribute}. That is, the player either chooses to contribute, or not. A mixed strategy would involve a weighting scheme determined by the player and some sort of randomization process. The player chooses an optimal weighting scheme, say 0.25*Contribute and 0.75*Don't Contribute, and uses a roulette wheel, coin flip, or some other randomization device to select among the pure strategies.

Threshold: If there is a certain number of individuals required for a collective effort to be successful, that number is often referred to as a threshold.

Tolerance Interval: As individuals decide whether or not to maintain their group memberships, they consider whether a group's policies are acceptable or not. The range of acceptable group policies defines one's tolerance interval. Group policies that would cause one to leave the group lie beyond one's tolerance interval.

Unraveling Problem: Any policy decision made by a group may cause a set of dissatisfied members to quit. If the remaining group members reconsider their earlier policy decisions, then the new policy decision made by this smaller group may prove to be intolerable for a set of members, causing them to quit. Once again, the group loses members. If this process continues unchecked, a group may completely unravel and lose all of its members.

Utility Function: Well-ordered preferences allow one to list a set of alternatives from best to worst. A utility function allows one to develop a metric for determining "how much" better one alternative is over another.

Voting Cycle: A voting cycle occurs when individuals with well-ordered preferences cannot, as a group, order a set of alternatives from best to worst. Suppose Uriah prefers A to B to C, Gwendolyn prefers B to C to A, and Horatio prefers C to A to B. As a group, Uriah, Gwendolyn, and Horatio prefer A to B, B to C, and C to A.

References

Books and Scholarly Articles

Aberbach, Joel D., and Bert A. Rockman. 1978. "Bureaucrats and Clientele Groups: A View from Capitol Hill." *American Journal of Political Science* 22: 818–32.

Adams, Douglas. 1979. *The Hitchhiker's Guide to the Galaxy.* New York: Harmony Books.

Ainsworth, Scott. 1989. *The Evolution of Interest Representation and the Emergence of Lobbyists.* Unpublished Ph.D. dissertation, Washington University, St. Louis, MO.

——. 1993. "Regulating Lobbyists and Interest Group Influence." *Journal of Politics* 55: 41–56.

——. 1995a. "Electoral Strength and the Emergence of Group Influence in the Late 1800s: The Grand Army of the Republic." *American Politics Quarterly* 23: 319–38.

——. 1995b. "Lobbyists as Interest Group Entrepreneurs and the Mobilization of Union Veterans." *American Review of Politics* 16: 107–29.

——. 1997. "The Role of Legislators in the Determination of Interest Group Influence in Legislatures." *Legislative Studies Quarterly* 22: 517–34.

——. 2000. "Modeling Efficacy and Interest Group Membership." *Political Behavior* 22: 89–108.

Ainsworth, Scott, and Fran Akins. 1997. "The Informational Role of Caucuses in the U.S. Congress." *American Politics Quarterly* 25: 407–30.

Ainsworth, Scott, and John Anthony Maltese. 1996. "National Grange Influence on the Supreme Court Confirmation of Stanley Matthews." *Social Science History* 20: 41–62.

Ainsworth, Scott, and Itai Sened. 1993. "Interest Group Entrepreneurs: Entrepreneurs with Two Audiences." *American Journal of Political Science* 37: 834–66.

Aldrich, John H., and David W. Rohde. 1997–98. "The Transition to Republican Rule in the House." *Political Science Quarterly* 112: 541–68.

Alinsky, Saul. 1971. *Rule for Radicals.* New York: Random House.

Aron, Joan B. 1979. "Citizen Participation at Government Expense." *Public Administration Review* 39: 477–85.

Arrow, Kenneth J. 1963. *Social Choice and Individual Values.* New Haven: Yale University Press.

Austen-Smith, David. 1987. "Interest Groups, Campaign Contributions, and Probabilistic Voting." *Public Choice* 54: 123–39.

——. 1993. "Information and Influence: Lobbying for Agendas and Votes." *American Journal of Political Science* 37: 799–833.

Austen-Smith, David, and John R. Wright. 1992. "Competitive Lobbying for a Legislator's Vote." *Social Choice and Welfare* 9: 229–57.

——. 1994. "Counteractive Lobbying." *American Journal of Political Science* 38: 25–44.

Axelrod, Robert. 1984. *The Evolution of Cooperation.* New York: Basic Books.

Bachrach, Peter, and Morton S. Baratz. 1962. "The Two Faces of Power." *American Political Science Review* 56: 947–52.

——. 1963. "Decisions and Nondecisions." *American Political Science Review* 57: 632–42.

Baker, Richard Allan. 1985. "The History of Congressional Ethics." In *Representation and Responsibility: Exploring Legislative Ethics,* edited by Bruce Jennings and Daniel Callahan. New York: Plenum Press.

Baker, Ross K. 1989. *House and Senate.* New York: W. W. Norton.

Banducci, Susan A. 1998. "Searching for Ideological Consistency in Direct Legislation Voting." In *Citizens as Legislators,* edited by Shaun Bowler, Todd Donovan, and Caroline J. Tolbert. Columbus: Ohio State University Press.

Banks, Jeffrey S., and Joel Sobel. 1987. "Equilibrium Selection in Signaling Games." *Econometrica* 55: 647–62.

Barker, Lucius J., and Twiley W. Barker Jr. 1975. *Civil Liberties and the Constitution: Cases and Commentaries,* 2nd ed. Englewood Cliffs, NJ: Prentice Hall.

Baron, Jonathon. 1997. "Political Action versus Voluntarism in Social Dilemmas and Aid for the Needy." *Rationality and Society* 9: 307–26.

Bauer, Raymond A., Ithiel de Sola Pool, and Lewis Dexter. 1963. *American Business and Public Policy*. New York: Atherton.

Baumgartner, Frank R., and Beth L. Leech. 1998. *Basic Interests: The Importance of Groups in Politics and in Political Science*. Princeton, NJ: Princeton University Press.

———. 1999. "Studying Interest Groups Using Lobbying Disclosure Reports." *VOXPOP: Newsletter of the Political Organizations and Parties Section of the American Political Science Association* 18: 13.

Baumgartner, Frank, and Jack Walker. 1988. "Survey Research and Membership in Voluntary Associations." *American Journal of Political Science* 32: 908–28.

Bentley, Arthur. 1967. *The Process of Government*, edited by Peter Odegard. Cambridge: Harvard University Press, originally published in 1908.

Berry, Jeffrey M. 1977. *Lobbying for the People*. Princeton: Princeton University Press.

———. 1978. "On the Origins of Public Interest Groups: A Test of Two Theories." *Polity* 10: 379–97.

———. 1984. *Feeding Hungry People*. New Brunswick: Rutgers University Press.

———. 1997. *The Interest Group Society*, 3rd ed. New York: Longman.

———. 1999. *The New Liberalism*. Washington, D.C.: Brookings Institution.

Berry, Jeffrey M., Kent E. Portney, and Ken Thomson. 1993. *Rebirth of Urban Democracy*. Washington, D.C.: Brookings Institution.

Bianco, William T. 1995. *Trust: Representatives and Constituents*. Ann Arbor: University of Michigan Press.

Biersack, Robert, John C. Green, Paul S. Herrnson, Lynda W. Powell, and Clyde Wilcox. 1999. "Individual Congressional Campaign Contributors: A Preliminary Report." Paper presented at the Annual Midwest Political Science Association Meeting, Chicago.

Black, Duncan. 1958. *Theory of Committees and Elections*. Cambridge: Cambridge University Press.

Blaug, Mark. 1978. *Economic Theory in Retrospect*. Cambridge: Cambridge University Press.

Bowler, Shaun, and Todd Donovan. 1998. "Direct Democracy and Minority Rights." *American Journal of Political Science* 42: 1020–24.

Bowler, Shaun, Todd Donovan, and Caroline J. Tolbert, eds. 1998. *Citizens as Legislators*. Columbus: Ohio State University Press.

Bowles, Nigel. 1987. *The White House and Capitol Hill*. Oxford: Oxford University Press.

Box-Steffensmeier, Jan M. 1996. "A Dynamic Analysis of the Role of War Chests in Campaign Strategy." *American Journal of Political Science* 40: 352–71.

Box-Steffensmeier, Jan M., and J. Tobin Grant. 1999. "All in a Day's Work: The Financial Rewards of Legislative Effectiveness." *Legislative Studies Quarterly* 24: 511–24.

Brady, Henry E., and Paul M. Sniderman. 1985. "Attitude Attribution: A Group Basis for Political Reasoning." *American Political Science Review* 79: 1061–78.

Brams, Steven J., D. Marc Kilgour, and William S. Zwicker. 1998. "The Paradox of Multiple Elections." *Social Choice and Welfare* 15: 211–36.

Brand, Stanley M., Stephen M. Ryan, and Margit H. Nahra. 1993. "Disclosing Lobbying Activities." *Administrative Law Review* Fall: 343–65.

Brown, Clifford W., Jr., Lynda W. Powell, and Clyde Wilcox. 1995. *Serious Money: Fundraising and Contributing in Presidential Nominating Campaigns.* New York: Cambridge University Press.

Browne, William P. 1995. *Cultivating Congress: Constituents, Issues, and Interests in Agriculture Policy Making.* Lawrence: University of Kansas Press.

——. 1998. "Lobbying the Public: All-Directional Advocacy." In *Interest Group Politics,* edited by Allan J. Cigler and Burdett A. Loomis. Washington, D.C.: CQ Press.

Browne, William P., and Won K. Paik. 1993. "Beyond the Domain: Recasting Network Politics in the Postreform Congress." *American Journal of Political Science* 37: 1054–78.

Buchanan, James M., and Gordon Tullock. 1967. *Calculus of Consent.* Ann Arbor: University of Michigan Press.

Caldeira, Gregory A., Marie Hojnacki, and John R. Wright. 2000. "The Lobbying Activities of Organized Interests in Federal Judicial Nominations." *Journal of Politics* 62: 51–69.

Caldeira, Gregory A., and John R. Wright. 1988. "Organized Interests and Agenda Setting in the U.S. Supreme Court." *American Political Science Review* 82: 1109–28.

——. 1990. "Amici Curiae before the Supreme Court: Who Participates, When, and How Much?" *Journal of Politics* 52: 782–806.

——. 1995. "Lobbying for Justice." In *Contemplating Courts,* edited by Lee Epstein. Washington, D.C.: CQ Press.

Calvert, Randall L., Mathew D. McCubbins, and Barry R. Weingast. 1989. "A Theory of Political Control and Agency Discretion." *American Journal of Political Science* 33: 588–611.

Carter, Lief, and Christine Harrington. 2000. *Administrative Law and Politics.* New York: Longman.

Chin, Michelle L., Jon R. Bond, and Nehemia Geva. 2000. "A Foot in the Door: An Experimental Study of PAC and Constituency Effects on Access." *Journal of Politics* 62: 534–549.

Clotfelter, Charles T. 1985. *Federal Tax Policy and Charitable Giving.* Chicago: University of Chicago Press.

Coase, Ronald H. 1960. "The Problem of Social Cost." *Journal of Law and Economics* 3: 1–44.

Corrado, Anthony. 1992. *Creative Campaigning: PACs and the Presidential Selection Process.* Boulder: Westview.

Cox, Gary W., and Jonathon N. Katz. 1996. "Why Did the Incumbency Advantage in U.S. House Elections Grow?" *American Journal of Political Science* 40: 478–97.

Cox, Gary W., and Eric Magar. 1999. "How Much is Majority Status in the U.S. Congress Worth?" *American Political Science Review* 93: 299–310.

Cunningham, Noble. 1978. *Circular Letters of Congressmen to Their Constituents, 1789–1829.* Chapel Hill: University of North Carolina Press.

Dahl, Robert A. 1956. *A Preface to Democratic Theory.* Chicago, University of Chicago Press.

——. 1961. *Who Governs.* New Haven: Yale University Press.

Danielian, Lucig H., and Benjamin I. Page. 1994. "The Heavenly Chorus: Interest Group Voices on TV News." *American Journal of Political Science* 38: 1056–78.

Davidson, Osha Gray. 1993. *Under Fire: The NRA and the Battle for Gun Control.* New York: Henry Holt and Company.

de Figueiredo, John M., and Emerson H. Tiller. 2001. "The Structure and Conduct of Corporate Lobbying: How Firms Lobby the Federal Communications Commission." *Journal of Economics and Management Strategy* 10: 91–123.

DeForest, J. W. 1960. *Honest John Vane.* State College, PA: Bald Eagle Press, originally published in 1875.

——. 1961. *Playing the Mischief.* State College, PA: Bald Eagle Press, originally published 1875.

DeGregorio, Christine. 1997. *Networks of Champions: Leadership, Access, and Advocacy in the U.S. House of Representatives.* Ann Arbor: University of Michigan Press.

DeGregorio, Christine, and Kevin Conway. 1999. "Some Consequences of Changing Majorities in the U.S. House of Representatives (1991–1996): Leaders and Advocates in Pursuit of Policy." Paper presented at the 1999 Annual Southern Political Science Association Meeting, Savannah, Georgia.

Dexter, Lewis Anthony. 1969. *How Organizations Are Represented in Washington.* Indianapolis: Bobbs-Merrill.

Donne, John. 1975. *Devotions upon Emergent Occasions,* edited by Anthony Raspa. New York: Oxford University Press.

Downs, Anthony. 1957. *An Economic View of Democracy.* New York: Harper & Row.

DuBois, W. E. B. 1993. *The Souls of Black Folk.* New York: Knopf, Random House.

Eastman, Hope. 1977. *Lobbying: A Constitutionally Protected Right.* Washington, D.C.: American Enterprise Institute.

Easton, David. 1953. *The Political System*. New York: Knopf.

Edwards, George C., III. 1980. *Presidential Influence in Congress*. San Francisco: W. H. Freeman.

Eggertsson, Thrainn. 1990. *Economic Behavior and Institutions*. Cambridge: Cambridge University Press.

Ellison, Ralph. 1992. *Invisible Man*. New York: Modern Library.

Epstein, David, and Sharyn O'Halloran. 1995. "Theory of Strategic Oversight." *Journal of Law, Economics, & Organization* 11: 227–55.

———. 1999. *Delegating Powers*. New York: Cambridge University Press.

Epstein, Lee. 1985. *Conservatives in Court*. Knoxville: University of Tennessee Press.

Epstein, Lee, and Jack Knight. 1998. *The Choices Justices Make*. Washington, D.C.: CQ Press.

Epstein, Lee, and C. K. Rowland. 1991. "Debunking the Myth of Interest Group Invincibility in the Courts." *American Political Science Review* 85: 205–17.

Esterling, Kevin. 2001. "Modeling Lobbyist Access: Ideology, Political Participation, and Specialized Knowledge." Paper presented at the Southern Political Science Association Meeting, Atlanta, Georgia.

Fenno, Richard F., Jr. 1959. *The President's Cabinet*. Cambridge: Harvard University Press.

———. 1978. *Home Style: House Members in Their Districts*. Boston: Little, Brown.

Fiorina, Morris. 1989. *Congress: Keystone of the Washington Establishment*, 2nd ed. New Haven: Yale University Press.

Fisher, David Hackett. 1970. *Historical Fallacies: Toward a Logic of Historical Thought*. New York: Harper & Row.

Fisher, Louis. 1993. "The Legislative Veto—Invalidated, It Survives." *Law and Contemporary Problems* 56: 273–92.

Foley, Edward B. 1994. "'Equal Dollars per Voter'—A Constitutional Principle of Campaign Finance Reform." *Columbia Law Review* May: 1204–57.

Follett, Mary P. 1918. *The New State*. Gloucester, MA: Peter Smith.

Freeman, J. Leiper. 1965. *The Political Process: Executive Bureau—Legislative Committee Relations*. New York: Random House.

Frendreis, John P., and Richard W. Waterman. 1985. "PAC Contributions and Legislative Behavior." *Social Science Quarterly* 66: 401–12.

Furlong, Scott. 1998. "The Lobbying Disclosure Act and Interest Group Lobbying Data." *VOXPOP: Newsletter of the Political Organizations and Parties Section of the American Political Science Association* 17: 4–6.

Gais, Thomas. 1996. *Improper Influence: Campaign Finance Law, Political Interest Groups, and the Problem of Equality*. Ann Arbor: University of Michigan Press.

Gais, Thomas L., and Jack Walker. 1991. "Pathways to Influence in American Politics." In *Mobilizing Interest Groups in America,* edited by Jack L. Walker. Ann Arbor: University of Michigan Press.

Galloway, George B. 1946. *Congress at the Crossroads.* New York: Thomas Y. Crowell.

———. 1951. "The Operation of the Legislative Reorganization Act of 1946." *American Political Science Review* 45: 41–68.

Garceau, Oliver. 1961. *The Political Life of the American Medical Association.* Hamden, CT: Archon Books.

Garson, G. David. 1978. *Group Theories of Politics.* Beverly Hills: Sage Publications.

Gartner, Scott Sigmund, and Gary M. Segura. 1997. "Appearances Can Be Deceiving: Self Selection, Social Group Identification, and Political Mobilization." *Rationality and Society* 9: 131–61.

Gerber, Elisabeth R. 1999. *The Populist Paradox.* Princeton, NJ: Princeton University Press.

Gerber, Elisabeth R., and Arthur Lupia. 1995. "Campaign Competition and Policy Responsiveness in Direct Legislation Elections." *Political Behavior* 17: 639–56.

Gibb, Corinne Lathrop. 1966. *Hidden Hierarchies: The Professionals and the Government.* New York: Harper & Row.

Godwin, R. Kenneth. 1988. *One Billion Dollars of Influence: The Direct Marketing of Politics.* Chatham, NJ: Chatham House Publishers.

Godwin, R. Kenneth, Nancy Kucinski, and John Green. 1993. "The Market for Publicly Supplied Goods." Paper presented at the Southern Political Science Association Meeting, Savannah, Georgia.

Goidel, Robert K., and Donald A. Gross. 1994. "A Systems Approach to Campaign Finance in U.S. House Elections." *American Politics Quarterly* 22: 125–53.

Goidel, Robert K., Donald A. Gross, and Todd G. Shields. 1999. *Money Matters: Consequences of Campaign Finance Reform in the U.S. House Elections.* Lanham, Maryland: Rowman and Littlefield.

Goldstein, Kenneth M. 1999. *Interest Groups, Lobbying, and Participation in America.* New York: Cambridge University Press.

Gray, Virginia, and David Lowery. 1996. *The Population Ecology of Interest Representation: Lobbying Communities in the American States.* Ann Arbor: University of Michigan Press.

Green, Donald Philip, and Jonathon S. Krasno. 1988. "Salvation for the Spendthrift Incumbent." *American Journal of Political Science* 32: 884–907.

———. 1990. "Rebuttal to Jacobson's 'New Evidence for Old Arguments.'" *American Journal of Political Science* 34: 363–72.

Grenzke, Janet M. 1989. "PACs and the Congressional Supermarket." *American Journal of Political Science* 33: 1–24.

Grier, Kevin B., Michael C. Munger, and Brian E. Roberts. 1991. "Industrial Organization of Corporate Political Participation." *Southern Economic Journal* 57: 727–38.

———. 1994. "The Determinants of Industry Political Activity, 1978–1986." *American Political Science Review* 88: 911–26.

Haire, Susan, and Stefanie Lindquist. 1997. "Social Security Disability Cases in the U.S. Court of Appeals." *Judicature* 80: 230–36.

Hall, Kermit. 1992. *Oxford Companion to the Supreme Court of the United States.* New York: Oxford University Press.

Hall, Richard L. 1998. "Lobbying as an Informational Subsidy." Paper presented at the Annual Meeting of the Midwestern Political Science Association, Chicago.

Hall, Richard L., and Frank W. Wayman. 1990. "Buying Time: Moneyed Interests and the Mobilization of Bias in Congressional Committees." *American Political Science Review* 84: 797–820.

Hammond, Susan W. 1998. *Congressional Caucuses in National Policy Making.* Baltimore: Johns Hopkins University Press.

Hammond, Susan W., Arthur G. Stevens, and D. P. Mulhollan. 1983. "Congressional Caucuses: Legislators as Lobbyists." In *Interest Group Politics*, edited by Allan J. Cigler and Burdett A. Loomis. Washington, D.C.: CQ Press.

Hansen, John Mark. 1985. "The Political Economy of Group Membership." *American Political Science Review* 79: 79–96.

———. 1987. "Choosing Sides: The Creation of an Agricultural Policy Network in Congress, 1919–1932." *Studies in American Political Development* 2: 183–229.

———. 1991. *Gaining Access.* Chicago: University of Chicago Press.

Hansen, Wendy L., and Neil J. Mitchell. 1999. "Is Corporate Political Activity Cumulative?" Paper presented at the Annual Meeting of the American Political Science Association, Atlanta, Georgia.

———. 2000. "Disaggregating and Explaining Corporate Political Activity." *American Political Science Review* 94: 891–905.

Hasen, Richard L. 1996. "'Clipping Coupons for Democracy'—An Egalitarian/Public Choice Defense of Campaign Finance Vouchers." *California Law Review* January: 1–59

Haskell, John. 2001. *Direct Democracy or Representative Government?* Boulder: Westview.

Haworth, Paul Leland. 1906. *The Hayes-Tilden Election.* Indianapolis: Bobbs-Merrill.

Heard, Alexander. 1962. *The Costs of Democracy.* Garden City, NY: Doubleday.

Heclo, Hugh. 1978. "Issue Networks and the Executive Establishment." In *The New American Political System,* edited by Anthony King. Washington, D.C.: American Enterprise Institute.

Heitshusen, Valerie. 2000. "Interest Group Lobbying and U.S. House Decentralization." *Political Research Quarterly* 53: 151–76.

Herbst, Susan. 1998. *Reading Public Opinion: How Political Actors View the Democratic Process.* Chicago: University of Chicago Press.

Herndon, James F. 1982. "Access, Record and Competition as Influences on Interest Group Contributions to Congressional Campaigns." *Journal of Politics* 44: 996–1019.

Herring, E. Pendleton. 1929. *Group Representation before Congress.* Baltimore: Johns Hopkins University Press.

Hertzke, Alan. 1988. *Representing God in Washington.* Knoxville: University of Tennessee Press.

Hess, Stephen. 1976. *Organizing the Presidency.* Washington, D.C.: Brookings Institution.

Hibbing, John. 1999. "Do Americans Care about and Trust Their Government? A Congressional Briefing." Consortium of Social Science Associations.

Hirschman, Albert O. 1970. *Exit, Voice and Loyalty: Responses to Decline in Firms, Organizations and States.* Cambridge: Harvard University Press.

———. 1982. *Shifting Involvements: Private Interest and Public Action.* Princeton, NJ: Princeton University Press.

Hojnacki, Marie. 1997. "Interest Groups' Decisions to Join Alliances or Work Alone" *American Journal of Political Science* 41: 61–87.

Hojnacki, Marie, and David C. Kimball. 1999. "The Who and How of Organizations' Lobbying Strategies in Committee." *Journal of Politics* 61: 999–1024.

Hoogenboom, Ari. 1988. *The Presidency of Rutherford B. Hayes.* Lawrence: University of Kansas Press.

Hula, Kevin W. 1999. *Lobbying Together: Interest Group Coalitions in Legislative Politics.* Washington, D.C.: Georgetown University Press.

Humphries, Craig. 1991. "Corporations, PACs, and the Strategic Link between Contributions and Lobbying Activities." *Western Political Quarterly* 44: 353–72.

Jacobson, Gary C. 1990. "The Effects of Campaign Spending in House Elections: New Evidence for Old Arguments." *American Journal of Political Science* 34: 334–62.

———. 1992. *The Politics of Congressional Elections,* 3rd ed. New York: HarperCollins.

———. 1999. "The Effect of the AFL-CIO's 'Voter Education' Campaigns on the 1996 House Elections." *Journal of Politics* 61: 185–194.

Jankowski, Richard, and Clyde Brown. 1995. "Political Success, Government Subsidization, and the Group Freerider Problem." *Social Science Quarterly* 76: 853–62.

Jenck, Christopher. 1987. "Who Gives to What." In *The Nonprofit Sector: A Research Handbook,* edited by Walter W. Powell. New Haven: Yale University Press.

Johnson, Paul E. 1987. "Foresight and Myopia in Organizational Membership." *Journal of Politics* 49: 678–703.

———. 1988. "On the Theory of Political Competition." *Public Choice* 58: 217–35.

———. 1990a. "Asymmetries in Political Entry." *European Journal of Political Economy* 6: 378–96.

———. 1990b. "Unraveling in Democratically Governed Groups." *Rationality and Society* 2: 4–34.

———. 1996. "Unraveling in a Variety of Institutional Settings." *Journal of Theoretical Politics* 8: 299–329.

Josephson, Matthew. 1938. *The Politicos: 1865–1896.* New York: Harcourt, Brace.

Kahneman, Daniel, and Amos Tversky. 1979. "Prospect Theory: An Analysis of Decisions under Risk." *Econometrica* 47: 263–91.

Kenny, Christopher, and Michael McBurnett. 1992. "A Dynamic Mode of the Effect of Campaign Spending on Congressional Vote Choice." *American Journal of Political Science* 36: 923–37.

Kernell, Samuel. 1984. "The Presidency and the People: The Modern Paradox." In *The Presidency and the Political System,* edited by Michael Nelson. Washington, D.C.: CQ Press.

———. 1986. *Going Public: New Strategies of Presidential Leadership.* Washington, D.C.: CQ Press.

Kerr, K. Austin. 1985. *Organized for Prohibition: A New History of the Anti-Saloon League.* New Haven: Yale University Press.

Kerwin, Cornelius M. 1994. *Rulemaking.* Washington, D.C.: Congressional Quarterly.

Kettl, Donald F. 1988. *Government by Proxy: (Mis?) Managing Federal Programs.* Washington, D.C.: CQ Press.

———. 1993. *Sharing Power: Public Governance and Private Markets.* Washington, D.C.: Brookings Institution.

Klein, Benjamin, Robert G. Crawford, and Armen A. Alchian. 1978. "Vertical Integration, Appropriable Rents, and the Competitive Contracting Process." *Journal of Law and Economics* 21: 297–326.

Knott, Jack H., and Gary J. Miller. 1987. *Reforming Bureaucracy: The Politics of Institutional Choice.* Englewood Cliffs, NJ: Prentice Hall.

Kobylka, Joseph F. 1987. "A Court Related Context for Group Litigation: Libertarian Groups and Obscenity." *Journal of Politics* 49: 1061–78.

Kollman, Ken. 1997. "Inviting Friends to Lobby: Interest Groups, Ideological Bias, and Congressional Committees." *American Journal of Political Science* 41: 519–44.

———. 1998. *Outside Lobbying: Public Opinion and Interest Group Strategies.* Princeton, NJ: Princeton University Press.

Krislov, Samuel. 1963. "The Amicus Curiae Brief: From Friendship to Advocacy." *Yale Law Journal* 72: 694–721.

Kumar, Martha Joynt, and Michael Baruch Grossman. 1984. "The Presidency and Interest Groups." In *The Presidency and the Political System*, edited by Michael Nelson. Washington, D.C.: CQ Press.

Lacy, Dean, and Emerson Niou. 2000. "A Problem with Referendums." *Journal of Theoretical Politics* 12: 5–31.

Laffont, Jean-Jacques. 1990. *Fundamentals of Public Economics.* Cambridge: MIT Press.

Langbein, Laura. 1986. "Money and Access." *Journal of Politics* 48: 1052–62.

———. 1993. "PACs, Lobbies, and Political Conflict: The Case of Gun Control." *Public Choice* 75: 254–71.

Langbein, Laura, and Mark A. Lotwis. 1990. "The Political Efficacy of Lobbying and Money." *Legislative Studies Quarterly* 15: 413–40.

Lasswell, Harold Dwight. 1958. *Politics: Who Gets What, When and How.* New York: Meridian.

Latham, Earl. 1952. "The Group Basis of Politics: Notes for a Theory." *American Political Science Review* 46: 376–97.

———. 1965. *The Group Basis of Politics.* New York: Octagon Books.

Leighley, Jan. 1996. "Group Membership and the Mobilization of Political Participation." *Journal of Politics* 58: 447–63.

Lipsky, Michael. 1968. "Protest as a Political Resource." *American Political Science Review* 62: 1144–58.

Lowi, Theodore J. 1969. *The End of Liberalism: Ideology, Policy, and the Crisis of Public Authority.* New York: W. W. Norton.

Lupia, Arthur. 1994. "Shortcuts versus Encyclopedias: Information and Voting Behavior in California Insurance Reform Elections." *American Political Science Review* 88: 63–76.

Madison, James. 1961. "Federalist #10." In *The Federalist Papers*, edited by Clinton Rossiter. New York: New American Library.

Magleby, David, ed. 2000. *Getting Inside the Outside Campaign.* Brigham Young University: Center for the Study of Elections and Democracy.

Maltese, John Anthony. 1992. *Spin Control: The White House Office of Communications and the Management of Presidential News.* Chapel Hill: University of North Carolina Press.

———. 1998. *The Selling of Supreme Court Nominees.* Baltimore: Johns Hopkins University Press.

Mansbridge, Jane. 1992. "A Deliberative Theory of Interest Representation." In *The Politics of Interests,* edited by Mark P. Petracca. Boulder: Westview.

Mathews, Donald R. 1960. *U.S. Senators and Their World.* Chapel Hill: University of North Carolina Press.

May, Kenneth O. 1952. "A Set of Independent Necessary and Sufficient Conditions for Simple Majority Decision." *Econometrica* 20: 680–84.

McAdam, Doug. 1982. *Political Process and the Development of Black Insurgency, 1930–1970.* Chicago: University of Chicago Press.

McCarthy, John D., and Mayer N. Zald. 1973. *The Trend of Social Movements in America: Professionalization and Resource Mobilization.* Morristown, NJ: General Learning Press.

McCarty, Nolan, and Lawrence Rothenberg. N.d. "Contributions, Candidates, and the Nature of Electoral Support." Mimeo, Princeton University.

McChesney, Fred S. 1997. *Money for Nothing: Politicians, Rent Extraction, and Political Extortion.* Boston: Harvard University Press.

McConnell, Grant. 1966. *Private Power and American Democracy.* New York: Alfred A. Knopf.

McCubbins, Mathew D., and Thomas Schwartz. 1984. "Congressional Oversight Overlooked." *American Journal of Political Science* 28: 165–79.

McFarland, Andrew S. 1984. *Common Cause: Lobbying the Public Interest.* Chatham, NJ: Chatham House Publishers.

Milbrath, Lester W. 1963. *The Washington Lobbyists.* Chicago: Rand McNally.

Milchtaich, Igal, and Eyal Winter. 2002. "Stability and Segregation in Group Formation." *Games and Economic Behavior* 38: 318–46.

Miller, Nicholas R. 1983. "Pluralism and Social Choice." *American Political Science Review* 77: 734–47.

Mitchell, William C., and Michael C. Munger. 1991. "Economic Models of Interest Groups." *American Journal of Political Science* 35: 512–46.

Moe, Terry. 1984. "The New Economics of Organization." *American Journal of Political Science* 28: 739–77.

Mollenkopf, John H. 1983. *The Contested City.* Princeton, NJ: Princeton University Press.

Monroe, James A. 1990. *The Democratic Wish: Popular Participation and the Limits of American Government.* New York: Basic Books.

Morton, Rebecca, and Charles Cameron. 1992. "Elections and the Theory of Campaign Contributions: A Survey and Critical Analysis." *Economics and Politics* 4: 80–107.

Mueller, John E. 1999. *Capitalism, Democracy, and Ralph's Pretty Good Grocery.* Princeton, NJ: Princeton University Press.

Nelson, Thomas E., and Donald R. Kinder. 1996. "Issue Frames and Group-Centrism in American Public Opinion." *Journal of Politics* 58: 1055–78.

Nownes, Anthony. 1999. "Solicited Advice and Lobbyist Power: Evidence from Three American States." *Legislative Studies Quarterly* 24: 113–23.

———. 2000. "Toward a Theory of Public Interest Group Collapse and Death." Paper presented at the Annual Midwest Political Science Association Meeting, Chicago.

Odegard, Peter C. 1928. *Pressure Politics: The Story of the Anti-Saloon League.* New York: Columbia University Press.

Olson, Alison Gilbert. 1992. *Making the Empire Work: London and American Interest Groups, 1690–1790.* Cambridge: Harvard University Press.

Olson, Mancur. 1965. *The Logic of Collective Action.* Cambridge: Harvard University Press.

———. 1982. *The Rise and Decline of Nations.* New Haven: Yale University Press.

Olson, Susan M. 1990. "Interest Group Litigation in Federal District Court." *Journal of Politics* 52: 854–82.

Ornstein, Norman J., and Shirley Elder. 1978. *Interest Groups, Lobbying, and Policymaking.* Washington, D.C.: CQ Press.

Page, Benjamin I., and Mark P. Petracca. 1983. *The American Presidency.* New York: McGraw-Hill.

Palfrey, Thomas R., and Howard Rosenthal. 1988. "Private Incentives in Social Dilemmas" *Journal of Public Economics* 35: 309–32.

Pateman, Carole. 1970. *Participation and Democratic Theory.* Cambridge: Cambridge University Press.

Peterson, Mark A. 1992. "Interest Mobilization and the Presidency." In *The Politics of Interests*, edited by Mark P. Petracca. Boulder: Westview.

Pika, Joseph A. 1983. "Interest Groups and the Executive." In *Interest Group Politics*, edited by Allan J. Cigler and Burdett A. Loomis. Washington, D.C.: CQ Press.

———. 1991. "Opening Doors for Kindred Souls: The White House Office of Public Liaison." In *Interest Group Politics*, 3rd ed., edited by Allan J. Cigler and Burdett A. Loomis. Washington, D.C.: CQ Press.

Pitkin, Hanna. 1967. *The Concept of Representation.* Berkeley: University of California Press.

Piven, Frances Fox, and Richard A. Cloward. 1977. *Poor People's Movements.* New York: Pantheon.

Posner, Richard A. 1977. *Economic Analysis and the Law*, 2nd ed. Boston: Little Brown.

———. 1993. "What Do Judges and Justices Maximize? (The Same Thing Everybody Else Does)." *Supreme Court Economic Review* 3: 1–41.

Potters, Jan. 1992. *Lobbying and Pressure.* Amsterdam: Tinbergen Institute.

Pratt, Cornelius. 1994. "Hill and Knowlton's Two Ethical Dilemmas." *Public Relations Review* 20: 277–93.

Putnam, Robert. 1995a. "Bowling Alone: America's Declining Social Capital." *Journal of Democracy* 6: 63–78.

——. 1995b. "Tuning in, Tuning out—The Strange Disappearance of Social Capital in America." *PS-Political Science & Politics* 28: 664–83.

——. 2000. *Bowling Alone: The Collapse and Revival of American Community.* New York: Simon & Schuster.

Rados, David L. 1996. *Marketing for Nonprofits,* 2nd ed. Westport, CT: Auborn House.

Rasmusen, Eric. 1990. *Games and Information.* Oxford: Basil Blackwell.

——. 1993. "Lobbying When the Decision Maker Can Acquire Independent Information." *Public Choice* 77: 899–913.

Regens, James L., and Ronald Keith Gaddie. 1995. *The Economic Realities of Political Reform.* New York: Cambridge University Press.

Rich, Andrew, and R. Kent Weaver. 1998. "Advocates and Analysts: Think Tanks and the Politicization of Expertise." In *Interest Group Politics,* edited by Allan J. Cigler and Burdett A. Loomis. Washington, D.C.: CQ Press.

Riker, William H. 1982. *Liberalism against Populism.* San Francisco: W. H. Freeman.

Roberts, Russell D. 1984. "A Positive Model of Private Charity and Public Transfers." *Journal of Political Economy* 92: 136–48.

Romer, Thomas, and James M. Snyder Jr. 1994. "An Empirical Investigation of the Dynamics of PAC Contributions." *American Journal of Political Science* 38: 745–69.

Roschwalb, Susanne. 1994. "The Hill & Knowlton Cases." *Public Relations Review* 20: 267–75.

Rosenstone, Steven J., and John Mark Hansen. 1993. *Mobilization, Participation, and Democracy in America.* New York: Macmillan Publishing.

Rosenthal, Alan. 1993. *The Third House: Lobbyists and Lobbying in the States.* Washington, D.C.: CQ Press.

Rothenberg, Lawrence S. 1988. "Organizational Maintenance and the Retention Decision in Groups." *American Political Science Review* 82: 1129–52.

——. 1992. *Linking Citizens to Government.* New York: Cambridge University Press.

Sabato, Larry J. 1985. *PAC Power: Inside the World of Political Action Committees.* New York: W. W. Norton.

St. James, Warren D. 1958. *The National Association for the Advancement of Colored People.* New York: Exposition Press.

Salisbury, Robert H. 1969. "An Exchange Theory of Interest Groups." *Midwest Journal of Political Science* 13: 1–32.

——. 1984. "Interest Representation: The Dominance of Institutions." *American Political Science Review* 78: 64–76.

——. 1986. "Washington Lobbyists: A Collective Portrait." In *Interest Group Politics,* 2nd ed., edited by Allan J. Cigler and Burdett A. Loomis. Washington, D.C.: Congressional Quarterly.

Salisbury, Robert H., and Kenneth A. Shepsle. 1981. "U.S. Congressman as Enterprise." *Legislative Studies Quarterly* 6: 559–76.

Scarsini, Marco. 1998. "A Strong Paradox of Multiple Elections." *Social Choice and Welfare* 15: 237–38.

Schattschneider, E. E. 1935. *Politics, Pressures and the Tariff.* Englewood Cliffs, NJ: Prentice Hall.

———. 1942. *Party Government.* New York: Holt, Rinehart, & Winston.

———. 1958. *Equilibrium and Change in American Politics.* College Park, MD: Bureau of Governmental Research, College of Business and Public Administration, University of Maryland.

———. 1960. *The Semisovereign People.* New York: Holt, Rinehart, & Winston.

———. 1969. *Two Hundred Million Americans in Search of a Government.* New York: Holt, Rinehart, & Winston.

Scheppele, Kim Lane, and Jack L. Walker Jr. 1991. "The Litigation Strategies of Interest Groups." In *Mobilizing Interest Groups in America*, edited by Jack L. Walker Jr. Ann Arbor: University of Michigan Press.

Schlozman, Kay Lehman, and John T. Tierney. 1983. "More of the Same: Pressure Group Activity in a Decade of Change." *Journal of Politics* 45: 351–75.

———. 1986. *Organized Interests and American Democracy.* New York: Harper and Row.

Schmidt, David D. 1989. *Citizen Lawmakers: The Ballot Initiative Revolution.* Philadelphia: Temple University Press.

Schroedel, Jean R. 1987. "Campaign Contributions and Legislative Outcomes." *Western Political Quarterly* 40: 371–89.

Segal, Jeffrey A., Charles M. Cameron, and Albert D. Cover. 1992. "A Spatial Model of Roll Call Voting: Senators, Constituents, Presidents and Interest Groups in Supreme Court Confirmations." *American Journal of Political Science* 36: 96–121.

Seidman, Harold. 1970. *Politics, Position, and Power: The Dynamics of Federal Organization.* New York: Oxford University Press.

Sened, Itai. 1997. *The Political Institution of Private Property.* Cambridge: Cambridge University Press.

Shaiko, Ronald G. 1998. "Reverse Lobbying: Interest Group Mobilization from the White House and the Hill." In *Interest Group Politics*, edited by Allan J. Cigler and Burdett A. Loomis. Washington, D.C.: CQ Press.

———. 1999. *Voices and Echoes for the Environment.* New York: Columbia University Press.

Sheets, Tara E. 1999. *The Encyclopedia of Washington Representatives*, 35th ed. Farmington Hills, MI: The Gale Group.

Shepsle, Kenneth A., and Mark S. Bonchek. 1997. *Analyzing Politics.* New York: W. W. Norton.

Shipan, Charles R. 1997. *Designing Judicial Review: Interest Groups, Congress, and Communications Policy.* Ann Arbor: University of Michigan Press.

Skocpol, Theda. 1992. *Protecting Soldiers and Mothers.* Cambridge: Harvard University Press.

Sloof, Randolph. 1998. *Game-theoretic Models of the Political Influence of Interest Groups.* Boston: Kluwer.

Smith, Hedrick. 1988. *The Power Game.* New York: Random House.

Smith, Steven Rathgeb, and Michael Lipsky. 1993. *Nonprofits for Hire: The Welfare State in the Age of Contracting.* Cambridge: Harvard University Press.

Snider, James H., and Benjamin I. Page. 1997a. "Does Media Ownership Affect Media Standards?" Paper presented at the Annual Meeting of the Midwest Political Science Association, Chicago.

———. 1997b. "The Political Power of TV Broadcasters." Evanston: Working Papers, Institute for Policy Research, Northwestern University.

———. 1999. "Measuring Information and Money as Interest Group Resources." Paper presented at the Annual Meeting of the Midwest Political Science Association, Chicago.

Snyder, James M., Jr. 1992. "Long-Term Investing in Politicians: Or, Give Early, Give Often." *Journal of Law and Economics* 35: 15–43.

———. 1993. "The Market for Campaign Contributions: Evidence for the U.S. Senate 1980–1986." *Economics and Politics* 5: 219–40.

Sorauf, Frank J. 1984. *What Price PACs?* New York: Twentieth Century Fund.

———. 1984–85. "Who's in Charge: Accountability in Political Action Committees." *Political Science Quarterly* 99: 591–614.

———. 1992. *Inside Campaign Finance: Myths and Realities.* New Haven: Yale University Press.

Steele, J. Valerie, ed. 1999. *Washington Representatives, 1999.* Washington, D.C.: Columbia Books.

Street, David, George T. Martin Jr., and Laura Kramer Gordon. 1979. *The Welfare Industry.* Beverly Hills: Sage Publications.

Suarez, Sandra L. 1997. "Explaining the Political Behavior of Business." Paper presented at the Annual American Political Science Association Meeting, Washington, D.C.

Talbert, Jeffrey C., Bryan D. Jones, and Frank R. Baumgartner. 1995. "Nonlegislative Hearings and Policy Change in Congress." *American Journal of Political Science* 39: 383–406.

Thomas, Lately. 1965. *Sam Ward: King of the Lobby.* Boston: Houghton Mifflin.

Thompson, Dennis F. 1995. *Ethics in Congress.* Washington, D.C.: Brookings Institution.

Thompson, Margaret Susan. 1986. *The "Spider Web": Congress and Lobbying in the Age of Grant.* Ithaca: Cornell University Press.

Tocqueville, Alexis de. 1961. *Democracy in America*, Volumes One and Two. New York: Schocken Books, first published in English in 1835 (Vol. I) and 1840 (Vol. II).

Truman, David B. 1971. *The Governmental Process*, 2nd ed. New York: Knopf, originally published in 1951.

Twain, Mark. 1892. *The American Claimant*. New York: C. L. Webster & Co.

van Winden, Frans. 1999. "On the Economic Theory of Interest Groups: Towards a Group Frame of Reference in Political Economics." *Public Choice* 100: 1–29.

Verba, Sidney, and Norman H. Nie. 1972. *Participation in America*. New York: Harper & Row.

Walker, Jack L., Jr. 1966. "A Critique of the Elitist Theory of Democracy." *American Political Science Review* 60: 285–95.

———. 1983. "The Origins and Maintenance of Interest Groups in America." *American Political Science Review* 77: 390–406.

West, Darrel M., and Burdett Loomis. 1999. *The Sound of Money: How Political Interests Get What They Want*. New York: W. W. Norton.

White, Leonard D. 1954. *The Jacksonians: A Study in Administrative History, 1829–1861*. New York: Macmillan Company.

———. 1956. *The Federalists: A Study in Administrative History*. New York: Macmillan Company.

Wiggins, Charles W., Keith E. Hamm, and Charles G. Bell. 1992. "Interest Group Influence and Party Influence Agents in the Legislative Process." *Journal of Politics* 54: 82–100.

Wilson, James Q. 1973. *Political Organizations*. New York: Basic Books.

Wittman, Donald A. 1995. *The Myth of Democratic Failure: Why Political Institutions Are Efficient*. Chicago: University of Chicago Press.

Wolfe, Tom. 1970. *Radical Chic and Mau Mauing the Flak Catchers*. New York: Farrar, Straus, and Giroux.

Woodward, C. Vann. 1951. *Reunion and Reaction: The Compromise of 1877 and the End of Reconstruction*. Boston: Little, Brown.

———. 1966. *The Strange Career of Jim Crow*. London: Oxford University Press.

Wright, John R. 1985. "PACs, Contributions, and Roll Calls." *American Political Science Review* 79: 400–14.

———. 1989. "PAC Contributions, Lobbying, and Representation." *Journal of Politics* 51: 713–29.

———. 1990. "Contributions, Lobbying, and Committee Voting in the U.S. House of Representatives." *American Political Science Review* 84: 417–38.

———. 1996. *Interest Groups and Congress*. Boston: Allyn & Bacon.

———. 2000. "Interest Groups, Congressional Reform, and Party Government in the United States." *Legislative Studies Quarterly* 25: 217–35.

Yoho, James. 1995. "Madison on the Beneficial Effects of Interest Groups." *Polity* 27: 587–605.

Court Cases

Brown v. Board of Education, 348 U.S. 886 (1954).

Buchanan v. Warley, 245 U.S. 60 (1917).

Buckley v. Valeo, 424 U.S. 1 (1976).

Chevron U.S.A. v. Natural Resources Defense Council, 467 U.S. 837 (1984).

Escobedo v. Illinois, 378 U.S. 478 (1964).

FEC v. Akins, 524 U.S. 11 (1998).

Friends of the Earth v. Laidlaw Environmental Services, 528 U.S. 167 (2000).

Grovey v. Townsend, 295 U.S. 45 (1935).

Guinn v. United States, 238 U.S. 347 (1915).

INS v. Chadha, 462 U.S. 919 (1983).

J. W. Hampton Jr. & Co. v. United States, 276 U.S. 394 (1928).

Mapp v. Ohio, 367 U.S. 643 (1961).

Miller v. California, 413 U.S. 15 (1973).

Miranda v. Arizona, 384 U.S. 436 (1966).

Moore v. Dempsey, 261 U.S. 86 (1923).

Meyer v. Grant, 486 U.S. 414 (1988).

National Association for the Advancement of Colored People v. Alabama, 357 U.S. 449 (1958).

National Society of Professional Engineers v. United States, 435 U.S. 679 (1978).

Nixon v. Shrink Missouri Government PAC, 528 U.S. 377 (2000).

Pacific Legal Foundation v. Jere Goyan, 664 F.2d 1221 (4th Cir. 1981).

Pipefitters Local Union No. 526 of St. Louis v. United States, 407 U.S. 385 (1972).

Plessy v. Ferguson, 163 U.S. 537 (1896).

Reitman v. Mulkey, 387 U.S. 369 (1967).

Sierra Club v. Morton, 405 U.S. 727 (1972).

Shelley v. Kraemer, 324 U.S. 1 (1948)

Smith v. Allwright, 321 U.S. 649 (1944).

United States v. Harriss, 347 U.S. 612 (1954).

United States v. Rumely, 345 U.S. 41 (1953).

Media Sources

Ablelson, Reed. "At Minnesota Public Radio, A Deal Way Above Average." *New York Times,* March 27, 1998a, D-3.

——. "Charities Use For-Profit Units To Avoid Disclosing Finances." *New York Times,* February 2, 1998b, A-1, A-12.

——. "Charity Led by Gen. Powell Comes Under Heavy Fire." *New York Times,* October 8, 1999, A-12.

Babcock, Charles R., and Richard Morin. "Following the Path of Self-Interest." *The Washington Post National Weekly Edition*, June 25–July 1, 1990, 14.

"Backers Hope Presidential Race Confers Front-Burner Status on Campaign Finance Overhaul." *CQ Weekly*, March 4, 2000, 464.

Berke, Richard L. "Sierra Club Ads in Political Races Offer a Case Study in Issue Advocacy." *New York Times*, October 24, 1998, A-12.

Bresnahan, John, and Damon Chappie. "Members Quit Weller Tech Group: Tax Structure Would Allow Companies to Write Off Membership Dues in Full." *Roll Call Monthly*, December 3, 2001.

Brinkley, Joel. "Cultivating the Grass Roots to Reap Legislative Benefits." *New York Times*, November 1, 1993, A-1, A-14.

Clymer, Adam. "GOP Filibuster Deals a Setback to Lobbying Bill." *New York Times*, October 7, 1994, A-1, A-13.

Codrescu, Andrei. "1 Man–1 Vote." *All Things Considered*, NPR, March 2, 2000.

Cushman, John H., Jr. "An Uncomfortable Debate for Sierra Club: Competing Views on Immigration Divide an Environmental Group." *New York Times*, April 5, 1998, A-12.

———. "Sierra Club Considers a Mutual Fund to Lure Investors." *New York Times*, July 20, 2001, A-17.

Davidson, Osha Gray. "Guns and Poses." *The New Republic*, October 11, 1993.

Dedman, Bill. "AMA Retains Chief Despite Sunbeam Furor." *New York Times*, June 18, 1998, A-24.

Delaney, Paul. "A Purge at the Top: Confusion in the Ranks." *New York Times*, March 29, 1992, wk-2.

Dreyfuss, Robert. "Which Doctors." *The New Republic*, June 22, 1998, 22–25.

Edsall, Thomas B. "Coming to Term Limits." *Washington Post*, May 12, 1998, A-4.

Eilperin, Juliet. "Hastert Drawing Crowds—of Lobbyists, With Eager Audience, Speaker Builds a Fund-Raising Machine." *Washington Post*, March 10, 1999, A-1.

Engelberg, Stephen. "A New Breed of Hired Hands Cultivates Grass-Roots Anger." *New York Times*, March 17, 1993, A-1, A-11.

Foerstel, Karen. "Grass Greener after Congress." *CQ Weekly*, March 11, 2000, 515–19.

Foerstel, Karen, and Peter Wallsten, with Derek Willis. "Campaign Overhaul Mired in Money and Loopholes." *CQ Weekly*, May 13, 2000, 1084–93.

Fritsch, Jane. "Donations from the Heart, Greetings from the Grave." *New York Times*, April 5, 1998, WK-7.

Goldberg, Carey. "Downsizing Activism: Greenpeace is Cutting Back." *New York Times*, Tuesday, September 16, 1997, A-1, A16.

——. "Court Upholds Maine Campaign Law." *New York Times,* November 9, 1999, A-13.

Grann, David. "Comeback Kid: Bill Paxon's Triumphant Return to Capitol Hill." *The New Republic,* November 1, 1999, 24–27.

Gray, Jerry. "1-Man Crusade over Lobbying Ensnares a Bill." *New York Times,* November 4, 1995, A-1, A-8.

Greenhouse, Linda. "Justices Reject Appeals in Two Cases Involving Limits on Political Money." *New York Times,* November 17, 1998, A-18.

——. "High Court Is Urged to Uphold 'Citizen Suit' to Curb Pollution." *New York Times,* October 13, 1999, A-18.

Holmes, Steven A. "Despite New Top, An Impatient NAACP." *New York Times,* May 19, 1995, A-6.

Honan, William H. "With Money Threatened, Colleges are Moving on all Lobbying Fronts." *New York Times,* June 28, 1995, B-11.

Johnston, David Cay. "How a Tax Law Helps Insure a Scarcity of Programmers." *New York Times,* April 27, 1998, C-1, C-12.

Kamen, Al. "Going the Distance for Medicare Money." *Washington Post,* December 6, 1999, A-25.

Kangas, Edward A. "Soft Money and Hard Bargains." *New York Times,* October 22, 1999, A-29.

Krauss, Clifford. "Clinton's Woes on Capitol Hill Spur Sharp Criticism of His Top Lobbyist." *New York Times,* May 25, 1993a, A-7.

——. "House Democrats Rush to Extinguish Rebellion." *New York Times,* May 19, 1993b, A-8.

Lacey, Marc. "NRA Stands by Criticism of President." *New York Times,* March 20, 2000, A-15.

Lee, Gary. "Robert Gray, 'Master of the Universe.'" *The Washington Post National Weekly Edition,* September 28–October 4, 1992a, 36.

——. "Ex-Lawmaker w/Hill Contacts Seeks Jobs w/Big Bucks, Prestige: Washington Headhunters' Advice: Get Real." *The Washington Post Weekly Edition,* October 5–11, 1992b, 32.

"A Letter and Its Response." *New York Times,* September 1, 1999, A-16.

Levy, Clifford J. "D'Amato Campaign Awash in Donations by Hopeful Lobbies." *New York Times,* June 2, 1998, A-1, A-18.

——. "Quietly, Tobacco Giant Philip Morris Lobbies against Local Efforts to Curb Smoking." *New York Times,* December 7, 1999, A-23.

Line, Les. "Birds in the Bush and Database: The Gadgets Needed to Spot Birds Becomes Ever More Sophisticated." *New York Times,* June 25, 1998, D-1, D-8.

MacArthur, John R. "Remember Nayirah, Witness for Kuwait?" *New York Times,* January 6, 1992, A-11.

McAllister, Bill. "Lobbied Out of a Cabinet Post." *The Washington Post Weekly Edition,* October 5–11, 1992, 14–15.

Mitchell, Alison. "Enron's Ties to the Leader of House Republicans Went Beyond Contributions to His Campaign." *New York Times*, January 16, 2002, C-1, C-8.

"NAACP's Julian Bond Sees a New Civil Rights Era Ahead." *New York Times*, July 13, 1998, A-12.

Nitschke, Lori. "Agriculture Has Muscle in Free-Trade Fight." *CQ Weekly*, March 2000, 444–48.

Ornstein, Norman. "Bad Contribution." *The New Republic*, June 10, 1995, 14–16.

Payne, Leslie. "After High Pressure Years, Contractors Tone Down Missile Defense Lobbying." *New York Times*, June 13, 2000, A-6.

Pear, Robert. "Health Industry Sees Wish List Made into Law." *New York Times*, December 6, 1999, A-1, A-26.

Powell, Michael. "The Revival of the NRA." *The Washington Post Weekly Edition*, August 28, 2000, 6–9.

Purdum, Todd S. "Ballot Initiatives Flourishing as Way to Bypass Politicians." *New York Times*, March 31, 1998, A-1, A-18.

Revkin, Andrew C. "Gun Lobby Helps States Train Young Hunters." *New York Times*, November 17, 1999, A-1, A-27.

Rohter, Larry. "Puerto Rico Fighting to Keep Its Tax Breaks for Business." *New York Times*, May 10, 1993, A-1, C-5.

Rosenbaum, David E. "Little Known Crusader Plays a Big Role in Tax Debate." *New York Times*, May 21, 2001, A-12.

Rosin, Hanna. "Whiplash." *The New Republic*, February 16, 1996, 17–20.

Sack, Kevin. "Mississippi Reveals Dark Secrets of a Racist Time." *New York Times*, March 18, 1998, A-1, A-16.

Schmitt, Eric. "Lott Pushes New Warship for Home State Contract." *New York Times*, June 23, 1998, A-12.

Schneider, Keith. "Selling Out? Pushed and Pulled, Environment Inc. Is on the Defensive." *New York Times*, March 29, 1992, section 4.

Seelye, Katherine Q. "Conservatives Hobble Lobbying Bill." *New York Times*, October 7, 1994, A-13.

———. "An Ailing Gun Lobby Faces a Bitter Struggle for Power." *New York Times*, January 1, 1997, A-1, A-9.

———. "President Hits the Golf Course, and the Books." *New York Times*, August 24, 1999, A-12.

Solomon, Burt. "Groups That Don't Cut the Mustard." *National Journal*, July 4, 1987, 1710.

Stout, David. "Tab for Washington Lobbying." *New York Times*, July 29, 1999, A-14.

Stricherz, Mark. "Any Volunteers." *The New Republic*, January 5 & 12, 1998, 12–13.

Taylor, Paul. "Superhighway Robbery." *The New Republic*, May 5, 1997, 20–22.

VandeHei, Jim. "Speaker Hastert's Inner Circle: Meet the Key Members, Staffers and Lobbyists Who Have the Boss's Ear." *Roll Call Monthly*, February 1999, 6.

———. "K Street Booms with Computer Cash: Technology Industry Emphasizing Lobbying over Campaign Giving." *Roll Call Monthly*, April 6, 1999, rollcall.com/newscoops/leadscoop.

Van Natta, Don, Jr., and Douglas Frantz. "Lobbyists are Friends and Foes to McCain." *New York Times*, February 10, 2000, A-23.

Wayne, Leslie. "Broadcast Lobby's Formula: Airtime + Money = Influence." *New York Times*, May 5, 1997, C1, C9.

Weiner, Tim. "Lobbying for Research Money, Colleges Bypass Review Process." *New York Times*, August 24, 1999, A-1, A-12.

Weisskopf, Michael. "Lobbyists Shift into Reverse." *Washington Post*, May 13, 1994, A-3.

Index